Alcohol and Crime

Alcohol and Crime

Gavin Dingwall

WILLAN
PUBLISHING

Published by

Willan Publishing
Culmcott House
Mill Street, Uffculme
Cullompton, Devon
EX15 3AT, UK
Tel: +44(0)1884 840337
Fax: +44(0)1884 840251
e-mail: info@willanpublishing.co.uk
website: www.willanpublishing.co.uk

Published simultaneously in the USA and Canada by

Willan Publishing
c/o ISBS, 920 NE 58th Ave, Suite 300
Portland, Oregon 97213-3786, USA
Tel: +001(0)503 287 3093
Fax: +001(0)503 280 8832
e-mail: info@isbs.com
website: www.isbs.com

First published 2006
Reprinted 2010

ISBN 1-84392-167-7 (hardback)

British Library Cataloguing-in-Publication Data

A catalogue record for this book is available from the British Library

Project managed by Deer Park Productions, Tavistock, Devon
Typeset by TW Typesetting, Plymouth, Devon
Printed and bound by TJ International Ltd, Trecerus Industrial Estate, Padstow, Cornwall

Contents

Acknowledgements

Many people have helped with this book. As I do not want to inadvertently cause offence by missing anyone out, most of the acknowledgements which follow are general. This approach has the added bonus that I can include past and present colleagues who may have had no direct input into this work, but whom I nevertheless wish to thank for their collegiality over the years.

In terms of this particular project, Shane Kilcommins and Ian O'Donnell first got me interested in alcohol and crime when they asked me to contribute a chapter to a collection that they were editing entitled *Alcohol, Society and the Law*. Willan Publishing shared my belief that this area merited an interdisciplinary monograph. I thank them for their enthusiasm and assistance throughout this project.

I worked at three universities during the process of researching and writing this book: the University of Wales, Aberystwyth; Flinders University of South Australia and De Montfort University, Leicester.

The University of Wales, Aberystwyth provided a stimulating working environment for nearly thirteen years and I am grateful to my former colleagues and students for their willingness to discuss my research over the years. I am also grateful for a period of research leave in 2004 which allowed me to undertake valuable comparative work for this book. Although I promised to keep my comments general, I am sure that no-one will take exception if I single out Neil Kibble for a particular mention. Neil and I have worked very closely over a number of years and his support and friendship have always been greatly appreciated. Despite a busy schedule, Neil took the time to debate many of the ideas in this book with me at length. The book benefits significantly from his input. Another former colleague, Laurence Koffman, also commented on some of the work in draft form and again I am grateful for his constructive contribution.

My stay at Flinders University of South Australia in Adelaide was far shorter than my stay in Aberystwyth but, similarly, proved to be enjoyable and productive. Again, I appreciate the time that colleagues took in discussing my work. Professor Mark Israel facilitated my visit in his capacity as Assistant Dean for Research and was ever ready to debate and refine my arguments. On a personal level, the friendship of Mark and his family enriched my time down under. My greatest debt in Australia by far is to Sue Lowe and her family and friends for making me feel so welcome. I will always treasure my time with them.

I moved to De Montfort Law School in Leicester as this project was reaching its conclusion. I wish to thank Professor Richard Ward, Head of Department, for ensuring that I could devote as much time as possible to the book and to my new colleagues for welcoming me into their fold.

The book benefits from the comments of those who listened to papers that I presented on various aspects of alcohol and crime at the Socio-Legal Studies Conference in Aberystwyth; the Sentencing and Society Conference at Strathclyde University; and staff seminars at the School of Law, Queens University, Belfast; the School of Law, Flinders University of South Australia; the Department of Criminology, the University of Melbourne; and the School of Law, Sussex University. I would like to thank all those who organised and participated in these sessions.

Finally, on a personal level, I wish to thank my family and friends for supporting me in this as in all previous ventures. Gary Wallace made a number of useful suggestions during what should have been a holiday in the United States. This book is dedicated to Sarah Goddard, for always giving me a good reason to get away from the computer and out of the library.

Gavin Dingwall
Leicester

Chapter 1

Alcohol and society

This work arose out of a belief that there was a need for a book which introduced readers to the debate about the relationship between alcohol and crime and the way in which the criminal justice system responds to those who offend after consuming alcohol. To many people, the link between alcohol and crime is self-evident. However, research (see Chapters 2 and 3) suggests that the link is far more complicated than is assumed both in popular discourse and in the official response to offences committed after the offender had been drinking. Consequently it is difficult to determine what the appropriate legal response should be. In England and Wales, as in other jurisdictions, the current legal position is controversial and appears in part to be based on assumptions that require, and lack, empirical verification (Dingwall 2003).

It is not the case that there has been a lack of research on the topic. As the references demonstrate, there is no shortage of valuable research but much of it is narrow in focus. What this work seeks to do is critically review this literature and then consider the policy implications that arise from it. The book therefore is not just an overview of existing research. Based on the available evidence, it suggests a principled approach to responding to those who offend after drinking alcohol. Given the variety of attitudes that people have towards drinking, this approach will no doubt lack universal approval. Nonetheless, if the book poses some difficult questions about the current approach and raises the issues that need more careful consideration then it will have served a valuable function.

Certainly, there could not be a more opportune time to consider alcohol and crime. Few could have anticipated the degree of political and media attention that has been devoted to the issue in the past two years. This attention is welcome for, as the next chapter demonstrates, there certainly appears to be a serious problem of alcohol-related crime in this country. However, the fact that alcohol consumption precedes many criminal events does not in itself prove that the drinking led to the offending. The governmental response to date does deal with some important issues, such as licensing and policing strategies (an overview is found in Department for Culture, Media and Sport *et al.* 2005). One of the arguments in this work though is that some enduring issues require further consideration. To take the two most notable arguments: what effect, if any, should an individual's intoxication have on whether the individual can be held criminally liable and, if he can, should it affect his sentence? The current law has been subject to considerable academic criticism (though practitioners generally find it acceptable: Law Commission 1995) but, in the current political climate, it is unlikely that any government would want to reform the law in a manner which may be seen to be unduly lenient to those who offend whilst intoxicated.

Substance abuse and crime

This work is, in one sense, narrower in focus than some research on this topic. Often work on alcohol and crime is considered as part of broader reviews of substance abuse and crime (e.g. South 2002; Wincup 2005). There are good reasons for adopting such an approach. First, the law is not concerned with whether the defendant's intoxication was caused by alcohol or by another substance (*DPP* v *Majewski* [1977] AC 443). Much of the legal analysis in Chapters 5 and 6, therefore, is equally applicable to those who offend after becoming intoxicated through the use of a substance other than alcohol. Similarly research shows that many individuals have taken a combination of alcohol and other (usually illegal) drugs prior to offending (see Chapter 2). Limiting the discussion in this book to alcohol does not mean that different substances can always be so neatly compartmentalised in practice or that there are not areas of common ground.

Why then is the discussion in this book limited to alcohol? There are a number of differences between alcohol and other substances which were felt to justify the approach taken. First, despite comparatively high rates of illegal drug use in society, alcohol use remains far more prevalent. Second, the use of alcohol, unlike most other types of recreational drug, is also generally legal. This difference means that research into the link between other drugs and crime have to consider the fact that an illegal market is in operation which, by necessity, involves determining a suitable response. This is obviously an important topic in its own right but not one that has any direct bearing on alcohol and crime. Third, the evidence tends to suggest that different types of offence are associated with the use of alcohol and the use of other drugs (see Chapter 2). Finally, given the government's recent concerns about alcohol-related crime (Department for Culture, Media and Sport *et al.*

2005), it was felt that narrowing the discussion to alcohol was appropriate. Readers who want to find out more about the link between illegal drugs and crime would be advised to consult Bean (2004).

A note on terminology

In a work which considers the causal link between drinking behaviour and offending behaviour it is important to give some thought to terminology. Many of the expressions commonly used in discussions of the topic are inherently problematic. 'Alcohol-induced' offending clearly states that there is a direct causal link between the consumption of alcohol and the crime; if the offender had remained sober, one is to presume that the offence would not have occurred. 'Alcohol-caused' assault, a term sometimes found in the Australian literature (e.g. Matthews *et al.* 2002; Chikritzhs *et al.* 1999), again denotes a direct causal link between drinking and offending. Terms such as 'alcohol-fuelled' and 'alcohol-related' crime, both of which were used in a recent British government document (Department for Culture, Media and Sport *et al.* 2005) are equally problematic because they imply that alcohol consumption was at least a contributory factor in the crime; the presence of alcohol is deemed to be 'relevant' to the offence.

More thoughtful analyses have sought to address this issue. In her study, Rumgay (1998) adopted the phrase 'intoxicated crime' in preference to the cumbersome 'crimes committed after the offender had been drinking alcohol', even though she recognised that crimes themselves do not become intoxicated. I too will seek to avoid using phrases such as 'alcohol-induced', 'alcohol-related' or 'alcohol-fuelled' crime, unless it is appropriate in the context (e.g. when asking what proportion of crimes committed by offenders who had been drinking alcohol were alcohol-induced). This will often be the case when considering strategies designed by others. For example, the government claim to be targeting 'alcohol-fuelled violence' (Department for Culture, Media and Sport *et al.* 2005) regardless of whether it would be more accurate to describe it as 'violence committed by those who had been drinking alcohol'.

Structure

In terms of structure, this introductory chapter will provide an overview of drinking habits in the UK. This is important for two reasons. First, if there is a link between alcohol consumption and crime, then patterns of consumption are obviously of direct importance. If such a causal link could be established, we could safely predict that crime rates would rise if there was a rise in alcohol consumption and that crime would fall if rates of consumption fell. However, even if such a link cannot be established, patterns of consumption are important. The government have introduced a number of measures designed to combat 'alcohol-related' crime, and have indicated that other measures are planned (Department for Culture, Media and Sport *et al.* 2005). Some of these measures are far-reaching (for a consideration see Chapters 4 and 7) and will affect all drinkers, whether or not they come into contact with the criminal justice system. It is important that our focus on alcohol and crime does not mask the fact that crime prevention measures in this field impact directly on an activity enjoyed by millions of people in the UK.

After reviewing patterns of alcohol consumption, the next two chapters consider the link between alcohol and crime. Chapter 2 analyses a number of important studies which have considered the extent to which offenders drink prior to offending. Chapter 3 then looks at some of the possible ways in which the consumption of alcohol may increase the likelihood of offending and concludes by considering some of the methodological problems that arise in trying to establish a causal link. Drawing on this, Chapter 4 looks at methods of preventing and policing alcohol-related crime and disorder. Chapters 5 and 6 provide a detailed critique of the legal response to alcohol-induced offending. Chapter 5 deals with substantive criminal liability whilst Chapter 6 is concerned with sentencing. Chapter 7 concludes by considering the government's recent strategy for tackling intoxicated crime and by suggesting areas which still need to be addressed.

Drinking habits in the UK

A considerable amount of data on how people in the UK drink has been published recently due to the government's commitment to provide an alcohol harm reduction strategy (Prime Minister's Strategy Unit 2003, 2004). The figures show that the vast majority of British adults, some 90 per cent, choose to drink alcohol (Prime Minister's Strategy Unit 2003: 6).

Those who do drink consume very different amounts, both generally and on specific occasions. Whilst general levels of consumption have always been a matter of interest to policy makers, the amount consumed on one-off occasions has also become a concern of late due to the increasing realisation that 'binge' drinking is a hazardous activity (Bondy and Rehm 1998; Wichstrom 1998), both because of the health risks that it carries and in terms of crime and disorder.

The data on consumption is based on government guidelines for weekly and daily drinking limits which, in turn, are based on units of alcohol. A unit is roughly equivalent to half a pint of ordinary strength beer, a small glass of wine or one measure of spirits (ibid.: 10) but this is far from exact as the alcoholic strength of some drinks, for example beer or wine, varies considerably. In 1992 the government recommended that men drink no more than 21 units per week and that women do not exceed 14 units per week. This advice was amended in 1995 to include recommended daily drinking levels. In addition to the limits set out above, men were advised not to drink more than three or four units per day and women two or three.

Using the criteria outlined above, men who drink up to 21 units a week are classified as low to moderate drinkers as are women who drink up to 14 units. Men who drink between 21 and 50 units a week and women who drink between 14 and 35 units a week are classified as moderate to heavy drinkers. Finally, men drinking in excess of 50 units and women drinking in excess of 35 units per week are classified as very heavy drinkers.

The government also adopt a unit-based approach to classify 'binge' drinking. Drinking at least double the daily guidelines – six units for women and eight for men – is classified as 'binge' drinking (Prime Minister's Strategy Unit 2003: 11). It was recognised that this definition was somewhat arbitrary and that 'binge' drinking is a problematic concept:

> [Binge] drinking is a debated term. Since alcohol will affect different people in different ways, there is no fixed relationship between the amount drunk and its consequences. So although many people understand 'bingeing' to mean deliberately drinking to excess, or drinking to get drunk, not everyone drinking over 6/8 units in a single day will fit this category. Similarly, many people who *are* drinking to get drunk, will drink far in excess of the 6/8 units in the unit-based definition. (ibid.: 11)

Using these classifications, the majority of British adults who use alcohol are low to moderate users. However, it is estimated that 6.4 million adults are moderate to heavy drinkers and an additional 1.8 million adults are classified as very heavy drinkers (ibid.: 12). On top of this, an estimated 5.9 million adults had been 'binge' drinking in the past week. So, despite the fact that most people drink within sensible limits, a significant minority of British adults drink in excess of both the suggested weekly and daily amount.

The statistics suggest that frequency of drinking varies according to income (Office of National Statistics 2004: Table 9.7). Fifty per cent of individuals (59 per cent of men, 45 per cent of women) with a gross weekly household income of less than £200 per week had drunk in the previous week compared to 81 per cent of people with household incomes of more than £1,000 a week (85 per cent of men, 76 per cent of women). Similarly 13 per cent of people who earned less than £200 a week (17 per cent of men, 10 per cent of women) drank on five or more days in the last week compared to 26 per cent of people (30 per cent of men, 21 per cent of women) with an income in excess of £1,000 per week.

This pattern is less marked with regards to 'binge' drinking. Those in the lowest income bracket (less than £200 per week) remain the group least likely to 'binge' drink regardless of gender (ibid.: Table 9.7) whilst the highest incidence of 'binge' drinking for both men and women is found in the top income brackets (ibid.: Table 9.7).

When the net is widened to include those who do not work, the proportion of 'binge' drinkers unsurprisingly reduces: 23 per cent of British men and 9 per cent of British women had done so on at least one occasion in the past week according to 2003 data (Office for National Statistics 2003). These figures hide notable national and regional variations. Scottish men were more likely to 'binge' drink than the British average (26 per cent as opposed to 23 per cent) and Scottish and Welsh women were slightly more likely to do so as well (10 per cent as opposed to 9 per cent). Within England, London had the lowest 'binge' drinking rates for both men (18 per cent) and women (5 per cent) whilst the Northwest and Yorkshire and the Humber had the highest rates for both men (28 per cent) and women (13 per cent). The next two sections will consider gender differences in more detail.

Drinking and women

Writing in 1902, Charles Booth was clear about why drinking had increased (though he offered no evidence to substantiate either the claim or the explanation):

> The increase in drinking is to be laid mainly to the account of the female sex. This latter phase seems to be one of the unexpected results of the emancipation of woman. On the one hand she has become more independent of man, industrially and financially, and on the other more of a comrade than before, and in neither capacity does she feel any shame at entering a public house. (cited in Waterson 1996: 176)

This statement is illuminating in two respects. Firstly it is an early example of a commonly held, chauvinist view of drinking – here the pub implicitly was the man's domain. Research suggests that male and female drinking are still perceived differently (Ettorre 1997). Drinking is seen as part of the male construct but contrary to standard notions of feminine behaviour. Women are thus stigmatised if they drink at home as this conflicts with widely held beliefs about female family responsibilities (Waterson 1996). Drunken, aggressive behaviour is deemed 'unfeminine' and is therefore seen as especially troubling when the aggressor is female (Robbins and Martin 1993). It is no coincidence that females who act in this way are popularly referred to as 'ladettes'.

This body of research reaches similar conclusions to feminist research in criminology which has found that female offenders are perceived to be 'doubly deviant': not only do they breach commonly accepted standards of behaviour, but their behaviour conflicts with gender stereotypes as well (Heidensohn 1985; Walklate 1995).

Booth also alleged that female drinking had increased by the early 1900s due to a combination of greater financial independence and a change in perceived gender roles. The link between greater female financial independence and alcohol consumption has been made again more recently.

Data suggests that women still drink considerably less than men (Office for National Statistics 2004; on female drinking see generally Breeze 1985; Department of Health and Royal College of General Practitioners 1992; Institute of Alcohol Studies 2005a; McConville 1995; Plant 1990, 1997). Women are both more likely not to drink than men (Lader and Meltzer 2002) and are less likely to drink above sensible limits (Waterson 1996: 171). At the same time, the average female drinker is drinking more than a decade ago whilst rates of heavy drinking by females are slowly rising (ibid.: 171). In 1988, 10 per cent of women were drinking in excess of the recommended 14 units per week. By 2002 this had risen to 17 per cent of women (Office for National Statistics 2004). Three per cent of women were drinking in excess of 35 units of alcohol per week, a level that can be classified as dangerous (ibid.: Table 9.12). There are marked regional variations in female drinking patterns: Scottish women are more likely to 'binge' drink than English women, but are less likely to exceed the recommended weekly limit (ibid: Table 9.10). To what extent this difference can be explained on economic grounds and to what extent it is due to cultural and social differences is difficult to ascertain.

If one moves away from the data on 'binge' drinking to consider instead aggregate levels of consumption, women who drink heavily do not generally conform to the popular 'ladette' stereotype:

> [Heavier] women drinkers have a high income, live in a profes-sional/managerial household, probably work (particularly in an occupation associated with heavy drinking), move in a social milieu where heavy drinking is a shared norm, have leisure pursuits which involve drinking and are less likely to be influenced by any health norms about restricted drinking. (Waterson 1996: 183)

According to data from the Office for National Statistics (2004), women from managerial/professional households were both more likely to drink regularly and to drink more frequently than women from routine/manual households: 71 per cent of women from professional households had drunk alcohol in the last week and 18 per cent had drank on five or more days that week compared to the 51 per cent of women from unskilled households who had drunk in the past week and the 9 per cent who had drunk on five or more days.

Age is also a significant factor in female drinking patterns. Women aged between 16 and 24 are more likely to 'binge' drink than older women – 28 per cent of women aged 16 to 24 had drunk over six units on at least one day in the previous week (ibid.: Table 9.3). This, in tandem with gendered stereotypes about 'acceptable' drinking behaviour (Ettorre 1997; Neve *et al.* 1997; Robbins and Martin 1993), may well give rise to the misleading perception that heavy female drinking is associated with a 'ladette' lifestyle.

Drinking and men

Unlike female drinking trends, alcohol consumption by adult males has remained reasonably constant since the early 1990s (Office for National Statistics 2003). Although, as men are still considerably more likely than women to drink excessively, it is important that the rise in female consumption does not disguise the fact that male problem drinking remains a significant issue (Alcohol Concern 2005).

In common with women, patterns of consumption vary markedly according to age. Younger men drink considerably more than older men (Harnett *et al.* 2000; Office for National Statistics 2004). There has, however, been a noticeable fall in heavy drinking by men aged between 16 and 24 between 1988 and 2002, despite the aggregate trend for men remaining constant (Office for National Statistics 2004: Table 9.2).

Despite the fact that consumption by men has remained constant while female consumption has increased, there are a number of similarities between male and female drinking patterns. As is the case with female drinkers, men in managerial or professional occupations consume more alcohol than those who have routine/manual occupations (Alcohol Concern 2005), though the discrepancy is not as marked as it is with females. Again in common with females, men who work in managerial or professional occupations drink more frequently than those in routine/manual occupations (Office for National Statistics 2004: Table 9.5). 'Binge' drinking is more common amongst those in routine/manual occupations, which may explain why those in lower socio-economic groups are significantly more likely to suffer from a range of alcohol-related harms (Harrison and Gardiner 1999; Makela 1999; Thom and Francome 2001).

Thom and Francome (2001) have found that there are a number of common predictors of alcohol misuse, crime and other risk-taking behaviour in men. These predictors include a disrupted family background, poor social skills, educational problems, having a risk-seeking personality, involvement with 'delinquents' and 'macho' cultural norms about drinking and subsequent behaviour (see also Andreasson *et al.* 1992; Neve *et al.* 1997).

Recently a considerable body of research has focussed on the values and practices which are commonly associated with 'masculine' behaviour (see e.g. Bowker 1998; Collier 1998; Connell 1995; Jefferson 1997; Messerschmidt 1993). There is an awareness that there are a variety of diverse forms of masculinity, and that each form displays different values and practices; some masculine identities, for example, engage in more criminality than others (Bowker 1998). Messerschmidt (1993) has argued that race and class interact with masculinity in that behaviour is justified with reference to norms within that race, class and gender. To some men, criminal activity would conform to their expectations of masculinity whilst, for others, such behaviour would be seen as unacceptable. Similarly, other forms of behaviour, such as 'binge' drinking, would be acceptable to some groups of men but not to others. Hobbs *et al.* (2003) have argued that some men who lack power in society may compensate for this by indulging in other activities, such as crime and excessive drinking, which increase their feelings of masculinity. Yet this behaviour would not be acceptable to all marginalised groups of men. For example, men from ethnic minority groups where abstinence is prized would be likely to find other forms of compensatory behaviour (see generally O'Donnell and Sharpe 2000). The next section considers drinking and ethnicity further.

Drinking and ethnicity

Rates of alcohol consumption vary considerably amongst different ethnic groups in the UK. Nazroo (1997) found that most ethnic minority groups reported far higher rates of abstinence than average: 40 per cent of the Chinese sample, 60 per cent of the Indian sample and more than 90 per cent of the Pakistani sample did not drink alcohol. Those with strong religious beliefs are most likely to abstain (Heim *et al.* 2004). As well as reporting higher rates of abstinence, studies have shown that members of ethnic minority groups who do drink tend to drink less than the British average (Erens *et al.* 2001; Heim *et al.* 2004; National Centre for Social Research and Department of Epidemiology and Public Health at the Royal Free and University College Medical School 2001; Purser *et al.* 1999).

There are also marked differences in alcohol consumption between drinkers from different ethnic minority groups. Although generally drinkers from ethnic minorities consume less alcohol than average (Cochrane and Howell 1995; Erens *et al.* 2001), Afro-Caribbean drinkers appear less likely to misuse alcohol than some South Asian drinkers (McKeigne and Karmi 1993; Wanigaratne *et al.* 2001). It has also been reported that, although comparative rates of consumption remain lower, there have been increases in alcohol consumption by ethnic minority young people in recent years (Denscombe and Drucquer 1997).

Researchers have warned that there are particular difficulties associated with measuring alcohol use amongst ethnic minority populations

9

(Subhra 2002; Wanigaratne *et al.* 2001). Many studies have limited samples which may be geographically-specific, making it potentially misleading to try and draw general conclusions (Subhra 2002). There is also the problem that members of ethnic minority groups may be unwilling to disclose alcohol use due to their religious beliefs or due to a sense of having shamed their family (Heim *et al.* 2004). Nonetheless, even allowing for these methodological difficulties, it would appear safe to conclude that most ethnic minority groups consume less alcohol than average.

Drinking and young people

It has already been mentioned with regard to both men and women that drinking patterns vary greatly according to age. This section considers alcohol use by young people in the UK. Before doing so, however, it is necessary to consider the legal framework for drinking. Although drinking is common amongst teenagers, and hardly exceptional amongst those younger, the law supposedly restricts the sale of alcohol to those below a certain age. The age is context-specific.

Save in the case of sickness or on prescription, it is an offence to give alcohol to a child under five years of age (Child and Young Persons Act 1933, s.5). Above the age of five there are a variety of offences designed to deal with particular issues. The Licensing Act 2003, not all of which is yet in force, is designed in part to simplify what is a confusing licensing system in England and Wales. Before the Act comes into force, the main offences were to be found in different statutes, most notably the Licensing Act 1964 and the Licensing (Young Persons) Act 2000.

The Licensing Act 2003 provides a number of offences relating to underage drinking. Section 146 makes it an offence for a person to sell alcohol to a person under 18. It is also an offence to knowingly allow the sale of alcohol to an individual under 18 if the individual works in a capacity that authorises him to prevent the sale (s.147).

An offence is also committed by someone under 18 who buys or attempts to buy alcohol in licensed premises (s.149) – unless the individual does so at the request of a police officer or a weights and measures inspector acting in the course of his duty. Additionally, there is an offence of buying or attempting to buy alcohol on behalf of an individual aged under 18 (s.149(3)) unless the purchaser is 18 or over, the drink was bought for a 16 or 17 year old, the alcohol is beer, wine or cider and it is purchased for drinking with a meal. An individual under 18 also commits an offence if he knowingly consumes alcohol on licensed premises (s.150) unless it is consumed with a meal and the conditions outlined in s.150(4) apply.

Provided that alcohol is not given to a child under 5, an adult commits no offence by supplying a young person with alcohol in the confines of the home. The legislation is primarily designed to regulate licensed premises. Similarly a young person will commit no offence just by drinking alcohol, though there are, of course, offences related to drunkenness with which they could be charged. However, this general position coexists with provisions in the Confiscation of Alcohol (Young Persons) Act 1997 which made it an offence for someone under 18 in a public place, or some other place to which he has gained unlawful access, to fail to surrender alcohol to a police officer without reasonable excuse. The Act does not make it an offence for a young person to drink alcohol in a public place (unless specific restrictions apply; see Chapter 4) – the offence is triggered by the failure to hand over alcohol – yet, in practice, the Act clearly is aimed at restricting drinking in public by those aged under 18.

Despite having a legal framework designed to restrict drinking by young people, research shows that many young people in the UK drink (Harrington 2000; Honess *et al.* 2000; Newburn and Shiner 2001). The data also suggests that young people are drinking more than they did a decade ago. Clearly there is need for empirical research into the effectiveness of current law enforcement strategies designed to curb underage drinking (Hafemeister and Jackson 2004). Goddard and Higgins (1999) report that, on average, 11–15 year olds drank 0.8 units of alcohol per week in 1990 but that this had doubled to 1.6 units per week by 1998 (although it is worth bearing in mind that this is still less than a pint of average strength beer or lager). Of far more concern is the apparent rise in 'binge' drinking among young people. Hibell *et al.* (2000) found that the proportion of 15–16 year old people who 'binge' drink had increased from 22 per cent in 1995 to 30 per cent in 1999.

A large study funded by the Rowntree Foundation, which drew on a sample of more than 14,000 secondary school students in England, Wales and Scotland, found that a small minority of pre-teen children drank regularly. Nine per cent of 11 and 12 year old boys and 5 per cent of 11 and 12 year old girls classified themselves as 'regular drinkers' (Beinart *et al.* 2002). With 15 and 16 year old students, the percentages rose to 39 per cent of boys and 33 per cent of girls. Fifty-nine per cent of boys and 54 per cent of girls aged 15 or 16 claimed to have taken part in 'binge' drinking in the previous month. The significant rise in consumption since 1990 by 11–15 year olds, particularly amongst girls, has coincided with the introduction onto the market of 'alcopops' (Becher *et al.* 2001), which has led the British Medical Association (2004) to call for more research into whether the introduction of 'alcopops' has encouraged more young people to start drinking, whether 'alcopops' have led to an increase in consumption and whether 'alcopops' act as a gateway to more traditional alcoholic drinks.

As with adults, rates of consumption by young people vary across the country. In one study (Anderson and Plant 1996), it was found, for example, that young people in the Western Isles of Scotland had distinctive drinking patterns from the rest of Scotland and the rest of the UK. In the Western Isles, a far higher proportion of young people reported not drinking alcohol; however, those who did drink reported drinking particularly heavily. This pattern may be explained by the unique blend of historical, cultural and religious factors found in the Hebrides.

Given the prevalence of drinking by young people which emerges from the research, one suspects that the law is rarely enforced. Although one does not know the circumstances in which the alcohol was obtained or consumed, it appears likely that many of the offences outlined above are committed frequently. Yet statistics, which admittedly are now dated, show that fewer than 2,000 individuals are convicted each year in England and Wales for underage alcohol purchase and less than 500 are convicted of selling alcohol to minors (Lister Sharp 1994). Central to the government's 'blitz' on 'alcohol-related' crime is a strategy of targeting those who supply alcohol to underage drinkers (Home Office 2004). On-the-spot fines of £80 have been introduced for this offence in April 2005 (Department for Culture, Media and Sport *et al.* 2005).

This policy followed the Alcohol Misuse Enforcement Campaign which ran in July and August 2004 in 90 police areas. Part of the campaign involved sending young people into licensed premises to see whether they could purchase alcohol. The campaign demonstrated the ease with which alcohol could be obtained: 45 per cent of on-licences and 31 per cent of off-licenses targeted were unlawfully selling alcohol to underage people (Department for Culture, Media and Sport *et al.* 2005: 10). The government have also recently proposed introducing a new power which will enable the police to close premises which persistently sell alcohol to underage people on a temporary basis (ibid.: 10). However, it is recognised that enforcing the criminal law has to be seen as part of a wider strategy to combat underage drinking:

> There does seem to be a general consensus that if sanctions are used, they should be just one part of a constellation of responses to underage drinking violations. Researchers and advocates are calling for comprehensive approaches to underage drinking that involve the youth, their families, and their communities. (Hafemeister and Jackson 2004: 524)

It is right that the government is concerned about the rise in 'binge' drinking by young people (Hingson and Kenkel 2004; Measham 1996). Nonetheless the statistics do need to be kept in perspective (May 1992). Whilst they show that the majority of teenagers do drink alcohol, there is nothing new about this and it is perhaps best to regard it as part of a socialisation process related to the coming of maturity in a society where the majority of adults use alcohol (Fossey *et al.* 1996; Lowe *et al.* 1993). In this context, most people 'learn to drink without serious mishap' (Fossey *et al.* 1996.: 61).

Drinking habits in an historical context

Just as there is nothing new in underage drinking, concern has been expressed before about the levels of alcohol consumption in Britain and the harm that this was causing to society. Consequently, it is instructive to situate current drinking habits in an historical context. So, are the British drinking more than in the past? The trend in alcohol consumption over the last century is interesting: British people are drinking less than they were 100 years ago, but considerably more than they were 50 years ago (Prime Minister's Strategy Unit 2003). The fact that drinking rates declined and then rose again merits further examination.

Alcohol has a rather inconsistent place in British history. Until the mid-nineteenth century, the majority of the population drank far more heavily than now. There was a widespread belief that alcohol was a source of goodness and not the cause of social problems. It was essentially an integral part of pre-industrial British life. There then followed a shift in attitude that started in the mid-nineteenth century.

This change is reflected in the history of the law associated with drunkenness. Although powers to punish drunkards had been in existence for centuries, by the mid-nineteenth century the law was haphazard and lacking in cohesion. A number of offences relating to drunkenness could be found in different statutes. These offences largely concerned particular situations where intoxication could prove particularly dangerous – for example there were a variety of offences concerned with intoxication and public transport.

The Licensing Act 1872 represented a major shift in emphasis. According to the preamble, it was designed in part for 'the better prevention of drunkenness'. It both codified and extended the existing offences relating to drunkenness. There was both a basic offence of being drunk on a highway, public place or in a licensed premises (s.12) and a number of aggravated offences, such as being drunk and disorderly and being drunk in charge of 'any carriage, horse, cattle, or steam engine' or in possession of a loaded firearm (s.12). For a first offence of being drunk on a highway, there was a maximum fine of ten shillings. The aggravated offences carried a maximum penalty of one month's imprisonment, with or without hard labour, or a maximum fine of 40 shillings (s.12). Punishment may have been seen as the most appropriate way to prevent drunkenness, but the punishments imposed remained modest compared with those for many other offences at the time.

Seven years later there was another notable change in policy. The Habitual Drunkards Act 1879 provided a framework for the voluntary treatment of habitual drunkards. This represented a shift away from a simple penal response towards a treatment model, although it was reserved for those with acute alcohol problems. 'Habitual drunkard' was defined in the Act as:

> [A] person who, not being amenable to any jurisdiction in lunacy, is notwithstanding, by reason of habitual intemperate drinking of intoxicating liquor, at times dangerous to himself or herself or to others, or incapable of managing himself or herself, and his or her affairs. (s.3)

The Act and its accompanying Schedules provided a detailed system for establishing and licensing retreats, although the Act was somewhat vague on the exact form that the treatment should take. Section 3 stated that retreats were licensed 'for the reception, control, care, and curative treatment of habitual drunkards' but that was all the detail given. As '[a] duly qualified medical man' had to be employed as a 'medical attendant' (s.6), it is clear that specialist treatment was envisaged.

Another dramatic reform was introduced less than 20 years later. The 'voluntary' treatment model was abandoned with the passing of the Inebriates Act 1898. Section 1(1) of the Act read as follows:

> Where a person is convicted on indictment of an offence punishable with imprisonment or penal servitude, if the court is satisfied from the evidence that the offence was committed under the influence of drink or that drunkenness was a contributory cause of the offence, and the offender admits that he is or is found by the jury to be a habitual drunkard, the court may, in addition to or in substitution for any other sentence, order that he be detained for a term not exceeding three years in any State inebriate reformatory or in any certified inebriate reformatory the managers of which are willing to receive him.

Section 2 of the Act was equally far-reaching. Habitual drunkards who committed any of the offences listed in the first Schedule to the Act and who had committed three or more similar offences in the past year could be detained for up to three years in a certified inebriate reformatory. This meant, for example, that an individual who, when drunk, had refused to leave licensed premises on four or more occasions and who was deemed to be an habitual drunkard could be involuntarily detained for up to three years.

In a time span of less than 30 years the official response to drunken offending had changed significantly. Not only had there been three significant Acts of comparatively general application instead of piece-meal legislation, but the underlying approach to persistent but often minor drunken offenders had hardened significantly. Explaining this shift is not easy. Like most attitudinal shifts, the process was gradual. Instrumental to the change was the formation and influence of the temperance movement in the early 1800s, but that has the potential to mislead. Despite the enormous popular support the movement undoubtedly attracted, one has to be wary of claiming that the views of its members reflected those of society more generally. Moreover, by focussing on the organisation, one can become distracted from the underlying issue; the degree of support that the temperance movement attracted merely demands a consideration of why it appealed to so many people at that particular time.

The most intuitive explanation for its success can be dismissed. People were not drinking more. However, drinking habits had changed. People were no longer just drinking beer but increasingly were drinking spirits instead or as well (indeed early temperance pioneers debated whether or not they objected to all forms of alcohol or just to spirits). Keller states that at this time, particularly in London, 'we get the overwhelming picture of gin as the instigator of all private and public mischiefs' (1976: 15).

Another potential explanation, the role of the church, also has to be considered carefully. Many members of the temperance movement were Protestants, and they were most commonly members of non-conformist churches, but Christianity's relationship with alcohol is complex. It may be the case that individuals from a non-conformist background were drawn to the temperance movement because they felt that it offered a lifestyle compatible with their religious beliefs. However, with the probable exception of Methodists, many non-conformists did not embrace the cause, nor did many members of the established church.

Religion did play a significant part in the rise of the temperance movement, but this explanation in itself is not sufficient for it fails to explain why the movement gained success at that particular time. Two sociological factors appear to be significant. First, the growth of temperance coincided with a process of industrialisation. It has been argued that employers were perfectly happy to supply farm workers with large amounts of alcohol to help them through their daily toil. In such an environment alcohol could cause little harm. However, in the context of industrialisation, the potential harm that alcohol could cause in the new workplace was greatly magnified. As such, alcohol became less part of the daily norm and people became more aware of its harmful qualities. This was especially true if the alcohol that they were drinking was stronger (Keller 1976).

Another trend was the emergence of a skilled working class. This group were keen to gain respectability in a society that was undergoing rapid and significant change. One way of obtaining respectability was to distance oneself from conduct that was seen as unbecoming. Again one must be careful not to exaggerate; it would be wrong to say that the temperance movement only gathered its support from this social group or that this group gave the organisation its wholehearted support. Yet, this increasingly powerful and militant group did form the bedrock of the movement.

Although the temperance movement's influence diminished from the 1920s it has had significant ramifications on alcohol policy in the UK and elsewhere to this day. Most directly, people now drink far less than they used to. Obviously medical advances and other factors have influenced lifestyle choices considerably but, for being the first mass organisation to warn of the dangers of drink, the temperance movement helped modify drinking patterns considerably. Its influence on nineteenth-century life was far-reaching:

> In the nineteenth century, the issue of temperance penetrated almost every important aspect of life – respectability and deviance, work and play, personal aspirations and political convictions. It affected the lives of our great-grandparents in a way which is now difficult for us to grasp. (Heather and Robertson 2004: 12)

And, whilst alcohol consumption continued to fall after the 1920s along with the temperance movement's direct influence, it would be wrong to say that its enduring legacy had no say on subsequent events.

Secondly, the movement's existence forced a debate about alcohol and alcohol policy. Unfortunately, because of the movement's extreme position, the debate became polarised. What opposition the temperance movement faced was largely supplied by the drinks industry. It became a debate between 'wets' and 'drys', and one which lacked impartial involvement. The nature of the debate had two unfortunate consequences. It meant that discussion on alcohol policy started from a presumption that alcohol was inherently beneficial or detrimental to society. Compromise, rational discussion and impartiality were always going to be hard to obtain. The temperance movement therefore opened, helped define and ultimately limited debate about alcohol and society in the late nineteenth century and throughout most of the twentieth century.

The wars clearly limited concern about alcohol in society and the inter-war years showed a significant reduction in alcohol consumption (Prime Minister's Strategy Unit 2003). In stark terms Britons were drinking 22 per cent less alcohol in 2001 than in 1901, but, if one takes 1951 as the base year, there was a rise in consumption of 121 per cent between then and 2001 (Prime Minister's Strategy Unit 2003: 13). This rise has been attributed to a combination of economic, legal and social factors which increased the availability of alcohol and hence resulted in a rise in consumption. At the same time there was a lack of a pressure group with the impact of the temperance movement to campaign for restrictions on availability. The temperance movement itself lacked its earlier mass support as its central ethos ran counter to the dominant climate of personal freedom (Thom 1999). Although it should not be forgotten that 10 per cent of British adults still choose not to drink alcohol (Prime Minister's Strategy Unit 2003), their motives vary and many abstainers believe that the decision whether to drink is a matter of personal choice. Nevertheless, the overall trend is clear – the per capita rate of alcohol consumption in the UK has risen in the last decade.

Drinking habits in an international context

As well as situating current trends in an historical context, it is important to compare British drinking habits with those in other countries. Many surveys have attempted to quantify the amount of alcohol consumed on average by citizens of different countries. Every year the World Advertising Centre collate the world drink trends from a variety of sources. The following table (adapted from Institute of Alcohol Studies 2005b: 2) shows the recorded per capita alcohol consumption in litres of pure alcohol for a variety of European countries in 2002:

Table 1.1 Per capita alcohol consumption (litres of pure alcohol)

Luxembourg	11.9
Hungary	11.1
Republic of Ireland	10.8
Czech Republic	10.8
Germany	10.4
France	10.3
Portugal	9.7
Spain	9.6
UK	9.6
Denmark	9.5
Austria	9.2
Cyprus	9.1
Slovakia	8.8
Netherlands	8.0
Belgium	7.9
Greece	7.8
Latvia	7.7
Finland	7.7
Italy	7.4
Poland	6.6
Estonia	6.2
Sweden	4.9
Malta	4.9

As well as having comparatively high per capita levels of alcohol consumption in a European context, the British also drink more litres of alcohol per capita than citizens of other English-speaking countries (ibid.: 2):

Table 1.2 Per capita alcohol consumption (litres of pure alcohol)

UK	9.6
Australia	7.3
New Zealand	6.9
Canada	6.9
USA	6.7

However, these per capita studies have the potential to mislead. For example, they would not show that different beverages are being consumed, nor would they differentiate between situations where drinking is spread out equally and situations where drinking is concentrated on a few particular incidents. Researchers have, therefore, sought to explore not just how much is being consumed but the nature both of the drink and of the drinking event.

Traditionally countries have been categorised as 'wet' or 'dry' depending upon the dominant cultural attitude to alcohol. In 'wet' cultures alcohol consumption is a common part of everyday activity. Mediterranean countries, where wine is often served with meals, are the usual examples given of this culture. Other factors common to such cultures are low rates of abstinence, low rates of drunkenness and the easy availability of alcohol. By contrast, 'dry' cultures have more restricted access to alcohol, abstinence is more common, alcohol is less a part of daily life but, when drinking occurs, it is more likely to be excessive and to lead to drunkenness. Northern European countries, and particularly Scandinavian ones, along with the United States and Canada have traditionally shown many of the characteristics of 'dry' cultures.

Some of the recent government proposals relating to alcohol licensing have been justified on a premise that drinking culture can be changed (Department for Culture, Media and Sport *et al.* 2005); effectively it is hoped that, by making alcohol more accessible, people will drink in what is seen to be a more responsible manner.

The data presented earlier in this chapter shows that frequent drinking in the UK is associated with those on comparatively high incomes (Office for National Statistics 2003). These individual's drinking habits are more in line with governmental expectations than those on lower incomes who exhibit more of the characteristics of a 'dry' culture. The new licensing regime (see Chapter 7) is designed to make it easier to drink frequently and will therefore prove attractive to those whose drinking habits already approximate to those found in a 'wet' culture, that is to say the comparatively affluent. Whether the changes prove sufficient to alter the 'binge' drinking habits of some drinkers remains a moot point (Association of Chief Police Officers of England, Wales and Northern Ireland 2005; Royal College of Physicians 2005).

It has been argued that there has been some degree of convergence in drinking habits on an international level. Countries which traditionally drank considerable amounts of wine with meals now drink less (Leifman 2001) whilst 'dry' cultures now drink more wine. What is concerning for policy makers here is that the UK has witnessed one of the most dramatic increases in per capita alcohol consumption in litres of pure alcohol between 1997 and 2002 (adapted from Institute of Alcohol Studies 2005b: 2):

Table 1.3 Increases in per capita alcohol consumption (litres of pure alcohol) 1997–2002

Cyprus	+2.5
UK	+1.4
Republic of Ireland	+1.1
Hungary	+1.0
Finland	+0.9
Latvia	+0.8
Canada	+0.8
Luxembourg	+0.5
Slovakia	+0.5
Czech Republic	+0.3
USA	+0.1

All of the other countries in the main table either witnessed a decrease in per capita alcohol consumption between 1997 and 2002 or there was insufficient data to allow a comparison to be made. It is notable that per capita consumption decreased in a number of traditionally 'wet' cultures: Italy, Greece, France, Spain and Portugal (ibid.: 2).

Gathering meaningful comparative data is fraught with methodological difficulty. Direct questions about how often people drink and how much they consume in say a given week may give an accurate representation of drinking habits in a 'wet' culture where drinking is spread out relatively evenly, but can be less accurate in a 'dry' culture as it can mask the fact that a disproportionate amount of the alcohol was consumed during a limited number of sessions.

Other variables also have to be considered. For example, it is difficult to measure the amount of alcohol consumed because drinks vary both in size and in alcoholic strength internationally. It makes the task easier if respondents are asked questions such as 'how many beers have you had in the last week?' but, as many Brits have woken up to discover, continental beers are often far stronger than those typically found in the UK. Researchers therefore have to balance the need to frame questions that are readily understandable with the need to produce reliable data.

Even once researchers have the raw data, assumptions have to be made. There are many thousands of varieties of alcoholic drink on sale and within beverage-type alcoholic strength varies considerably. It is also difficult to calculate exactly how much was consumed, particularly with drinks poured at home and/or when a number of people were sharing a large bottle of alcohol. These difficulties exist when looking at the domestic data but obviously become compounded when one attempts international comparisons due to both cultural differences relating to drinking habits and to international variations in strength and size of alcoholic drinks.

The World Health Organisation (2000) has recognised these difficulties and has made a number of recommendations, including the need for research to measure not only the overall volume of alcohol consumed but patterns of drinking. It also recommended that, where possible, researchers should adopt a variety of methodologies to compare drinking habits internationally.

Having recognised the difficulties associated with gathering and interpreting international data, it is nonetheless instructive to see how drinking habits in the UK compare with other countries. In terms of frequency of drinking, Hupkens et al. (1993) found that, out of 12 European Union member states, Spain had the highest frequency of drinking for men and Italy for women. Ireland had the lowest frequency rates for both men and women. This finding would confirm that Spain has a 'wet' culture whilst Ireland has a classically 'dry' alcohol culture. A more recent study by Ahlström et al. (2001) found that France had the highest rate of frequency of drinking whilst Finland had the lowest.

Ahlström et al. (ibid.) also found that Italians reported the highest total monthly alcohol consumption. Finland had the lowest total. This contrasts with a study by Leifman (2002) which concluded that the UK had the highest mean alcohol consumption in a study of six European Union member states. Sweden had the lowest mean consumption rates. Despite the government's desire to change British drinking culture, it is suggested that methodological differences between the studies are a more likely explanation for their different conclusions!

What is perhaps less of a surprise from Leifman's research is that the UK has the highest reported rate of 'binge' drinking (ibid.). The lowest rate was found in France. Other studies have shown that 'binge' drinking behaviour still appears to be more commonly found in 'dry' cultures. Wilsnack et al. (2000) concluded that Canadian men and Swedish women were most likely to self-report 'binge' drinking.

Ramstedt and Hope (2004: 5) found that in countries which tradition-ally exhibited many of the characteristics of a 'wet' culture, high frequency of drinking was still common; in Italy, 42 per cent of men and 26 per cent of women drank every day as did 21 per cent of French men and 9 per cent of French women. This compared with 9 per cent of British men and 1.6 per cent of Irish men and 5 per cent of British women and 0.2 per cent of Irish women. However, higher proportions of men and women from 'dry' cultures engaged in 'binge' drinking on at least one occasion a week. Both the British sample (38 per cent of men and 12 per cent of women) and the Irish sample (48 per cent of men and 16 per cent women) reported higher rates than the French (8 per cent of men and 2 per cent of women) or Italian (11 per cent of men and 7 per cent of women) sample.

Surveys also suggest that young British people generally consume more alcohol than their European counterparts (Hibell *et al.* 2000). The figures are striking. Forty-seven per cent of British 15–16 year olds surveyed have drunk alcohol at least 40 times, more than double the percentage of French and more than three times the percentage of Portuguese young people of an identical age (ibid.). This finding certainly lends credence to claims that drinking habits in what traditionally were 'wet' cultures are changing dramatically. It is probable that the differences in consumption rates are explained both by an increase in drinking by British young people and by a decrease in drinking by young people in many other countries.

The UK is certainly not alone in witnessing a rise in problem drinking by young people. According to Lash (2002) the proportion of 14–15 year olds and 16–17 year olds in New Zealand who drank did not change significantly between 1995 and 2000; however, for both age groups, there was a significant increase in both the frequency of drinking and in the amount consumed amongst the drinkers (paragraphs 2.1–2.2). Further evidence that 'binge' drinking is becoming far more common among young New Zealanders is provided by Wilkins *et al.* (2002), who found that the proportion of females aged 15–17 who drank four or more drinks at least once a week had risen from 15 per cent in 1998 to 28 per cent in 2000. The proportion of males in the same age range who drank four or more drinks at least once a week had also increased from 43 per cent in 1998 to 58 per cent in 2000. American data also suggests that there is no decrease in alcohol consumption by young people (Flewelling *et al.* 2004), although it has to be borne in mind that the minimum age for drinking in the United States is 21 and that the category of underage drinkers is correspondingly wider.

Conclusion

This introductory chapter has provided an overview of drinking patterns in the UK generally and in terms of gender, age and ethnicity. It has then compared these figures with regard to both historical drinking patterns and international trends. Although men aged above 24 are drinking similar levels to a decade ago (Office for National Statistics 2003), there have been significant increases in alcohol consumption by young people and by females. This trend runs counter to the experience of most other countries which have seen either a decline in alcohol consumption or a rise of more modest proportions (Institute of Alcohol Studies 2005b).

There are two things to take from this which may, at first glance, appear somewhat paradoxical. First, we have to recognise that this increase in per capita consumption has *the potential* to lead to an increase in a variety of harms. This book is concerned with one of them – crime. There are others which come to mind such as accidents (Hingson and Howland 1993; Raistrick *et al.* 1999; Royal Society for the Prevention of Accidents 1998) – whether generally or specifically related to motor vehicles; physical health problems (Britton and McPherson 2001; Guntjahr *et al.* 2001; World Health Organisation 2002), mental health problems (Institute of Alcohol Studies 2004; Weaver *et al.* 1999), domestic problems (Kroll and Taylor 2002; Velleman and Templeton 2003) and the burden to business caused by absenteeism (Confederation of British Industry 2004; Health and Safety Executive 1998). If there is a causal link between the consumption of alcohol and either aggregate social harm or any specific harm then it is right that we should be concerned by the increases in alcohol consumption.

The related point is that we should be aware that increases in consumption, and the effects of intoxication, lead not to one but to a variety of consequences. In an editorial entitled 'The Yin and Yang of Alcohol Intoxication' (2003: 1021), Graham highlights how alcohol intoxication gives rise to both positive and negative social consequences. Some of these consequences are minor in character while others are anything but. Although most research on alcohol 'treats these two outcomes as separate, unrelated, phenomena' (ibid.: 1021), positive and negative social consequences can co-exist in the same incident. While the remainder of this book is concerned with one of the most significant potential harmful consequences of alcohol intoxication, it is imperative to keep Graham's title in mind so that, in attempting to address this negative outcome, we do not forget that intoxication is not always a problematic phenomenon.

Chapter 2

Alcohol use and crime

This chapter reviews the data on the links between alcohol and crime. It does not seek to look at *why* there might be a link if one is established. Some possible explanations for a link are explored in the next chapter. To many, this chapter will appear unnecessary. Whilst writing this book, I have been met with the frequent response that a link between alcohol and crime is self-evident. As this view is commonly held it is worth speculating on why this view exists.

Research has shown that people are particularly frightened about street crime (Hale 1996; Ross and Polk 2003). Crime occurs in other environments as well – and alcohol may also be a factor in these environments, e.g. in domestic violence – but the enduring perception of the street, especially an urban street at night, is as a place of unpredictability and danger. One unpredictable, threatening, and potentially dangerous aspect of this environment is the possibility of coming across intoxicated individuals. Makkai comments:

> In part, fear of crime comes from perceptions of disorder in the local community. Disorder is a term within criminology that is used primarily to refer to behaviour that is not necessarily criminal but is considered by the community as deviant behaviour . . . Research in the United States has shown that within communities there is agreement on what behaviours are constituted as disorderly, regardless of ethnicity, class or other characteristics. Much of this disorder is perceived to be associated with both licit and illicit drugs. Thus, excessive consumption of alcohol in public places can contribute to disorder, and sometimes violence, that heightens fear of crime. (2001: 86)

In part, of course, this fear is wholly rational. The likelihood of victimisation may be low compared to other types of crime, but the harm if one were victimised in this manner generally would be greater. Criminologists may caution that violence by strangers is relatively low, but we too avoid certain places at particular times for exactly the same reason.

However, the reality according to both official criminal statistics and victim surveys is that street crime is comparatively rare. Objectively people should be more concerned about other types of crime. Similarly one should not always assume that crime committed by intoxicated people is a particularly metropolitan phenomenon. Australian research (Matthews *et al.* 2002) shows that hospitalisations for 'alcohol-caused' assault were far more frequent in non-metropolitan areas than metropolitan areas (6.6 per 100,000 population compared with 3.5 per 100,000 population; ibid.: 2) as were rates of reported serious 'alcohol-caused' assaults (20.7 per 100,000 population compared with 14.5 per 100,000 population; ibid.: 2). In Australia, the Northern Territory, a predominantly rural state, has by far the biggest problem of 'alcohol-related' violence. In 1998–99, one in every 263 adults in the Northern Territory was admitted to hospital with a serious 'alcohol-related' injury, a rate five times higher than the next worse state, Western Australia, and 19 times worse than the Australian Capital Territory which had the lowest rate (Cain 2002).

The public's concern about street crime may be partly explained by the media concentration on reporting violent offences committed by strangers. A study by Williams and Dickson (1993) found that 64.5 per cent of crime stories reported in British newspapers over a one month period in 1989 concerned violent crimes whereas, for the same period, the British Crime Survey found that 6 per cent of crimes involved violence. This imbalance is common. Marsh (1991) reviewed 56 analyses of crime news from 15 different countries and found there to be a consistent over-representation of violent offences. It is noticeable that the British media have recently given considerable attention not only to violent offences but to 'binge' drinking and have often linked it to crime and disorder.

Whilst it is straightforward, if time-consuming, for researchers to show that the media's focus on violence misrepresents the fact that most crime is both minor and property-related, it is more problematic to show what effect, if any, this has on the public's fear of crime (Ditton *et al.* 2004). Most people rely heavily on the media for information on crime (Herz and Kania 2002). Smith (1984) found that 52 per cent of her sample got most of their information from media sources compared to 3.2 per cent who got it from personal experience. Yet, as Reiner comments (2002: 396–397) '[the] armoury of possible research techniques for assessing directly the effects of media images on crime is sparse, and suffers from evident and long-recognised limitations'.

One British study (Williams and Dickinson 1993) did report a relationship between reading newspapers with a particular tendency to focus on violent crime and fear of violent crime but there was no association between reading such papers and subsequent behaviour designed to reduce the possibility of victimisation. However findings are inconsistent. Some studies into newspapers and the fear of crime do find a relationship (for a survey see Ditton *et al.* 1994). Others do not (ibid.). The same is true for studies looking at the link between viewing television and fear of crime (ibid.). We cannot say with any certainty, therefore, that people's perceptions of crime are actually influenced by a selective, and potentially misleading, media concentration on violent offences (Livingstone 1996; Ditton *et al.* 2004).

Even if we do not know the cause, we should recognise that most people intuitively believe that there is a link between alcohol and crime. Light (1994), in a chapter which specifically addresses the link between alcohol and crime, explains the appeal of mono-causal explanations for crime; they are simple to understand, they accord with common sense and they satisfy the media's demand for short explanations.

It is important that researchers and policy makers are aware of this so that they can try and remain as objective as possible for it is possible that they too share popular assumptions. Collins (1981) highlights the danger. He has argued convincingly that there is a pervading 'malevolent assumption' regarding alcohol: if any socially disadvantageous event happens after alcohol has been consumed, it is assumed that alcohol was the direct cause. This assumption may be false; the event may have occurred regardless. In the present context, therefore, one cannot assume that an offence occurred because of the presence of alcohol if the offender had been drinking prior to the incident. It may have happened anyway. There is also the possibility, and this is almost invariably forgotten, that alcohol may *stop* some offences from taking place. The individual, for example, may become too intoxicated to carry out an offence that would otherwise have occurred.

This chapter aims to assess the results and the limitations of empirical studies which have sought to investigate the possible link between alcohol and crime. Due to the enormous international literature on the topic, it has been necessary to be highly selective in my coverage. Unlike some of the later chapters, which are concerned with different legal systems, there has been no deliberate decision to focus on British research. As we are concerned with a universal problem (albeit one with marked regional variations) the studies that are discussed have been selected for the contribution that they make to our understanding of the problem rather than for reasons of geography.

The picture that will emerge is a complex one. Whilst studies consistently document that a very high proportion of offenders had drunk alcohol prior to offending, it remains difficult to find any direct link between alcohol and crime (which should perhaps come as little surprise if one remembers that most drunk people do not commit criminal offences). Anyone who is familiar with the literature might be tempted to follow the advice of the American comedian Henny Young who once said that, when he read about the evils of drinking, he gave up reading.

Alcohol-related crime: a profile

My belief that a book on alcohol and crime was both important and timely came from research I undertook for a comparative collection on legal responses to intoxication (Dingwall 2003). The statistics that I found made alarming reading. To take but one example, evidence to the All Party Group on Alcohol Misuse (1995) from the British Medical Association claimed that alcohol use is associated with 60–70 per cent of homicides, 70 per cent of stabbings, 70 per cent of beatings and 50 per cent of fights or assaults in the home. In Australia, it has been calculated that 'alcohol-caused' violence led to 124 deaths with a total of 4,381 years of lost life and 26,882 hospital bed-days in 1997 (Chikritzhs *et al.* 1999).

The Home Office study into alcohol and violence

The Home Office undertook detailed, specific research into alcohol and violence in 2003 (Budd 2003). The research was based on the results of the 1996, 1998 and 2000 British Crime Surveys. The British Crime Survey interviews a random sample of the population in England and Wales about their experiences of victimisation in the last year. Criminologists believe that the results are more accurate than the official crime statistics which depend upon victims reporting and police recording offences.

In each of these surveys victims of violent offences were specifically asked '[as] far as you know, at the time it happened, was the person/were any of the people who did it under the influence of drink?'. If the victim responded positively the incident was classified as 'alcohol-related'. Incidents which took place in or around licensed premises were also categorised as alcohol-related. This is, as the author admits (ibid.: 1–2), a pragmatic decision but one which is potentially problematic. The determination depends upon both the respondent's interpretation of the question and the respondent's perception of the offender. A subjective determination has to be made both as to what constitutes being 'under the influence of drink' and then, following this, the respondent has to decide whether the attacker met that standard. There are dangers that the latter determination may be unduly influenced by factors such as where the incident took place or how the assailant was dressed. In short the classifications may not be perfect but, as they remain constant, they do allow a comparison to be made between the three surveys to ascertain whether any particular trends emerge from the data.

According to victims' perceptions in the 2000 survey, the offender was 'under the influence of drink' in 40 per cent of violent incidents (ibid.: 2). This proportion varied depending on the relationship between the parties: 53 per cent of incidents where the attacker was not known to the victim occurred where the offender was 'under the influence of drink' compared to 44 per cent of domestic incidents and 36 per cent of assaults involving an acquaintance (ibid.: 2). The 2000 survey showed that 19 per cent of all violent incidents took place 'in or around a pub, bar, or club', a proportion that is consistent with both of the earlier surveys (ibid.: 3). Of the incidents that were classified as 'alcohol-related', about a third involved a stranger, a third involved an acquaintance, a quarter were domestic assaults and a twentieth were muggings (ibid.: 5). The report estimates that 795,000 people were the victim of 'alcohol-related' violence in England and Wales during 1999 (ibid.: 7) and that there were a total of 1,246,000 incidents of 'alcohol-related' violence (ibid.: 5).

Turning to a comparison of the three surveys, Budd (ibid.: 24, Table A2.2) notes a significant fall in the number of 'alcohol-related' incidents of violence reported by each successive sample. Between 1995 and 1999 'alcohol-related' incidents of violence fell by 24 per cent. The most significant drop related to 'alcohol-related' incidents between strangers which fell by 46 per cent. This trend mirrors those observed for 'non-alcohol-related' assaults with the result that the proportion of incidents involving an offender 'under the influence of drink' has remained reasonably constant.

Another useful aspect of the report is the detail that it provides about the nature of 'alcohol-related' violence. As is the case with violent incidents generally, extreme violence was comparatively rare (ibid.: 29, Table A4.6). This does not mean that 'alcohol-related' violence is any less serious than violence inflicted by sober offenders. There is evidence that in domestic violence cases alcohol use is associated with greater injury severity (Martin and Bachman 1998).

According to the study (Budd 2003) most 'alcohol-related' violence involved the victim either being grabbed/pushed (43 per cent of stranger and 49 per cent of acquaintance assaults) or punched/slapped (64 per cent of stranger and 53 per cent of acquaintance assaults: the figures come from a combined sweep of the 1998 and 2000 surveys). Nonetheless a weapon, most commonly a glass or bottle, was 'used' in 19 per cent of 'alcohol-related' incidents involving both strangers and acquaintances (ibid.: 29, Table A4.6). According to the text of the report the victim was not hit by the weapon in a single case, its use had always been threatened (ibid.: 17). This seems remarkable, not least as 12 per cent more strangers and 6 per cent more victims of 'alcohol-related' violence received cuts and scratches than victims in 'non-alcohol-related' incidents despite the proportion of incidents involving weapons remaining the same (ibid.: 29, Table 4.6). Whilst it is true that the types of weapon varied according to whether the offender was 'under the influence of drink', this would not appear to be of particular relevance if the weapons were used to threaten. Generally the physical consequences of an 'alcohol-related' assault were not severe – minor bruising was the most common injury (ibid.: 19) – but 75 per cent of respondents in stranger cases and 81 per cent of respondents in acquaintance cases reported being emotionally affected by the incident (ibid.: 30, Table A5.2).

Incidents of violence by those who had been drinking most commonly occur on weekend evenings or nights (54 per cent of those involving strangers and 61 per cent of those involving acquaintances: ibid.: 27, Table A4.2) or on weekday evenings or nights (33 per cent of those involving strangers and 25 per cent of those involving acquaintances: ibid.). Although the proportion of incidents occurring on weekday evenings or nights is remarkably similar to the proportion of assaults where the attacker was sober (ibid.), there is a very marked discrepancy when it comes to incidents on weekend evenings or nights when only 17 per cent of assaults on strangers by those who had not been drinking alcohol and 5 per cent of assaults between acquaintances who had not been drinking take place (ibid.).

Certain factors were identified which heightened the risk of becoming a victim of 'alcohol-related' violence. First, men were significantly more likely to be victimised than women: men were 5.9 times more likely to become the victim of an 'alcohol-related' incident involving a stranger and 1.9 times more likely to become the victim in an incident involving an acquaintance (ibid.: 25, Table A3.1). With respect to both men and women, younger age groups were most at risk. Both of these findings are consistent with other studies (e.g. Borges *et al.* 1998; Brismar and Bergman 1998; Homel *et al.* 1992). Men aged between 16 and 19 were 11.3 times more likely to be victimised by a stranger and 12.2 times more likely to be victimised by an acquaintance than a man aged 45 or older (ibid.: 25, Table A3.1). The corresponding figures for females in the same age brackets are 31.4 times and 9.7 times more likely (ibid.). A gender difference also emerged with regard to marital status. Men who were single had the highest rates of victimisation from both strangers and acquaintances but, whilst single women also had the highest risk of victimisation from strangers, women who were separated or divorced had the highest risk of victimisation by an acquaintance (ibid.: 9).

Those who were unemployed were 2.6 times more at risk of an 'alcohol-related' attack by a stranger and 3.7 times more likely to be attacked by an intoxicated acquaintance than someone in work (ibid.: 25, Table A3.2).

Finally, the drinking habits of victims appear to be highly relevant, both in terms of the units of alcohol that they consume and in terms of the frequency with which they visit licensed premises. Taking incidents involving strangers by way of example, someone who drinks more than ten units on a typical 'drinking day' is 10.5 times more likely to be victimised than someone who usually drinks between one and four units and 1.9 times more likely to be victimised than someone who drinks nine or ten units (ibid.: 26, Table A3.3). Those who had visited a pub or wine bar on nine or more occasions in the last month were 12.7 times more likely to be assaulted by a stranger than those who had not been at all (ibid.). Those who had visited a nightclub on more than three occasions in the last month were similarly 12.9 times more likely to be the victim of an 'alcohol-related' attack by a stranger than someone who had not frequented a nightclub in that period (ibid.). There is also evidence that 'binge' drinkers are particularly at risk: those who drink alcohol on three or four days a week are actually twice as likely to be assaulted by an intoxicated stranger than someone who drinks every day (ibid.).

One thing is worth bearing in mind about the data. As Levi (1997: 846, n.14) points out 'the risk of street victimisation should be a proportion of the occasions on which people go out'. It might be the case that those over 45 are far more likely to be attacked if they go out *as a proportion of the times they go out* compared to younger age groups. It is hardly surprising that the groups most likely to be in the vicinity of intoxicated people are most likely to be assaulted by them.

Alcohol-related violence in Cardiff

The British Crime Survey measures 'alcohol-related' violence in all locations, but a study into 'alcohol-related' violence and disorder in central Cardiff (Maguire and Nettleton 2003) provides further information about patterns of victimisation in that particular setting. This is of specific interest given the recent Home Office 'blitz' on 'alcohol-related' violence and disorder on the street (Home Office 2004a). The new initiatives (discussed in Chapters 4 and 7) were clearly influenced by the findings of this study. The Cardiff study concentrated on two central police sectors. Data was gathered from police records of incidents in conjunction with records of incidents at the Accident and Emergency department of the hospital which covered the district.

This methodology could be expected to exclude some incidents that would be mentioned by respondents in the British Crime Survey. For example, the police are only likely to be notified of more serious incidents of disorder whilst victims of minor assaults may not report the incident to the police or attend hospital. Similarly, some incidents might be included which would have been excluded by the British Crime Survey. By way of example, some individuals might choose not to mention an incident for which they had received hospital treatment.

Of the incidents recorded, 61 per cent were classified as 'violent' and 39 per cent as incidents of 'disorder' (Maguire and Nettleton 2003: 38). The incidents generally happened in different locations. Violent incidents were over twice as likely to occur inside licensed premises as incidents of disorder (ibid.: 39, Table 3.4). Disorder was more likely to happen outside. As the authors explain, this is hardly surprising; incidents of disorder will frequently be dealt with by staff if they happen inside the venue and, if the offender refuses to leave, the incident will often change in character to one of violence.

In common with Budd's research, the Cardiff study found that 'alcohol-related' incidents of violence and disorder occurred predomi-nantly late on Fridays and Saturdays: 49.6 per cent of all recorded incidents happened between 6pm and 6am on a Friday/Saturday or a Saturday/Sunday (ibid.: 35).

One thing that did differ, and this may in part be explained by the different methodologies employed, was the severity of the injuries received. Although the types of violence inflicted were broadly similar – a glass or bottle was used in an identical 10 per cent of cases – the injuries sustained in the Cardiff study were more severe. 65 per cent of violent incidents resulted in a hospital visit (ibid.: 41). And, whilst 54 per cent of the injuries sustained were minor cuts, bruises or blows, 30 per cent of all those assaulted received 'severe' injuries (ibid: 41). In two cases the injuries were classified as life-threatening.

The police data provides a profile of those arrested for 'alcohol-related' violence and disorder in Cardiff: 90 per cent were white, 88 per cent were male, 72 per cent were aged under 30, 48 per cent had previous convictions and 39 per cent were unemployed (ibid.: 37, Table 3.3; the employment status of 5 per cent of those arrested was not known or unclassified). Less data was available with regards to the profile of victims but again the majority were white, male and aged under 30 (ibid.: 37).

Another recent British study (Richardson and Budd 2003) has sugges-ted that 'binge' drinkers commit a disproportionate number of offences. The authors noted that:

> [Binge] drinkers were almost three times more likely to admit to committing an offence in the previous 12 months than regular drinkers. The difference was particularly marked for fights, with binge drinkers five times more likely to admit to an incident ... Frequency of drunkenness was strongly associated with violent crime and fighting, even after other factors were taken into account ... Frequency of drinking was not associated with any offence, suggesting it is binge drinking rather than frequent drinking *per se* which is important. (ibid.: 2)

The United States Department of Justice study

Studies in other jurisdictions reveal similar patterns. The United States Department of Justice compiled statistical data for the Assistant

Attorney-General prior to a national symposium on alcohol abuse and crime (Bureau of Justice Statistics 1998). On average there were 11.1 million violent victimisations of American citizens aged 12 or over each year between 1992 and 1995. Victims were asked whether they thought that the person who had attacked them had been drinking or using drugs prior to the incident. In the majority of cases (69.3 per cent) the victim claimed to have been able to tell whether or not the person had been drinking or taking drugs (ibid.: 2). Based on these perceptions, about 2.7 million violent crimes took place every year in the US where the victim was sure that the offender had been drinking. In about 0.5 million of these cases the victim believed that the offender was also taking drugs at the time (ibid.: 3). Nearly a quarter of victims of violence, therefore, were certain that the offender had been drinking prior to offending.

When one removes the 30.6 per cent of victims who were not sure whether the offender had been drinking or taking drugs, 37 per cent believed that the offender was using alcohol either alone or in combination with another drug. The victim–offender relationship was highly important. With regard to intimate victims (defined as current or former spouses, boyfriends and girlfriends) 67 per cent believed that the offender had been using alcohol either alone or in combination with other drugs as opposed to 50 per cent of non-marital relatives, 38 per cent of acquaintances and 31 per cent of strangers (ibid.: 3). This finding is supported by statistics from the FBI's National Incident-Based Reporting System. About half of the incidents of violence where it was reported that the offender had been drinking prior to the offence recorded in the 1995 dataset involved intimate victims (ibid.: 8). Of the incidents recorded 6.3 per cent involved child victims under the age of 18 (ibid.: 9). This differs from the British data (Budd 2003) where alcohol-use was more prevalent before attacks on strangers than intimates.

There were also marked differences between offence type in the American study. So that, whilst 65 per cent of the victims of violence who perceived that the offender had committed the offence whilst using alcohol were victims of a simple assault (23 per cent had been victims of an aggravated assault, 7 per cent of a rape or sexual assault and 6 per cent of a robbery; ibid.: 5), the proportion of simple assaults committed by those whose victims thought they had been drinking (25 per cent) was lower than the proportion of both aggravated assaults (28 per cent) and rape/sexual assaults (37 per cent; ibid.: 4). According to the FBI's National Incident-Based Reporting System, 61 per cent of victims of alcohol-related violence received an injury. The figures for male victims (61 per cent) and female victims (62 per cent) were nearly identical but males were more than twice as likely to suffer a major injury (16 per cent compared with 7 per cent; ibid.: 10).

The Australian National Drug Strategy surveys

An Australian study by Makkai (2001), based on the results of three national drug strategy surveys, demonstrated similar results to Budd's (2003) profile of alcohol-related offending in Britain. The surveys took place in 1993, 1995 and 1998 and again had large initial samples (3,500, 3,850 and 10,030 respectively; Makai 2001: 87). Respondents were asked whether they had been the victim of five types of behaviour by people who had been 'affected by alcohol' in the past 12 months. The most recent survey revealed that about a third of the sample had been verbally abused, nearly a quarter had been put in fear, 13 per cent had property damaged, 9 per cent had been physically abused and 6 per cent had property stolen by someone 'affected by alcohol' (ibid.: 91).

As with Budd's (2003) study there was a decrease in all types of victimisation between 1993 and 1998, although the decrease was most marked between the 1993 and the 1995 surveys. Patterns of victimisation were also remarkably similar. Taking the 1998 figures once again, men were considerably more likely to be the victim of verbal abuse from someone 'affected by alcohol' and were more likely to be physically abused or the victim of theft or criminal damage than women (ibid.: 92). Women though were more likely than men to report that they had been put in fear by someone 'affected by alcohol' (ibid.: 92). In common with the British research, those between the ages of 14 and 24 are far more likely to report victimisation than those aged over 25 (ibid.: 93).

Makkai (2001: 92) reports that employed people have a greater probability of experiencing physical and verbal abuse and of being put in fear by a person 'affected by alcohol' than unemployed people. This finding contrasts with the British research which found that unemployed people reported higher rates of victimisation. She attributes this finding to the greater financial freedom enjoyed by those in work and their greater ability to go out. This explanation is consistent with the fact that those with a post-secondary qualification are 'significantly more likely' to be the victim of property damage, verbal abuse and being put in fear by an intoxicated person (ibid.: 95).

Those who engaged in 'binge drinking' were particularly likely to be the victim of an offence committed by someone who had been drinking (ibid.: 97). However, it is noted that this finding should not lead to the conclusion that there is a direct causal link between drinking and alcohol-related victimisation because '[personal] drinking may be associated with other lifestyle behaviours that increase the risk of victimisation' (ibid.: 98).

The Australian surveys also asked respondents if they had engaged personally in any of the listed activities whilst under the influence of alcohol. Unlike the data on rates of victimisation, the data on offending would not suggest that there has been a decrease in alcohol-related offending in Australia between 1993 and 1998. In all of the surveys the majority of respondents claimed never to have committed any of the listed disorders, however, in 1998, 18 per cent self-reported drink-driving, 10 per cent verbally abusing somebody, 3 per cent damaging property and 2 per cent physically abusing somebody (ibid.: 99). Overall, 23 per cent of respondents self-reported at least one of the categories in the past 12 months, whilst 7 per cent reported that they had committed one of the disorders on at least two occasions in the past year (ibid.: 100). Around 3 per cent of the sample self-reported committing between three and six of the listed activities on six or more occasions (ibid.: 104). Based on population estimates, this means that approximately 1,000,000 Australians (roughly the population of Adelaide) aged over 14 commit one of the above disorders on two or more occasions a year (ibid.: 100). Young males self-report the highest rates of alcohol-related disorder (ibid.: 101) and are the group that are most likely to be multiple offenders (ibid.: 105).

So, according to the rather rough-and-ready question put to victims of violence, a high proportion, though usually a minority, reported that the offender had been under the influence of alcohol at the time of the offence. The proportion varied depending upon the relationship between the parties and the nature of the offence charged. How do these victims' perceptions compare with evidence obtained from convicted offenders?

Offender self-report studies

An alternative method of obtaining data is to ask convicted offenders about their drinking habits in the period immediately preceding the offence. This methodology has proved to be very popular and has generated a huge body of research. As we shall see, some studies suffer from a multitude of methodological flaws. To take but one obvious example, many of the earlier studies asked a binary question along the lines of 'had you drunk alcohol in the x hours prior to arrest?'. Such a question fails to discriminate between an individual who drunk a pint of lager x hours before the offence and someone who drunk a bottle of whisky immediately beforehand. The studies referred to in this section are included because they either avoid falling into such methodological traps or because, warts and all, they add something important to our overall knowledge of alcohol and crime.

One of the largest and most important studies of this type drew on data from the US (National Institute of Justice 1991). A sample of 17,753 offenders, of whom 13,143 were male and 4,610 were female, were asked about their use of legal and illegal drugs both generally and in the three days before arrest. In the three days prior to arrest, 59 per cent of males and 47 per cent of females reported using alcohol. No significant difference in alcohol usage was found between different racial groups. The figures for male offenders were broken down according to charge in the following manner:

Table 2.1 Percentage of male offenders who had drunk alcohol in the hours prior to offence type

Offence type	Percentage of male offenders who had drunk alcohol in the 72 hours prior to arrest by offence type
Public disorder	69
Family offence	67
Assault	64
Homicide	64
Sexual assault	60
Weapons	60
Robbery	60
Burglary	60
Drug offences	58
Theft/stolen property	56
Flight/warrant	55
Auto theft	53
Forgery/fraud	51

As the study also considered the offenders' use of other drugs, it allows comment to be made on the types of offence that those who used alcohol only committed compared to those who had not taken alcohol or drugs, those who had taken another type of drug and those who had taken both alcohol and an illegal drug. It is important to note that, although 59 per cent of males reported taking alcohol in the three days prior to arrest, only 19 per cent of the sample reported taking alcohol alone: 19 per cent reported taking both alcohol and cocaine while 21 per cent reported taking both alcohol and another illegal drug. In fact, as 25 per cent of the males in the sample reported not using alcohol but using another illegal drug, a higher proportion of men had used illegal drugs (66 per cent) than alcohol (59 per cent) in the three days prior to arrest.

This statistic though has the potential to mask an important finding. Those who drank and didn't use any other drug committed a disproportionate number of violent offences (a finding replicated elsewhere; e.g. Bureau of Justice Statistics 1998; Farabee et al. 2001). A group which comprised 19 per cent of the sample committed 29 per cent of the offences of violence. The study suggests two things worth noting at this point. Many offenders consume not just alcohol but other drugs in the period prior to offending. This obviously adds a further methodological problem in that it is difficult to separate the effects, or the perceived effects, of alcohol from the other substance or substances taken. Second, certain categories of offence, most notably public disorder offences and offences of violence, appear to be committed disproportionately by offenders who have drunk in the period prior to arrest compared with offenders who have not drunk and compared with offenders who have taken illegal drugs alone or in combination with alcohol.

The Bureau of Justice Statistics (1998) referred to earlier also reviewed data from offenders. About 40 per cent of violent offenders reported that they had been drinking at the time of the offence; a figure almost identical to the victims' perceptions (ibid.: 1998). This proportion is also remarkably similar to victims' perceptions in the British Crime Survey but, as will be shown, is substantially lower than that found in some British studies with offenders (e.g. Jeffs and Saunders 1983). More generally, of the 5.3 million convicted adult offenders in the US who were under the jurisdiction of probation authorities, jails, prisons, or parole agencies in 1996, 36.3 per cent had been drinking at the time of the offence (Bureau of Justice Statistics 1998: 20). On an average day in America, therefore, there were just under two million individuals serving sentences for an offence where alcohol 'had been a factor' (ibid.: 20). This should not, of course, be taken to mean that none of these offences would have occurred were it not for the fact that the offender had been drinking.

The percentages of offenders who had been drinking varied according to both disposition and offence type. Convicted offenders in local jails and adults on probation were more likely to have been drinking than convicted offenders in State or Federal prisons (ibid.: 21). Those who had committed a public order offence or a violent offence were also more likely to have been drinking than property or drug offenders (ibid.: 21).

Regardless of disposition, most offenders who had drunk prior to offending had been drinking beer. However, the amount drunk again differed depending on both disposition and offence type. In the eight hours prior to the offence, probationers consumed an average of 8 beers compared with 11 beers for jail inmates and 15 beers for prisoners. When it comes to offence type, property offenders have the highest average consumption rates amongst probationers, jail inmates and prisoners (ibid.: 22).

The Bureau of Justice Statistics also show an interesting gender difference. Far fewer women than men on probation had been drinking at the time of the offence (25 per cent compared to 41 per cent; ibid.: 36). Similarly, far fewer female local jail inmates had been drinking prior to offending than their male counterparts (29 per cent as opposed to 41 per cent; ibid.: 36). However, female State prisoners report higher levels of intoxication than male State prisoners at the time of the offence (ibid.: 28). This finding may not be as inconsistent as it first appears. State prisoners, it will be recalled, were generally less likely to have used alcohol prior to offending than jail inmates or probationers. The smaller group of drinkers were, however, likely to have drunk more than jail inmates or probationers who had been drinking. It is perfectly possible for a smaller proportion of women to have been drinking but for that proportion to have drunk more excessively than the male drinkers. It is also possible that the difference is sufficient to reverse the order of the overall consumption figures for male and female State prisoners relative to probationers and jail inmates.

A number of other researchers have studied the proportion of American inmates who had drunk prior to offending (e.g. Blount et al. 1994; Collins and Schlenger 1988; Greenfield and Weisner 1995; Holcomb and Anderson 1983; Hollis 1974; Miller and Welte 1986; Spunt et al. 1994; Wieczorek et al. 1990; Wiley and Weisner 1995; Wolfgang and Strohm 1956; Yarvis 1994). Some of these studies (e.g. Wolfgang and Strohm 1956) only considered alcohol consumption whilst others (e.g. Miller and Welte 1986) also looked at the use of other drugs. A number of the studies also looked at the proportion of victims who had been drinking prior to the offence: the proportion generally was between 40–50 per cent (Abel 1987; Abel and Zeidenberg 1985; Goodman et al. 1986; Welte and Abel 1989) although Hollis (1974) found that 74.7 per cent of homicide victims in an eight year period in Tennessee had been drinking prior to their death. Studies in Denmark (Moller-Madsen et al. 1986) and the Netherlands (Kingma et al. 1992) show that rates between 40 per cent and 50 per cent are common internationally (although Shepherd et al. 1989 found that 74 per cent of male victims in a British study had been drinking).

The American studies generally report a lower use of alcohol than that reported in the National Institute of Justice Report (1991). The proportion of offenders who had been drinking is also lower than that commonly found in European studies, particularly those from Scandinavia. This is most probably explained by the fact that generally you have to be older to buy alcohol legally in the US than in Europe and that other forms of drugs are often more readily available in the US. The proportion of offenders in the US who had taken other drugs either alone or in combination with alcohol before offending is notable (Holcomb and Anderson 1983; Miller and Welte 1986; National Institute of Justice 1991; Yarvis 1994). Finally, it would appear from both victim surveys and offender surveys that a decreasing share of violent crime is attributable to offenders who had been drinking prior to the offence being committed (Greenfeld and Henneberg 2001).

Canadian studies also traditionally reported comparatively low rates of alcohol consumption by offenders prior to the offence. For example, Tardif (1968) reported that 27 per cent of violent offenders had consumed alcohol whilst Gerson (1978) put the figure at 35 per cent. Two trends in the Canadian statistics though give cause for concern. First, more recent studies show that a far greater proportion of offenders had been drinking. For example, Loza and Clements (1991) found that 71 per cent of a (comparatively small) sample of incarcerated offenders had been drinking prior to the offence. Secondly, studies have also shown that a comparatively high proportion of Canadian offenders have taken drugs other than alcohol either in isolation or in combination with drink (Lightfoot and Hodgins 1988).

British research has often shown higher rates of alcohol consumption. Jeffs and Saunders (1983) study to ascertain the proportion of offenders in an English seaside town who had drunk in the four hours prior to arrest provides an interesting contrast. The results are summarised in the following table:

Table 2.2 Percentage of offenders who had drunk alcohol in the four hours prior to arrest by offence type

Offence	Per cent reporting alcohol intake
Criminal damage	88
Breach of the peace	83
Assault	78
Theft	41
Miscellaneous	37
Burglary	26
TOTAL	64

Cookson (1992) undertook research with 24 randomly selected offenders in each Young Offender Institution in England. Part of each interview dealt with whether the respondent had been drinking at the time of the current offence as well as the offender's general drinking habits. Of the total sample of 604, 25 per cent said that they had been drunk at the time of the current offence and a further 16 per cent said that they had been drinking but were not drunk. A total of 41 per cent had therefore been drinking. These percentages were broadly comparable to those in an earlier study by the Young Offender Psychology Unit (Thornton *et al.* 1990) as well as more recent Home Office research (Richardson and Budd 2003). Cookson (1992: 353) found a significant association between claiming to be under the influence and a violent current offence, again replicating the earlier study (Thornton *et al.* 1990). This finding is also consistent with the National Institute of Justice (1991) study in the US (and also in the American context with the Bureau of Justice Statistics 1998 and Farabee *et al.* 2001) and with Jeffs and Saunders. It is also consistent with figures from a 1977 Australian Senate Standing Committee Report (Mason and Wilson 1989) and other Australian research (White and Boyer 1985; Taylor 1988).

Those who claimed to have been drinking were also asked how much and what they had been drinking prior to committing the offence. The totals were then converted into standard units of alcohol. Those claiming to have been drunk had consumed a mean of 20.06 units as compared to a mean of 11.51 for those who had been drinking but were not drunk. In terms of the type of alcohol that had been consumed, Cookson (1992: 355) found that it was the excessive drinking of spirits which distinguished the violent offenders in the sample from the acquisitive offenders; the excessive consumption of beer, cider or lager merely distinguished the drunk group from the drinking group. Cookson's study also found no significant association between habitual drunkenness and the number of previous convictions for offences of violence however there was a significant positive association between habitual drunkenness and acquisitive offences.

All of these studies consider alcohol use by those either arrested or convicted of criminal offences. An Australian study by Ireland and Thommeny (1993) adopted a different approach and measured instead police officers' assessment of alcohol involvement in all incidents. Whilst this could perhaps be criticised for involving subjective determinations, what the officers were being asked to determine was no different to the type of questions asked in victim surveys. In the officers' view, 77 per cent of street offences involved alcohol. Such a methodology is interesting as it would be useful to know if the police are more or less likely to arrest individuals in such situations.

There are dangers in drawing direct comparisons between the studies as the offences are categorised differently – criminal damage, for example, would come under the miscellaneous heading in the National Institute of Justice (1991) research. Not all of these studies had a distinct category for sexual offences, however studies of sexual offenders have shown that a high proportion had drunk prior to the offence (e.g. Cordner *et al.* 1979). A related problem is that differences in the criminal law between different jurisdictions mean that even where the categories look identical they may not be. The time scale also varies between the studies. Finally, some studies differentiate between those who drank and those who drank and had taken another form of drug as well. Yet, despite these notes of caution, a surprisingly consistent overall pattern emerges: a far higher proportion of those who had committed criminal damage, public disorder or violent offences reported drinking prior to arrest than those who committed property or other offences.

Comparing official crime statistics and alcohol consumption statistics

Studies which analyse the relationship between regularly collected data series, such as crime statistics and alcohol consumption statistics, are highly useful for the reasons outlined in a report by the United States Department of Heath and Human Services (2000: 55):

> [When] data are collected regularly over time, studies can reveal such associations as two variables rising and falling in synchrony. Demonstrations of this kind of relationship would provide more persuasive evidence of an underlying causality than, for example, the finding of a one-time connection among variables through a cross-sectional study.

This type of study has been particularly favoured in the US but one of the most important British studies also adopted this approach. Field (1990) analysed the link between recorded offences of violence in England and Wales since the Second World War and rates of alcohol consumption. He found that there was a strong relationship between the growth in beer consumption by volume and the growth in recorded offences of violence. However, when he substituted other consumption variables, such as total alcohol consumption, no corresponding relationship was found (ibid.: 48; compare with Lenke 1982 who found a correlation between aggregate alcohol consumption in a Scandinavian study and with Parker and Cartmill 1998 who found a general correlation in the US).

Field's study raises the intriguing question of why there is a correlation between offences of violence and beer but not between offences of violence and alcohol generally? One possible explanation which Field puts forward is that beer may be drunk in a different setting to other forms of alcohol. It might be the case, for example, that beer is drunk more frequently in pubs and clubs whilst other types of alcohol are consumed at home. However, when Field tested this hypothesis by adding the growth in the number of off-licences and the growth in the number of on-licences since the war as additional variables, he found no correlation (ibid.: 49). In conclusion he ruled out the possibility of a direct causal link between alcohol and crime:

> The most convincing explanation of these findings is that, although the consumption of alcohol itself is not a cause of violent crime, the drinking activities of particular social groups – those who drink beer – probably combined with a particular set of social circumstances, may be a factor in offences against the person. (ibid.: 49)

Field's findings differed from the results of an American study by Parker and Cartmill (1998). Here the researchers conducted a time-series analysis of annual homicide rates (unlike Field who used the annual statistics for offences of violence) and annual estimates of beer, wine and spirits consumed between 1934 and 1994. They found that there was a general link between rates of alcohol consumption and homicide, although the link was stronger with whites than with non-whites. Unlike Field, Parker and Cartmill found that homicide rates appeared to be unconnected to beer consumption but were related to the consumption of spirits and wine, though in different ways. Homicides by white offenders rose with increases in the amount of spirits consumed but *decreased* as wine consumption increased. This again raises the obvious question of why different types of alcoholic beverage have different relationships to crime patterns.

Another American study (Cook and Moore 1993a; 1993b) used data collected over both time and different locations to ascertain if there was a link between alcohol consumption and reported assaults, homicides, rapes and robberies. Data on alcohol sales, state-level beer taxes and crime reports from 48 states between 1979 and 1998 were pooled. The authors concluded that there was a statistically significant relationship between alcohol consumption and assault, rape and robbery but, unlike Parker and Cartmill (1998), found no significant link between alcohol consumption and homicide. Australian research has also generally found a statistically significant link between alcohol consumption and levels of violence (Stevenson *et al.* 1999; Stockwell *et al.* 1998).

It will be recalled that Field's (1990) study found no statistically significant relationship between the number of licensed premises and the number of reported offences of violence in England and Wales. Parker and Rebhun (1995) reviewed the data from 256 large American cities to see if there was a link between the number of stores selling alcohol per 1,000 of the population and the reported homicide rate. This methodology obviously excludes on-licenses. A number of other variables such as poverty and racial composition were controlled for. The data for 1960, 1970 and 1980 was analysed but only in 1970 was there a statistically significant link. One issue which both of these American studies (Cook and Moore 1993a; 1993b; Parker and Rebhun 1995) raise is why the link between alcohol availability and/or consumption and homicide appears to be weaker than less serious forms of violent offence despite the fact that offender self-report studies would suggest that a similar proportion of offenders had been drinking prior to the offence (National Institute of Justice 1991; United States Department of Health and Human Services 2000).

Occasionally policy changes mean that criminologists are afforded a rare opportunity to witness the effect that a change will have on crime. This has occurred, for example, with regards to a period in New Zealand history when the death penalty was or was not in operation (Walker 1991). A similar natural experiment arose in the village of Barrow, Alaska. Over the course of three years, the citizens voted first to ban alcohol, then to withdraw the ban and then to reimpose it. It was reported (Chiu *et al.* 1997) that the initial ban led to a significant decrease in the number of accident and emergency cases at the local hospital, including those which arose out of violent offences. When the ban was lifted, the level of accident and emergency visits returned to the original level. When the ban was reintroduced the level fell once again. The results of this study were stark, but a degree of caution is required. Barrow is a small, remote community and there are questions about the extent to which the experience there 'should be generalised beyond the particular culture and social setting in which the study was done' (United States Department of Health and Human Services 2000: 61).

The Alaskan study demonstrated a decrease in hospitalisations for assault following a policy of restricting alcohol availability. Smith and Burvill (1987) studied the effects of increasing alcohol availability to young people. They surveyed the effects of reducing the legal age to 18 in three Australian states and found that, in two of the states male juvenile crime increased by between 20–25 per cent. Data for the third state was more limited, but again suggested a sizable increase in juvenile crime. A British study (Duffy and De Moira 1996) also found that reported offences of violence increased at the same time as a change in the licensing law, but cautioned that any causal relationship is purely speculative. After reviewing a number of studies, Cook and Moore (1993b) concluded that interventions that reduce alcohol availability may also reduce violent crime. Research from jurisdictions which liberalised their licensing laws will be reviewed in the last chapter when the current government plans are being assessed.

The criminal histories of those with alcohol problems

Another approach which researchers have taken is to look at whether those with recognised alcohol problems have disproportionately bad criminal histories. In a study of 269 people who had been admitted to an alcohol-rehabilitation unit in the Western Cape in South Africa, 104 (39 per cent of the sample) had criminal convictions (Allan et al. 2001). Most of these offences had occurred when the individual had been drunk. The authors of the study also considered the types of offence that had been committed and found that the most frequent group, perhaps unsurprisingly, were driving-related offences (where 17 per cent of the sample had convictions) followed by offences of violence (where 15 per cent of the sample had convictions). With regard to the latter, they found that violent crime was associated with a particularly early onset of initial, regular and problem drinking and with maternal alcohol abuse.

A Swedish study (Bergman and Brismar 1994) studied a group of 53 men who were undergoing an alcohol detoxification programme. Fifty-seven per cent of the sample said that they had been physically violent towards another person and 86 per cent of these incidents had occurred when the offender was drunk. Whilst this figure is far higher than the

South African study, this can partly be explained by differences between the studies. Allan *et al.* (2001) considered convictions whilst Bergman and Brismar asked the sample about incidents rather than incidents which had resulted in a conviction. Many violent incidents do not result in a conviction for a variety of reasons ranging from the lack of a report to the authorities to a technical acquittal in a court of law.

Neither of these studies differentiated between different types of problem drinkers unlike Platz (1994) who compared the criminal histories of two groups of problem drinkers: 41 men who were receiving treatment after having committed a criminal act and 55 men who had been voluntarily admitted to a forensic hospital because of alcohol-dependency. Both groups had committed a disproportionate amount of offences compared with the general population, however, the group who were receiving treatment in connection with an offence had committed two to three times the number of offences that the other group had committed, depending upon the nature of the offence.

O'Farrell and Murphy (1995; see also Murphy and O'Farrell 1996; Murphy *et al.* 2001) also found that half of their sample of men undergoing treatment for alcoholism had been violent towards an intimate partner in the year before they commenced their treatment. They found that incidents of domestic violence decreased significantly if the individuals successfully completed their treatment and received marital therapy.

Dar *et al.* (2002) studied the case notes of 200 consecutive attendees at a Community Drug Treatment Unit in outer London. The primary purpose of the study was to compare ethnicity, patterns of substance misuse and criminality amongst White and Asian patient populations. The researchers found that the Asian sample contained more opiate users than the White sample, and that the Asian sample reported lower levels of alcohol consumption than the White sample. It was also found that the Asian sample reported lower rates of criminal activity than the White sample. One does not know to what extent the lower rates of criminality reported by the Asian sample can be explained by that group's lower alcohol consumption and to what extent it is explained by other factors.

That problem drinkers have worse criminal histories than the general population may, however, not take us very far forward. It may be the case that problem drinkers are not representative of the general population. If, for example, problem drinkers are more likely to come from a background that increases the likelihood of criminality then factors other than their drinking may explain their abnormal criminal histories. Collins and Schlenger (1988) found that there was no significant association between a diagnosis for alcohol abuse or dependence and incarceration for a violent offence amongst convicted male offenders in North Carolina. Indeed there was a stronger association between light to moderate drinking and incarceration for a violent offence.

Taking account of other variables

One objection that can be raised to all of the above studies is that they test the linkage between two factors – alcohol and crime. However (United States Department of Health and Human Services 2000: 55):

[An] apparent relationship between two variables may actually be caused by a third, unknown factor. Thus, studies that attempt to establish causality must not only determine the timing of events, but also identify and measure the effects of any intervening factors that may have affected the outcome.

It is essential then to consider whether there are other factors common to individuals who are more likely to offend and drink excessively. Studies have shown (Hawkins *et al.* 1992; Farrington and Loeber 1999; Gottlieb *et al.* 1990) that those with an increased rate of offending and an increased rate of alcohol consumption share certain common characteristics. Young people who are socially disadvantaged, come from dysfunctional families and whose own parents have a history of deviancy have increased rates both of offending and of drinking more than average. Poldrugo (1998) has similarly argued that people with learning difficulties are over-represented in the prison system and are also more likely to have alcohol problems. There are also further complications if individuals with mental health problems drink and offend (Russell 1993).

It is also important to remember that, if the sample is drawn from arrestees or convicted offenders, the potential interaction is not just between alcohol and offending but between alcohol, crime and the criminal justice system. For example, alcohol use may affect the probability of detection (Ensor and Godfrey 1993) or that the incident is reported. The danger of just looking at two factors is that the drinking may mask other more important correlations such as those listed above.

Lipsey *et al.* (1997) reviewed 129 studies concerned with the link between alcohol and crime published between 1950 and 1994. The studies generally concluded that alcohol use preceded a high proportion of violent offences and that this was particularly marked with domestic violence. However, when the authors considered those studies which included a number of control variables, they found that the inclusion of these variables weakened the apparent relationship between alcohol and crime. For example, 14 studies on criminal violence had data on control variables and in six of these studies there was no statistically significant relationship between alcohol and the offence after the influence of these variables were taken into account. Even once these variables were taken into account, there was a statistically significant association between alcohol and domestic violence in 11 out of the 13 studies which took account of other variables.

Two studies from New Zealand have attempted to take account of these additional factors. Fergusson *et al.* (1996) analysed a sample of 16 year olds and found that those who abused or used alcohol in a hazardous manner were five to six times more likely to say that they had committed either property or violent offences than those who did not drink in such a manner. It would be easy when faced with such a statistic to come to the conclusion that there was a very direct link between alcohol and crime. However, when the researchers introduced some of the further variables listed above they found that the odds ratios between alcohol abuse and crime ranged between 1.4 and 3.2. This is far less of an association than the first figure, but still demonstrated a heightened risk which, again, was most marked for violent offences.

The second New Zealand study (Fergusson and Horwood 2000) looked at the relationship between crime and alcohol abuse in a birth cohort of over 1,000 people born in Christchurch in 1977. They were asked about the period when they were aged between 15 and 21 years. Depending on their age at the time, between 5 per cent and 20 per cent of the sample admitted committing either an offence of violence or a property offence. Information was also collected about a range of other factors that may be associated with alcohol abuse and crime, such as measures of family socio-economic background. After undertaking a sophisticated fixed-effects regression analysis, Fergusson and Horwood concluded (ibid.: 1533) that much of the apparent link between alcohol and crime could be attributed to factors associated with both alcohol abuse and crime but that, even after these factors were taken into account, alcohol abuse was still significantly related both to violent offences and to property offences. One of the advantages of this study is that it used two regression methods with different strengths and weaknesses yet the conclusions were remarkably similar. As the authors conclude:

> This . . . provides generally compelling evidence for the view that it is unlikely that the relationship between alcohol abuse and crime is due solely to the effects of confounding factors. The results suggest that increasing alcohol abuse is associated with increasing rates of crime with every symptom of alcohol abuse being associated with in the region of a 1.1–1.2-fold increase in rates of crime. (ibid.: 1534)

Conclusion

A multitude of studies from various jurisdictions have shown that a high proportion of offenders have drunk alcohol before offending. This is particularly marked for some offences, not all of which are serious in nature (e.g. criminal damage), but, generally speaking the proportion of offenders who had been drinking is higher for violent offences than for property offences. This finding cannot be ignored and it is right that policy makers consider ways of reducing such offending through prevention measures and through effective policing strategies (see Chapter 4). At the same time though this finding tells us little, if anything, about the nature of the link between alcohol and crime. Such a link may be deeply rooted in the popular contemporary psyche but needs further investigation. The next chapter will consider some explanations that have been offered by academics and by offenders themselves for the impact that drinking has on subsequent behaviour.

Chapter 3

Explaining the frequent coexistence

The previous chapter reviewed a number of studies which ostensibly would suggest that alcohol consumption and crime are somehow linked. But one has to be careful in ascribing direct causality. Just because, for example, a high proportion of offenders had drunk alcohol prior to the offence does not mean that we can categorically conclude that alcohol consumption leads directly to offending. Such a conclusion is patently flawed as offending behaviour does not follow the majority of incidents where alcohol is consumed. Similarly many offences are committed by those who have not drunk alcohol. The link, if one does indeed exist, is therefore complex.

Unsurprisingly, a number of potential explanations for the comparatively high rates of alcohol use before offending have been offered, both by academics and by offenders themselves in interviews or in mitigation in court (for further information see Chapter 6). This chapter will review a number of them. It will start with a consideration of some of the academic explanations before looking at some of the accounts offered by offenders who had been drinking.

Academic explanations

Given the multitude of explanations that have been offered it is useful to have some kind of framework for the ensuing discussion. Commentators have adopted different frameworks for categorising explanatory theories. Graham (1980), for example, distinguished between direct cause theories, indirect cause theories, motivational theories and predispositional-situational factor theories, even though he recognised that these categories were not necessarily mutually exclusive. By way of contrast,

Rumgay (1998) distinguished between substance-focussed theories, dispositional theories and situational theories. Whichever scheme one adopts is problematic as there is a real danger of oversimplification and arbitrariness. The approach taken here starts with a general consideration of the research methodologies employed to research whether alcohol consumption is causally linked to offending. As will be seen, rather than testing the link between alcohol and crime (a legally defined concept), research has tended to focus on the link between alcohol consumption and aggression. Even if research suggested that there was a link between alcohol consumption and aggression, we would need to then consider the link between aggression and criminality.

Research on alcohol and aggression

By far the most common form of research involves clinical experimentation. The participant is typically told that he or she is in competition with a fictional opponent. In order to win the competition, the participant can subject the 'opponent' to a number of objectively unpleasant experiences such as an electric shock. The researchers can assess the participant's levels of aggression by measuring both the frequency with which the participant was prepared to administer the unpleasant experience and/or the intensity of the experience. A frequently used measure is the Point Subtraction Aggression Paradigm. The fictitious contest in this type of experiment is the accumulation of money. This can be achieved either by amassing money yourself or by taking money away from the 'opponent'. The researchers provoke the participants periodically by taking money from their 'accounts' and the number of times that the participant retaliates by taking money from the 'opponent' is used to measure the participant's aggression. This methodology has demonstrated that, when provoked in this manner, offenders convicted of violent offences demonstrate more aggressive tendencies than college students (Wolfe and Baron 1971) or those convicted of non-violent offences (Cherek et al. 1996).

It has also been used on many occasions to assess whether alcohol is likely to make someone react in a more aggressive manner. One of two methodologies is typically employed: the placebo design or the balanced placebo design (Bushman and Cooper 1990). In the former, all of the participants are told that they will be given alcohol, although some of the participants will in fact be given a non-alcoholic beverage. Some studies modify this approach by informing some of the participants that they will be given a non-alcoholic drink, which they are then given. By comparing the placebo group with this subgroup, researchers can measure the impact of alcohol-related expectancies on aggression.

The balanced placebo design differs in that half of the group who are told that they will be given alcohol and half of the group who are told that they will not be drinking alcohol are given alcohol. The remaining half are given a non-alcoholic drink. This methodology allows a comparison to be drawn between the group who do not believe that they are drinking alcohol when they are (the 'antiplacebo' condition) and the group who believe they are not drinking alcohol and who are not drinking alcohol. Such a comparison allows researchers to measure the pure pharmacological effect of alcohol on aggression.

Bushman and Cooper (1990) reviewed the results of 30 studies that used the Point Subtraction Aggression Paradigm to assess whether there was a link between alcohol consumption and aggression. Although the findings of the studies were mixed, they concluded that alcohol consumption does increase aggression. They did however caution that this finding was not universal. Some studies did not arrive at this conclusion and, even when studies concluded that there was a statistically significant link, not all individuals acted in a more aggressive manner after consuming alcohol.

One factor which may be relevant is that the Point Subtraction Aggression Paradigm, along with some other methodologies, measures responses to detrimental actions made by a fictional opponent. What it therefore measures is how individuals react when they have been provoked. As a consequence, studies which use this methodology may demonstrate that those who drink alcohol are more likely to react aggressively *if they are provoked* (Bennett et al. 1969; Bushman 1999; Lipsey et al. 1997).

Studies which have employed methodologies which are not intrinsically provocative though have sometimes arrived at similar conclusions, suggesting that the existence or the degree of provocation may not be crucial factors. For example, a study by Wieczoerek and Welte (1994) found that there was a link between the extent of the attacker's intoxication and the severity of injury inflicted. A similar correlation between levels of intoxication and degree of injury in domestic violence cases has also been reported (Fagan et al. 1983; Leonard and Quigley 1999; Martin and Bachman 1997; Stets 1990).

Not all research, however, supports such a link. There is, for example, research to suggest that such a link is not marked with regards to adolescents (Osgood 1994; for possible explanations see Huang et al. 2001) – a highly criminogenic group who are also drinking far more prevalently than previously (see Chapter 1). Similarly, despite laboratory research which suggests that intoxication impacts on aggression in a similar way for men and women (Bond and Lader 1986; Bushman and Cooper 1990; Dougherty et al. 1996), outside of this setting there would appear to be sizeable differences (Giancola and Zeichner 1995; Gustafson 1991; Rohsenow and Bachorowski 1984).

Hoaken and Pihl's (2000) research into the effects of alcohol intoxication on aggressive responses in men and women came to some interesting and thought-provoking conclusions. They found, unsurprisingly in light of the studies mentioned above, that intoxicated men acted more aggressively than sober men. There was also little difference between the responses of intoxicated and sober women but what was surprising was why this was the case. It was not because intoxicated women failed to act in an aggressive manner when provoked but because sober women reacted in a manner which was wholly unanticipated: '[both] groups acted with considerable aggression in response to provocation, and did not differ from intoxicated males' (ibid.: 474). The least aggressive group in this study were sober men, a surprising finding given the fact that violent offending is carried out predominantly by males.

There are a number of interesting questions raised by these findings. Perhaps most fundamentally, why did the women react differently to alcohol than men? The authors cite a study by Bettencourt and Miller (1996) which concluded that the nature and intensity of any provocation was the most important predictor of female aggression. According to Hoaken and Pihl:

[Inconsistencies] in the literature may be the result of the various experimental paradigms used, in that some may be more provocative than others. In the present study, for example, the fictitious opponent moves rather abruptly from a series of 'low provocation' shocks to considerably more provocative attacks, regardless of the behaviour of the participant. As such, the paradigm is clearly physically provocative, and retaliatory aggression may be considered 'justified'. (2000: 475)

Therefore, there may not be any contradiction in the studies if it is accepted that provocation is the primary predictor of female aggression and if the studies differ in the extent to which participants are provoked. Studies, such as this, where aggression appears high for women regardless of whether they had drunk alcohol, can be explained on the basis of the type of provocation inherent in the methodology. Similarly, studies which use less provocative methodologies can be expected to find lower rates of female aggression. Studies which use particularly provocative methodologies therefore are likely to find less difference between the rates of aggression for sober and intoxicated women due to the fact that sober women are more likely to react aggressively to provocation of this nature than sober men.

Attempts then to find a causal link between alcohol and aggression in a laboratory setting have met with mixed results, even if several meta-analyses have concluded that such a link is generally consistent with research findings (Bushman and Cooper 1990; Hull and Bond 1986; Taylor and Leonard 1983; Steele and Southwick 1985). One obvious question is the extent to which results from clinical experiments equate to the 'real life' situations where acts of violence and disorder occur. A more immediate concern though is to explain both this general conclusion, and why it is not universal.

Pharmacological explanations

There is no doubt that the pharmacological properties of alcohol (or more specifically ethanol) produce a range of physiological changes in the brain, central nervous system and hormonal systems, and that these are complex and non-specific in character. What has to be assessed is whether these physiological and cognitive changes (Gibbs 1986; Pernanen 1991; Steele and Joseph 1990) are more likely to make an intoxicated individual act in an aggressive manner. Contrary to popular claims (Rumgay 1998), it is not appropriate to talk of direct causation, save in the most extreme of cases:

> No psychoactive drug itself is a 'cause' of complex human behavior; yet any drug is likely to modify that complex behavior, although such modification need not be constant over time, since processes of adaptation, sensitisation, interaction, and the like occur. Insofar as drugs are administered which allow 'normal' behavior to continue, the role of a compound is necessarily but one element affecting that behavior; as dosage increases such that visible limitations on the behavior repertoire occur (e.g. motor decrement, reduced information processing, sedation, coma, death), the contribution of the drug is seen to be the greater ... [The] observer interested in complex events, as, for example, interpersonal violence, will have the task of identifying and measuring more modest effects, those that interact with neurophysiological processes as well as social behaviors. (Blum 1981: 113)

Alcohol is, by turns, a stimulant and a sedative. After the consumption of alcohol, there is an increase in blood alcohol concentration (BAC) followed by a subsequent decrease in BAC. During the initial increase, the alcohol has a stimulating effect. However, when the BAC subsequently decreases, the alcohol has a sedative effect (Martin *et al.* 1993). Higher levels of aggression are shown during the first stage than in the second stage of the process (Giancola and Zeichner 1997).

If we consider the methodological techniques outlined in the previous section, we can see that, for there to be a convincing pharmacological explanation, one would need to find statistically significant results from studies which sought to measure the pure pharmacological effects of alcohol on aggression. These studies would have adopted a balanced placebo design for the reasons outlined above. Bushman and Cooper

(1990) found that the average effect size for studies employing this methodology in their analysis was 0.06 and, as this was not statistically different from zero, they concluded that there was no evidence to suggest that the pharmacological effects of alcohol directly affects levels of aggression.

Psychopharmacological explanations

A body of research (e.g. Chermack and Giancola 1997; Ito *et al.* 1996; Parker and Auerhahn 1998; White and Gorman 2000) has considered some of the other possible ways in which the use of alcohol could make the commission of an offence more likely. Given the finding that intoxicated people are likely to act in a more aggressive manner if they have been provoked (Bushman 1997; Lipsey *et al.* 1997), it is worth considering why this might be the case. The suggestion (Ito *et al.* 1996) is that intoxication leads to impaired communication which, in turn, makes individuals both more likely to give offence and more likely to take offence. When situational factors, such as a noisy bar, are included then the problem is further compounded.

Psychologists have studied the effect of alcohol on executive cognitive functioning (ECF). Baddely and Della Sala (1997) have defined ECF as a subset of cognitive capacities including abstract reasoning, self-monitoring and the ability to take cognisance of external feedback. Phil *et al.* (2003) reported that alcohol consumption affected ECF both during the initial stage after consumption when there was an increase in the BAC and subsequently when the BAC decreased. In the context of criminal behaviour, it has been argued that low ECF accounts for the apparent relationship between alcohol consumption and aggression (Hoaken *et al.* 1998). However, Phil *et al.* (2003) found that ECF was actually lowest when the BAC was decreasing, which would appear to conflict with findings that levels of aggression are highest during the first stage (Giancola and Zeichner 1997).

Another possibility is that intoxication has the effect of making individuals take greater risks than normal. This theory has a lot of popular currency and is used in a variety of situations as an explanatory factor for supposedly abnormal behaviour. To take one example, it is commonly accepted that people are more likely to engage in risky sexual behaviour after consuming alcohol.

Expectations regarding behaviour

The problem with all of the above is that the effect could be attributed to the intoxication or, alternatively, the behaviour could stem from an expectation about how intoxicated people behave. Individuals have beliefs about the effects of drinking and about the possible outcomes of drinking. Goldman *et al.* (1987) have argued that these expectancies develop through a process of vicarious learning and other conditioning mechanisms, indeed children as young as six years old have been found to articulate alcohol expectancies that are similar to those of adults (Miller *et al.* 1990). There is debate about the exact role of expectancies. Goldman and Rather (1995) argue that expectancies are stored as memory processes. A more complicated account is offered by Oei and Baldwin (1994). They believe that there is a two stage process:

> The early, or acquisition, phase of drinking behavior is seen as dominated by controlled processing, during which alcohol expectancies are acquired by the process of instrumental learning and decisions to drink or not to drink are made on the basis of these expectancies. Repeated association of drinking behavior with internal and external cues, however, produces classical conditioning of the response to the stimulus, such that decisions to drink no longer require conscious effortful thought but become incorporated into an automatic process. In this maintainance phase of drinking behavior, specific expectancies about reinforcement from drinking are no longer open to conscious scrutiny and refutation. (ibid.: 525)

Research generally suggests that expectations regarding drinking outcomes are highly significant (Connors and Maisto 1988; Goldman *et al.* 1987; Hull and Bond 1986; Leigh 1989). A number of studies have shown that individuals who believed that they had been drinking acted in a manner associated with someone who had drunk alcohol, even when they had been given a placebo (Evans 1986; Goldman *et al.* 1987). However, this finding has not been universal. In their meta-analysis, Bushman and Cooper (1990) found that the data did not support a statistically significant link between expectancy and aggression. Nonetheless, Rohsenow, amongst others, has been prepared to assert that:

> [Mere] belief that alcohol has been administered is sufficient to result in loss of control and craving in alcoholics and changes in social anxiety, aggression, sexual arousal, and mirth in social drinkers, independent of actual consumption. (1983: 752)

Rohsenov cited aggression as one area in which there was a relationship between drinker expectations and displayed aggression. Other researchers have supported this conclusion (e.g. Lang *et al.* 1975). Research has also suggested that high-risk drinkers have different expectancies about alcohol than low-risk drinkers (McMahon *et al.* 1994; Oei *et al.* 1998).

So-called 'expectation theory' also helps bolster a number of competing explanations as to why alcohol may lead to crime:

Expectancy theory has particular advantages for the different theoretical approaches ... Firstly, the variability of intoxicated behaviour may be explained by postulating expectancies, themselves modified by dose, setting and individual differences, as mediating factors between consumption and response. Secondly, learned expectancies may explain the links between prior life experiences and later alcohol-related behaviour. Thirdly, the significance of situational factors for alcohol-related behaviour may derive from learned associations, or expectancies. (Rumgay 1988: 44)

However, assuming it could be established that expectations do indeed affect how people act after they drink alcohol, it does not offer a complete explanation as individuals tend to react differently to alcohol on different occasions; why do some incidents involving alcohol result in an aggressive outcome whilst others involving the same individual do not (Maisto *et al.* 1981; Steele and Southwick 1985)? For this it is worth considering the explanations offered by offenders themselves.

Offender explanations

A number of studies of convicted offenders have employed qualitative methodologies in order to try and explore how offenders who had been drinking prior to the offence accounted for their subsequent behaviour. Those engaged in this type of research believe that quantitative studies, such as those discussed in the previous chapter, can only tell us so much about the link between alcohol and crime. Parker (1996: 295), for example, argues that current quantitative research in this area is 'locked into unproductive paradigms and modes of investigation' with the result that future studies are 'unlikely to be veracious or productive'.

The qualitative studies differ from the quantitative ones in that they almost invariably have a far smaller sample. However, the nature of the studies allows a more in-depth exploration of the offender's motivations for drinking. The material generated by these studies is rich but complex. Like the quantitative studies discussed in the previous chapter, they demonstrate that many offenders are heavy drinkers but, at the same time, they show how difficult it is to generalise about why offenders drink and the impact that their drinking has on their offending.

This complexity is shown in McMurran and Hollin's (1989) study of 100 young offenders at Glen Parva Young Offenders' Centre in Leicester. The sample generally were heavy drinkers: 12 per cent were abstainers, 6 per cent light drinkers (1–10 units per week), 39 per cent moderate drinkers (11–50 units per week) and 43 per cent were heavy drinkers (over 50 units per week). To put this into context, nearly half of the sample had been drinking in excess of the equivalent of 25 pints of beer a week.

The sample were interviewed by a trained prison psychologist. During the interview the offender was asked whether he saw a link between his drinking and his offending. Of those who drank, 44.3 per cent said that they saw a connection (ibid.: 389). What the study was designed to do was explore the offenders' perceptions of this link further. At this point the offenders were shown seven cue cards, each containing a statement about drinking and crime. The cards were designed to cover all possible causal links between alcohol and crime. When the offenders were shown the cards a higher proportion of the drinkers in the sample identified at least one link between their drinking and their offending (69.3 per cent as opposed to 44.3 per cent). Quite why this is the case is interesting to speculate. Some offenders clearly agreed with the cue card that said that they didn't think that drinking had anything to do with the offence but then went on and selected a card which suggested that a link existed. Of the drinkers in the sample (88 per cent of the total), the following percentage selected each of the seven cue cards (ibid.: 390):

(1) 46.59 per cent said that they didn't think that drinking had anything to do with the offence;

(2) 37.50 per cent said that they had been drinking and then do things that they wouldn't do if they hadn't been drinking;

(3) 21.59 per cent said that they have the same reason for drinking as they do for offending, but that drinking and offending were not really related;

(4) 0.46 per cent said that they drank after they offended;

(5) 20.46 per cent said that the place they went to for a drink was where they got the idea of committing the offence;

(6) 17.05 per cent said that drinking gave rise to problems which made them offend;

(7) 12.50 per cent said that they offended so that they could drink.

Four points are worth making. First, despite the fact that the sample of offenders contained a high proportion of heavy drinkers, many of those questioned said that there was no connection between their drinking and their offending. When a direct question was asked, the majority of drinkers claimed that there was no connection. And, although the proportion of offenders who saw a connection rose when cue cards were used, the card selected most frequently was that there was no connection.

Second, one has to remember that the study measures the offenders' *self-perceptions* of the link between their drinking and their offending. It is difficult to know how accurate these perceptions are. It is possible that some offenders may see alcohol as a way of explaining their offending whilst others may believe that they have greater control over their actions than they do. Perceptions, however, are important for they may impact on the potential effectiveness of measures designed to help offenders with alcohol problems.

Third, the causal link most subscribed to by the drinkers in the sample was that their drinking had led them to do things that they otherwise would not have done. As McMurran and Hollin (1989: 391) note, this category is especially problematic for two reasons. Drunkenness may simply be a convenient excuse for the offender's behaviour and there may in fact be no causal link at all. Furthermore, it is unclear whether any genuine behavioural change is actually caused by alcohol or is caused by the *expectation* that alcohol will have that result.

Finally, the study found no significant association between the type of offence and the offender's self-reported relationship between drinking and offending unlike the conclusion drawn by Cookson (1992, see above). There are though a number of important methodological differences between the studies which could account for this (ibid.: 358–359). As Cookson comments:

> When criminals are the focus of study, it seems from all the data sources that drinking and delinquency tend to go together, and this is true for all types of crime. When criminal incidents are examined, alcohol is clearly involved more frequently in crimes of violence than in crimes of acquisition. These two findings are not in opposition. The impulsive, sensation-seeking, extravert personality may well be attracted to crime as to alcohol, and indulge in both frequently and heavily; and most crime is acquisitive in nature. Alcohol may well have the effect of making the drinker more violent, and this will occur for moderate and heavy drinkers alike. In fact, the habitual drinker may be less likely to be affected since his tolerance will be higher. The violent current offenders did not necessarily drink more heavily than others, but they were more likely to have been drinking on the particular occasion in question. (1992: 359)

Despite the fact that this study highlights the complexity of the link between alcohol and crime and the corresponding difficulties of responding to it effectively, there is cause for some optimism. The study suggests that many of the young offenders were aware of the problems caused by their drinking and were amenable to offers of assistance and treatment (ibid.: 392). The challenge may not be one of motivation but may be one of designing effective rehabilitative schemes given the variety of different links between alcohol and offending.

Parker's study (1996) of young adult offenders in the North West of England again showed a refusal by the drinkers to accept 'the simple or the universal' (ibid.: 291). Parker offered his sample a greater range of options than McMurran and Hollin so it is difficult to make direct comparisons. Once again, of the drinkers in the sample the following percentage selected each of the following options:

(1) 65 per cent said that drinking made them impulsive and that they then offended;

(2) 62 per cent said that drinking had nothing to do with their offending;

(3) 37 per cent said that drinking caused problems which led them to offend;

(4) 37 per cent said that the places where they drank led them to offend;

(5) 35 per cent said that drink had made them change their mind about avoiding crime;

(6) 31 per cent said that they drank after offending;

(7) 19 per cent said that they offended to get the money to buy alcohol;

(8) 19 per cent said that crime and drinking were not linked but the causes were identical;

(9) 15 per cent blamed drink for crime but said that drink was not the cause;

(10) 14 per cent said they drank in order to get courage.

Parker's methodology exposes the complex nature of the link between alcohol and crime. His conclusion highlights this:

> The quantification and search for linkage via frequency counts and correlations from these semi-structured interviews clearly produces a daunting complexity. Even among such a criminogenic, heavy drinking sample, statistical significance is hard to find and a multiplicity of factors appears relevant but difficult to sort and shape into reliable explanations or conclusions. Given the opportunity, these research subjects insisted on qualifying and complicating their conclusions, making significant correlations hard to secure. For the positivists this 'flatness' will suggest methodological flaws. The explanation offered here however is that the more reflexive methods used are veracious and the statistical flatness and dissonance in the findings is indicative of the complexity and multi-variate nature of social and in this case criminal behaviour. (ibid.: 292)

Conclusion

In order to understand why it is difficult to find a direct link between alcohol and crime, we need to understand some of the problems associated with this type of research. Although many of the studies would appear to suggest a link because of the high rates of alcohol consumed by offenders and the incidence of drinking prior to offending, many other individuals who do not engage in criminal activity drink equally heavily. Designing studies that help tease out the relevance of alcohol to an individual's behaviour is fraught with difficulty. Many common problems persist. Writing over twenty years ago, Greenberg (1981: 71; see also Hore 1988) identified six common weaknesses with research in this area:

- multiple and loosely defined concepts of alcohol use;

- lack of uniformity in definitions of crime;

- biased samples;

- failure to control for relevant variables;

- lack of information on the context in which drinking and crime co-occur; and

- inability to distinguish subgroups of alcohol users and offenders.

These are significant flaws and it is apparent that some studies still fail to address some of these issues. The first concern serves as a useful example. Some of the studies that we have considered do not address the issue of how intoxicated offenders had been at the time of the offence once it has been established that they had been 'drinking', others ask for a completely subjective assessment either by the offender or by a victim that the offender was 'under the influence of alcohol' at the time of the offence whilst others have relied upon arbitrarily drawn categories. This means that some studies are simplistic: whilst the results might show high rates of alcohol consumption by a sample of offenders, it is difficult to draw any meaningful conclusions from it. One extreme example comes from research by the West Midlands police into the effectiveness of a bylaw banning alcohol in the centre of Coventry (see Chapter 4 for further information). To do this the researchers had to devise a way of classifying offences as being 'alcohol-related'. Any incident which took place outside a licensed premises was one category of offence which was to come within this classification. As Marsh and Fox Kibby (1993) comment, an incident involving a total abstainer outside a pub would therefore have to be recorded as an 'alcohol-related' offence!

The differences between definition also make it problematic to compare different studies. Apparent differences could be accounted for by the use of different terminology whilst apparent similarity could in fact mask quite different patterns of alcohol use. It is clear that research studies have shown quite different rates of alcohol usage by offenders. We quite simply do not know how much of this is accounted for by methodological disparity but it is difficult not to agree with Cordilia (1985): the categories of alcohol use and crime lack sufficient specificity. Unfortunately such methodological difficulties are not always taken on board by politicians who want to be able to offer direct solutions to easily explained problems.

Another real problem is that other factors are often common both to those who drink heavily and to those who offend (Farrington and Loeber 1999). Some research therefore suffers from the problem that only one factor – drinking – is analysed in relation to offending. Other equally plausible connections are marginalised or ignored. Despite the fact that many studies therefore document extensive use of alcohol one has to be wary of assuming that this fact proves that the offence was caused by alcohol. Pernanen and Brochu describe the danger well:

> One of the necessary conditions for ascribing a causal connection is that the cause (alcohol or drug intoxication) occurs before the effect (the criminal act). This condition is almost invariably fulfilled in the studies. The fact that 50 per cent of assaults in one jurisdiction were committed under the influence of alcohol is then taken to imply that 50 per cent of assaults are directly caused by alcohol use, and the attributable fraction therefore being .50. A simple way of showing where this type of thinking leads us is to consider that many other factors that were present in the situation, such as the occurrence of provocative behaviour on the part of one of the people involved in a violent episode, have an equal claim to a sizeable attributional fraction. By this logic we soon arrive at a situation where the combination of attributable fractions exceeds unity. This defeats the whole idea of a share or fraction of the combined causal impact that can be attributed to a specific factor. (1997: 3)

As was shown in the preceding chapter, research which deliberately takes account of these additional factors tends to suggest that there is still a relationship between alcohol and crime, but that the association is considerably weakened (Fergusson *et al.* 1996; Fergusson and Horwood 2000).

One of the most sophisticated multi-variate analyses was undertaken by Norström (1993). He studied a variety of factors in Sweden to calculate the attributable fraction of alcohol on assaults in the 1980s. One of the key factors related to the amount of alcohol sold. This variable can be calculated more easily with regard to alcohol than to many other drugs due to alcohol's legal status. Once these variables had been considered, he found that the attributional fraction of alcohol on assaults was .40. His research found that the offender had drunk before approximately 80 per cent of assaults had taken place. Norström therefore concluded that the attributable fraction of alcohol in assault cases is about half the figure one would obtain by simply converting the percentage of offenders who had been drinking prior to the offence. Other researchers caution that such a conclusion is dangerous. Room and Rossow (2001) believe that cultural differences mean that there is no single invariant attributable fraction for alcohol in cases of assault.

What conclusions then can one take from the studies referred to in this chapter? Research consistently shows that a high proportion of offenders drink alcohol prior to offending yet this does not 'prove' that alcohol caused the offence to take place. Rumgay comments:

> The repeated finding of an association between alcohol consumption and a problematic event explains very little about the relationship between the two phenomena. Nevertheless, the tendency to assume cause from association pervades much of the literature. Indeed, the presence of alcohol, where it is found, is often treated as the sole cause for criminal events which are, in their sober manifestations, recognised to be complex, multi-factored phenomena. (1998: 13)

Even if the methodological problems discussed above that are present in many of the studies are addressed, and it is fair to say that more recent studies have in most cases been somewhat more sophisticated, we would have to ask what can be gained from knowing the proportion of offenders who had been drinking. Research also shows that problem drinkers have more extensive criminal histories than the population at large. Again though, what does this prove? Many problem drinkers are not offenders just as many intoxicated people do not offend. Having said that, it would be wrong to conclude that these studies are worthless or for that matter prove that there is no link between alcohol and crime. What the better studies prove is that the link is both weaker and more complex than is often assumed. Parker's conclusion is accurate and apt (1996: 296): 'alcohol is an accessory, but both to crime and a lawful good time. There is perhaps no definitive criminological message in a bottle.'

There is, however, a very practical dimension to this. Strategies have to be designed to prevent crime being committed by those who have been drinking and suitable ways of dealing with those who offend whilst intoxicated have to be found. The next three chapters will address these issues. The danger is that the complexity of the link (or links) between alcohol and crime (if any) will mean that finding universally effective solutions to the problem will prove difficult. At the same time, the public, who generally subscribe to the view that there is a direct causal link between alcohol consumption and offending, are likely to judge a lack of success harshly. It is perfectly understandable then that the government are keen to adopt the popular conception of 'alcohol-induced' crime whilst introducing a comprehensive range of measures to deal with what they know to be a complex phenomenon. One cannot blame politicians for being politicians (Freiberg 2003).

Chapter 4

Crime prevention and policing

[The] situation at night in our towns and city centres raises serious concerns about the control of alcohol-related crime and disorder. (Extract from a leaked letter from the Home Secretary to the Prime Minister, cited in Innes 2004)

Whilst the previous chapters show that it can be difficult to attribute criminal events directly to the consumption of alcohol, a plethora of measures or strategies which are designed to prevent or reduce alcohol-related offending have been introduced. This chapter will review and evaluate a number of strategies that have been employed either to prevent alcohol-related crime or to police areas where drunken disorder is a particular problem. Given the then Home Secretary's assessment of the situation in Britain's towns and cities at night, this assessment could hardly be more timely.

In the past two years the government have introduced a range of new measures as part of a 'blitz' (Home Office 2004a) on alcohol-related violence and disorder. These new measures operate in tandem with existing measures such as CCTV, changes to licensing laws and Zero Tolerance Policing.

Many people would welcome such initiatives. Despite evidence that alcohol-related violence is on the decrease (Simmons and Dodd 2003), the popular perception is that the situation is getting worse. Research by the marketing company MORI in 2001 (cited in the Prime Minister's Strategy Unit 2003: 57) showed that 61 per cent of the sample believed that alcohol-related violence was becoming more prevalent in the street, 52 per cent believed that it was increasing in pubs, clubs and bars and 40 per cent believed it to be on the rise in the home. Those aged between 55 and 64 appeared to be particularly concerned: 71 per cent believed that alcohol-related street violence was getting worse (ibid.: 57). The fact that concern has risen despite evidence that the problem has decreased should not come as a surprise. Research on public perceptions of crime has consistently shown that people believe that crime is on the increase even in periods when official statistics and victim surveys have shown that crime has in fact decreased (Roberts and Hough 2002).

Respondents in the British Crime Survey also expressed concern about alcohol-related crime and disorder (Simmons and Dodd 2003). Twenty-three per cent of respondents claimed that 'drunk' or 'rowdy' behaviour was either a 'very' or a 'fairly' big problem in their area – although it is worth noting that the figure is noticeably lower than those for vandalism (35 per cent) and for teenagers 'hanging around on the street' (33 per cent). The percentage of respondents concerned about drunken or rowdy behaviour varied markedly depending upon the type of area in which they lived: 33 per cent of inner city residents stated that drunkenness or rowdiness was a 'very' or 'fairly' big problem in their area compared to 26 per cent of urban residents and 12 per cent of rural residents. The Aberystwyth crime survey (Koffman 1996: 101) also found that very few people regarded drunks as a problem in a rural town, albeit one with a sizeable student population and which serves as the entertainment centre for a large hinterland.

What these studies suggest is that, regardless of the reality, and despite the fact that evidence from the most recent British Crime Survey suggests that a smaller proportion of the public are 'very worried' by violent crime (Dodd *et al.* 2004: 18, Table 2d) or are personally troubled by drunken and rowdy behaviour (ibid.: 19, Table 2e) than the year before, the public remain concerned about alcohol-related crime. A sizeable majority believe that alcohol-related violence is increasing and a substantial minority believe that drunken or rowdy behaviour is a problem in their locality. This is the reality which informs political decision-making.

Crime prevention and insecurity

It is important though not to be too dismissive of these findings on the basis that they appear to be ill-informed. Zedner (2003) argues that we must recognise both an objective and a subjective dimension to feelings of security. Whilst objective risk can be a valuable focus for designing strategies to protect the public, there is an additional subjective fear or apprehension caused by certain types of crime. People do not feel safe even if, objectively, there is little likelihood of the harm coming to fruition. This subjective fear remains a powerful political force. Alcohol-related crime may be a good example of an area where the unpredictability of intoxicated behaviour allied with popular perceptions of a malevolent causal link between alcohol and crime make people feel at risk. This perception of risk may be heightened when it is linked to the street, a location which criminologists have suggested is perceived as unfamiliar and dangerous (Hale 1996; Ross and Polk 2003). To compound matters further, research has also shown that fear of crime is increased when it is dark (Hough 1995), a time people would often be concerned about coming across intoxicated people on the street.

Criminologists now recognise that fear of crime, as distinct from crime itself, is a serious social harm that needs to be addressed. Yet herein lies a problem which Williams explains well:

> Such awareness can produce policy conflicts: thus many of the crime prevention schemes raise the public's awareness of the risks and so tend to increase rather than decrease fear of crime, even where the programme may lead to some decrease in actual crime. (2004: 105)

Policy makers, therefore, need to be aware that measures designed to address alcohol-related crime may have the undesirable effect of increasing the public's fear of that type of crime. How best to reconcile this conflict is a key challenge.

Crime prevention and civil liberties

Another challenge for policy makers is to ensure that, in a desire to protect the public from crime, fundamental freedoms are not breached or that, if they are, such a breach can be justified as a proportionate response to the problem (Ashworth 2004; Wilson and Sutton 2003). Experience has shown that knee-jerk reactions to a perceived problem, be it dangerous dogs, joyriding or terrorism, can result in legislation that unnecessarily restricts civil liberties and often appears to have had little impact on the underlying 'problem'.

Let us take an admittedly extreme example. If the sale of alcohol was to be prohibited (and this has happened and continues to happen in some jurisdictions) one may well reduce the overall number of crimes committed. However, such a measure would deny millions of people pleasure (over 90 per cent of adults in Britain drink alcohol: Prime Minister's Strategy Unit 2003: 6), severely reduce public revenue (by £7bn a year: ibid.: 8) and would carry other dangers (such as the possibility that illegal drinking dens would flourish making criminals rich and making drinking difficult to police). This far-fetched scenario may raise the issue in unrealistically stark terms but seemingly less invasive measures also need to be fully scrutinised. Proof of age cards serve as a useful example. They may seem like a sensible measure to tackle underage drinking but is it acceptable to require someone engaged in an otherwise lawful activity to show proof of their identity? And whilst CCTV may be useful to the police does it not raise important questions about civil liberties? It is not then just a question of assessing whether particular strategies or measures *work* in terms of crime reduction but also of deciding whether they can be *justified* even if crime is successfully reduced (see further Duff and Marshall 2000; Kleinig 2000).

Calculating whether a measure reduces crime can be difficult, as we shall see, and demands careful attention to methodology. Calculating whether a measure can be justified in civil libertarian terms is equally problematic, but for different reasons. Crime prevention and policing are inherently political activities. Decisions therefore have to be taken on a national and/or local level, by state agencies and by private organisations about prioritisations. Should public resources be put into tackling drunken disorder or domestic violence? Should licensed premises be given the choice about whether to offer drinks promotions which may lead to disorder? Any decision-making in this field (and any subsequent evaluation of it) will inevitably be partly evaluative, partly ethical and partly political in nature.

Both crime prevention and policing have a considerable literature. This comprises not only of studies which evaluate various measures but also a body of more theoretical work which seeks to place these developments in a broader socio-political context. As in previous chapters it is necessary to be selective. A decision has been taken to concentrate on the British literature, although certain key studies from elsewhere will be mentioned. Another decision that had to be taken relates to terminology. Commentators have debated the accuracy of the term 'crime prevention' and have come to prefer the term 'crime reduction'. Like the *Oxford Handbook of Criminology* (Pease 2002) this chapter will use the phrases interchangeably. This is not to ignore the significance of terminology but is rather a recognition that dictates of space preclude further discussion of a debate which is analysed more fully elsewhere (Crawford 1998).

Defining crime prevention

There is nothing inherently new about taking measures to protect one's person and property. Yet it is only comparatively recently that crime prevention has become a major topic of political interest and criminological study. The broad context behind the new interest in crime reduction was the massive rise in recorded crime in the 1980s. As a result an increasing range of measures have been employed to try and reverse this trend. Whereas there had previously been broad cross-party consensus on crime control, it became an increasingly divisive and political issue.

At the same time crime reduction was becoming more complex as an increasing number of actors acquired some kind of crime prevention function. All of this created a rich site for criminological debate about the extent and the nature of the state's involvement in crime control in post-modern society. This academic activity means that we are joining a vibrant debate with much complexity and disagreement. We therefore need to consider some of the definitions and typologies of crime prevention in order to differentiate between different types of activity which could come within this overall heading.

Tonry and Farrington (1995) argue that all types of crime prevention activity fall within one of four categories: law enforcement, developmental crime prevention, communal crime prevention or situational crime prevention. What is unusual about this model is that law enforcement is seen as an essential ingredient in preventing crime and hence should be categorised as a form of crime prevention. The criminal law, in Tonry and Farrington's analysis, aims to reduce criminal victimisation through sentences which deter potential offenders or incapacitate those who would otherwise re-offend (for further discussion see Layton Mackenzie 2002 and, more generally, Chapters 5 and 6 of this book). As such it is an integral part of state crime prevention. Their other categories are less contentious. Developmental strategies are designed to arrest criminogenic tendencies that have emerged in studies on human development. Community crime prevention is concerned with changing environmental factors associated with crime. Situational crime prevention encompasses measures designed to stop crimes happening by either making them harder to commit or increasing the risk of detection.

The inclusion of law enforcement differentiates this model from others. Whilst this could be seen as more holistic, others see crime prevention as an activity *other* than law enforcement which is designed to reduce criminal harm (Van Dijk and De Waard 1991). Cherney and Sutton, who agree with this distinction, adopt a useful metaphor to describe the process of crime prevention:

> Crime prevention is about dealing with issues 'upstream', before they have a chance to develop into 'downstream' problems that require justice agencies to be invoked. (2003: 332)

This is not to suggest that the police do not have a role to play in crime prevention, they do and it is often crucial. The argument is rather that the involvement comes prior to an offence being committed. It is, therefore, convenient to consider crime prevention and policing strategies together. One strategy which will be considered later, Problem Oriented Policing, demands that the police address the underlying causes of particular problems in an attempt to avert or reduce subsequent offending. And even Zero Tolerance Policing, which makes extensive use of law enforcement tactics, could be said to fit within Cherney and Sutton's definition. Advocates of the Zero Tolerance model argue that there is a direct causal link between minor offences and more major offences (Wilson and Kelling 1982): dealing with minor matters 'upstream' will stop more serious problems developing 'downstream'. If Zero Tolerance strategies prove effective, the more serious offences will never occur. This is different from attempting to prevent repetitions of offences by sentencing convicted offenders in a particular manner (see Chapter 6 for further information).

Primary, secondary and tertiary crime prevention

The most commonly used crime prevention model draws on public health terminology to distinguish between primary, secondary and tertiary crime prevention measures (Brantingham and Faust 1976). Primary crime prevention measures are designed to affect the population as a whole. Quite simply the aim of such measures is to make the general population less likely to offend. Secondary crime prevention measures are narrower in focus and seek to make a specific subgroup less likely to offend, for example those from economically marginalised backgrounds or those with alcohol-related problems. Tertiary crime prevention is concerned with those who already offend, or are believed to offend. Such measures are designed either to make such individuals stop offending or to make their offending less frequent or less serious.

Crawford (1998: 15) claims that Brantingham and Faust's classifications are useful in 'framing the lens of crime prevention'. They make us think about the target audience of crime prevention measures and are sufficiently wide to include many different forms of crime reduction activity performed by different individuals and agencies, whether or not they form part of the 'official' criminal justice system. However, they do not say anything about the nature of the different types of activity designed to achieve that effect. Van Dijk and de Waard (1991) addressed this deficiency by adding a further dimension to Brantingham and Faust's approach. Their revised model distinguishes not only between primary, secondary and tertiary approaches but between approaches orientated towards the victim, the community or the offender.

Situational and social crime prevention

An alternative distinction that is often drawn in the literature is between situational and social measures. Unlike the framework above, this distinguishes between types of crime prevention activity rather than the target audience. Situational crime prevention is designed to stop crimes occurring by reducing the opportunities to offend (see Clarke 1995). Underlying situational crime prevention is a belief that individuals operate rationally. It is assumed that those who may be tempted to offend try to balance the perceived benefits against the perceived costs of offending and that successful crime prevention can positively alter the result of this calculation either by reducing the perceived benefit or by increasing the perceived cost of offending. All situational crime prevention measures share this basic assumption. Once again, situational crime prevention measures can be further classified depending on how they are designed to make individuals desist from offending.

Cornish and Clarke (2003) have attempted to classify various situational crime prevention measures into five main types: those which increase the effort, those which increase the risks, those which reduce the rewards, those which reduce provocations and those which remove excuses. Each of these in turn has been subdivided into five additional categories. Measures designed to prevent alcohol-related offending share a distinct category with those concerning the control of drugs. However, strategies to deal with alcohol-related offending are also found in other categories. Dispersing pubs is an example of the first category – 'increasing the effort' – whilst efficient queues, polite service, expanding seating, soothing music, muted lights and reducing overcrowding in pubs all fall within the fourth category of 'reducing provocation'. The examples provided by Cornish and Clarke in the subgroup of controlling drugs and alcohol are the provision of breathalysers in pubs, server intervention and alcohol-free events.

It should be clear from the above discussion that crime reduction is a complex subject due to both the variety of approaches and the variety of individuals that the measures are aimed at. Given the complexity of the link (if any) between alcohol and crime, it is hardly surprising that a diverse range of crime reduction strategies are in use or have been suggested.

It is undoubtedly the case that some situational crime prevention measures have led to a reduction in crime (Clarke 1997). However, results have been mixed. This has made it difficult to determine what measures work in what situations. By way of example, two crime prevention measures will be assessed in this chapter: CCTV and restricting the consumption of alcohol in public places.

These examples were chosen for very different reasons. In the UK CCTV is the most heavily funded form of crime prevention (if one excludes law enforcement from the definition). According to Koch (1998: 49) expenditure on CCTV between 1996 and 1998 amounted to more than three quarters of the total expenditure on crime prevention. The sums of money involved are significant. Between 1999 and 2001, the government spent £170 million on CCTV schemes primarily in town and city centres, in car parks, in crime 'hot spots' and in residential areas (Welsh and Farrington 2002: 44).

CCTV also serves as a useful example for the purposes of this book as cameras are often situated in places where alcohol-related offending is a particular concern. Often the type of criminal behaviour that CCTV is designed to prevent is loosely defined – 'anti-social behaviour' is a particularly common target (Wilson and Sutton 2003) – but there are schemes that have been specifically designed to target violence around licensed premises. What we are witnessing therefore is a concentration of governmental crime prevention resources on a particular, if somewhat loosely defined, type of behaviour associated with disorder in public spaces. This represents a deliberate political decision, and one, as we shall see, that attracts a considerable degree of consensus. It is important to see if this investment is warranted.

Restricting the consumption of alcohol by contrast is designed specifically to counter alcohol-related disorder. By its very nature, such a measure cannot prevent any form of crime other than that which is alcohol-related. It is also an interesting example because its monetary costs, unlike CCTV, are fairly limited. It therefore promises a lot for minimal outlay. However, there is a non-monetary cost to all crime reduction measures and this example serves as a useful reminder that a cost-benefit analysis should not just consider financial outlay when it comes to measuring costs.

Closed circuit television

Imagine what the reaction would be if a new crime prevention measure was introduced and, after a year, research showed that 3,156 fewer crimes and offences had been committed than the average for the two years before the measure was introduced. This is exactly what happened when 32 CCTV cameras were installed in the centre of Glasgow in 1994 (Scottish Office 1999b). Although such a positive fall in crime is obviously welcome, one has to be careful of automatically attributing it to the new measure. Research on the Glasgow scheme (ibid.) concluded that the CCTV cameras could not be said to have made a significant difference to crime after account had been taken of a general downward trend in crime in the area in question both before and after the cameras were installed.

What emerged was complex. After allowing for the general downward trend, CCTV did appear to make a difference to certain types of offence (ibid.). These offences were primarily comprised of those categories which research suggests are committed by a disproportionate number of offenders who had been drinking (see Chapter 2): breach of the peace, vandalism, minor offences of violence and offences relating to drunkenness. Decreases in these areas though were offset by a very significant increase in crimes of dishonesty and a lesser, but still marked, increase in drug and prostitution offences. CCTV also appeared to have little effect on the clear up rate.

The CCTV in Glasgow city centre was tested alongside another scheme in Scotland. Twelve open street cameras had been put into operation in Airdrie in 1992. Again crime fell after CCTV was introduced (Scottish Office 1995). However, as in Glasgow, this had to be seen in the context of a general decrease in recorded crime which made it difficult to determine the impact that the introduction of CCTV had made. As the report (ibid.: 3) states:

> Assessing the success of crime prevention measures is always problematic because, in effect, what is being attempted is to measure the extent to which certain events did not happen and to attribute causal explanations to those 'non-events'. Whilst it is possible to measure changes in the incidence of crime within the target area and to hypothesise a connection between these changes and the CCTV initiative, it is not possible to state with absolute certainty that the latter is entirely, or even partially, responsible for the former. (p. 3)

Despite this note of caution, the Airdrie study was generally more optimistic than the Glasgow study about the effect of CCTV. In Airdrie it was estimated that CCTV was responsible for a 21 per cent fall in total recorded crimes and offences in the two years after CCTV was introduced compared to the two years before, even allowing for the general decrease in recorded crime over the period in question. There were other differences from Glasgow. Firstly, CCTV led to 16 per cent more offences being cleared up by the police in Airdrie in the two years after installation compared with the two years before. Second, the category of offences which saw the largest decrease in Airdrie was offences of dishonesty. It will be recalled that there was a significant increase in offences of dishonesty in Glasgow after CCTV was introduced.

What do these Scottish studies show? First, they demonstrate the real difficulties in calculating how effective situational crime prevention measures are. Second, they demonstrate that success is not universal. It is difficult to see why one scheme crudely appears to have had little effect on crime whereas another in a neighbouring town 'has led to a real reduction in the level of crime and to an improvement in the detection of crime' (Scottish Office 1995). Given these mixed results, it is interesting to note that the Scottish Office have concluded that 'CCTV appears to have been effective in cutting crime, and in not simply displacing it' (Scottish Office 1999a: para 18). This belief is also borne out by the fact that 30 CCTV projects received grants amounting to almost £1.9 million in 1997/98 in Scotland and a further 23 projects received £1.5 million in 1998/99 (ibid.). This is a large financial commitment given the ambiguous empirical evidence that CCTV 'works' but demonstrates that it has clear political support. Researchers have been concerned that such decisions have often been made on the basis of apparently successful evaluations that contain serious methodological flaws (Welsh and Farrington 2002: 44). It is for this reason that the following meta-analysis is particularly useful.

Welsh and Farrington's review of the crime prevention effects of CCTV

The authors (2002) undertook a systematic review of the effectiveness of CCTV for the Home Office in England and Wales. They reviewed 22 CCTV evaluations from the UK and the US which met their methodological criteria for inclusion. The Airdrie scheme was included whilst the Glasgow scheme was excluded. Of the 22 schemes, 11 had a desirable effect on crime, five had no effect on crime, five had an undesirable effect on crime and one had an uncertain effect on crime (ibid.: vi). The study looked at the operation of CCTV in three particular locations: city centre/public housing; public transport; and car parks. As the first would appear to be particularly relevant to alcohol-related offending, though such incidents may well occur in the other two environments as well, it is worth considering their conclusions on CCTV in city centre/public housing locations in more depth. Thirteen of the evaluations came within this category of which 11 were city centre schemes.

The authors found that five of the schemes had resulted in a decrease in crime, four had no impact on the crime rate, three had resulted in an increase in crime and the evidence about the remaining scheme was unclear as to the effect that it had (ibid.: 13). Taking data from nine of the evaluations – the other four had to be discarded due to deficiencies in the data – the odds ratio was calculated for each of the evaluations. From this, Welsh and Farrington (ibid.: 26) concluded that CCTV had a statistically significant effect in all five of the British evaluations, three of which were desirable (Birmingham, Doncaster and Burnley) and two of which were undesirable (Newcastle and Cambridge). Statistically CCTV had no effect in the remaining four American evaluations (ibid.: 26).

Pooling data from all nine studies showed that there was no evidence that CCTV had led to a reduction in crime in city centre/public housing locations (ibid.: 27). When the American studies were removed, the pooled data from the remaining British evaluations showed that CCTV had a 'small but significant effect on crime' (ibid.: 27). The results, therefore, were mixed and failed to show a significant overall drop in crime when CCTV systems were installed. The report also concluded that CCTV had been more effective when it came to preventing vehicle crime than when it came to preventing violence: CCTV appeared to have had no significant effect on violent crime (ibid.: 42). If the government wish to prioritise violent offences one has to question the effectiveness of spending so high a proportion of their crime prevention budget on CCTV.

Given the results of this research, why is CCTV so popular a crime prevention strategy? It has been suggested that CCTV commands support from four key groups and that that support has nothing to do with its actual effectiveness at reducing crime (Williams *et al.* 2000). The police support CCTV because it can help their work but they do not have to fund it out of their budget. Central government supports it because they can be seen to be responding to crime yet, once they have contributed to it financially, they are not responsible for it thereafter. At a local level, there is support for it due to the commercial rivalry between different town centres. Finally, public support legitimises CCTV, even if that support often comes from reports of evaluations that lack methodological rigor.

Welsh and Farrington came up with a number of useful suggestions for future research into the effectiveness of CCTV. Given the variety of results that they encountered one suggestion seems particularly important:

> Research ... is needed to help identify the active ingredients of effective CCTV programmes. One-third of the included programmes involved interventions in addition to CCTV, and this makes it difficult to isolate the independent effects of the different components, and interactional effects of CCTV in combination with other measures. Future experiments are needed which attempt to disentangle elements of effective programmes. (2002: 43)

Banning the consumption of alcohol in public

CCTV is one measure that has been used specifically to target crime in public places. Another relevant initiative has been the increased use of measures to ban or restrict the consumption of alcohol in various public locations. Such a measure again has the potential to be discriminatory in character as it targets those who drink on the streets. These people may not be able to afford to pay the additional premium associated with drinking in licensed premises or may be refused admittance because of their appearance. There is also the potential for further discrimination in that certain minority groups, such as some aboriginal communities in Australia, have a culture of communal public drinking. These issues have to be borne in mind, especially as it is easy to say that, unlike CCTV, there is little cost associated with such a measure. These issues will be considered again in the next section after consideration has been given here to the claim that banning drinking in public reduces crime.

Traditionally bylaws were used in England and Wales to ban public drinking. A useful starting point for analysis is the bylaw passed in 1989 which effectively banned the public consumption of alcohol in Coventry city centre. The police claimed that the bylaw had been a resounding success: 87.4 per cent of public order incidents had been alcohol-related (according to some highly suspect categorisation) in the city centre in 1988 as compared to 58.19 per cent in 1989 (figures from Marsh and Fox Kibby 1983, Appendix A). However, Marsh and Fox Kibby (1993) demonstrate how the figures can be interpreted in a rather different way.

According to the police statistics, crime and disorder increased overall in the period in question yet the proportion of alcohol-related incidents decreased. This makes evaluation problematic. One could argue that the scheme was successful in that the number of alcohol-related incidents decreased. On the other hand, the bylaw appeared to have no effect on the overall crime rate (Ramsay 1991b). As a measure designed to reduce the proportion of alcohol-related crimes it succeeded. As a crime prevention measure it had no effect.

These two conclusions are not necessarily in conflict. The bylaw was based on a premise that there is a direct link between alcohol and crime, a notion that may have popular acceptance but one which research would suggest is problematic (see Chapter 3). This study serves as further evidence that the link between alcohol and crime is complex. As Marsh and Fox Kibby (1993: 57) note, '[if] an effect increases while an assumed cause decreases there is no option but to reconsider the attribution of causality'.

More recently the government have made it easier for local authorities to ban public drinking. Section 13 of the Criminal Justice and Police Act 2001 allows local authorities to designate public places if they are satisfied that there has been 'nuisance or annoyance to members of the public or a section of the public' or 'disorder' that was 'associated with the consumption of intoxicating liquor in that place'. Once the area has been so designated, it is a criminal offence for a person without reasonable excuse not to comply with a request from a police officer to stop consuming alcohol or to surrender alcohol in his possession (s.12). An individual does not commit an offence merely by drinking in the designated area. The offence is only committed if he or she then refuses to stop drinking if asked to do so by the police. It could be argued that this is a more sensible approach than an outright ban. Officers could, for example, enforce it more strictly at particular times. However, by giving the police wide discretion, there is an associated danger that subjective assessments will discriminate against particular groups in society.

The Criminal Justice and Police Act has made it easier for an authority to designate an area than was previously the case with bylaws. Although s.13 of the Act stipulates that the authority have to be satisfied that nuisance, annoyance or disorder has been associated with drinking in the area, they are no longer under a legal obligation to conduct a formal assessment of the area over a period of time. In the guidance letter issued by the Home Office to police chiefs and chief executives of local authorities (2001b) it was stated that '[clearly] there should be evidence of an existing problem, with an assessment as to the likelihood that the problem will continue unless these powers are adopted'. Nonetheless, 'it is possible that a single, serious incident might be sufficient to justify adoption of the powers'. The Local Authorities (Alcohol Consumption in Designated Public Places) Regulations 2001 require the authority to consult with various people, such as the police, parish councils and licensees who may be affected although, obviously, the local authority is at liberty to make whatever determination it sees fit thereafter. Existing bylaws have largely ceased to exist. Under s.15 of the Act, bylaws cease to have effect either after the local authority designate the area under s.13 or, if they fail to do this, the bylaw will automatically cease to have effect five years after the section came into force on 1 September 2001.

Crime prevention: some concerns

Despite the fact that crime reduction measures have undoubtedly reduced crime on occasions, sometimes significantly, there are important issues that need to be addressed (Crawford 1998; Duff and Marshall 2000). Often these do not lend themselves to easy quantification unlike an apparent reduction in crime.

The first concern has already been mentioned in the introduction to this chapter. Situational crime prevention measures such as CCTV may reassure members of the public or, alternatively, the presence of such measures may lead to a heightened sense of fear. The mere fact that the cameras are there suggests that there is a problem, heightening the public's demand for yet more protection. When asked a direct question, the public usually state that CCTV makes them feel safer. So to take two Australian examples, 85.4 per cent of those aware of CCTV in Sydney reported that the presence of cameras made them feel safer and 61 per cent of those surveyed in Fairfield also said that CCTV made them feel safer (Wilson and Sutton 2003).

Yet it would appear that the public's apparent satisfaction with CCTV is not incompatible with an increased sense of fear. In the Glasgow study, 72 per cent of a sample of around 3,000 thought that CCTV would prevent crime and disorder, 81 per cent thought that it would be effective in catching perpetrators and 79 per cent thought that it would make people feel that they would be less likely to become victims of a crime (Scottish Office 1999b) but, after the cameras were installed, a higher proportion of the public said that they would avoid the city centre than before (50 per cent before CCTV was installed, 59 per cent three months after CCTV was installed and 65 per cent 15 months after installation). What this means is that '[the] desire for security and the absence of fear may be insatiable and unattainable, as the quest itself fuels anxiety' (Crawford 1998: 12). An 'entertainment' environment characterised by heavily-built door staff, CCTV cameras both inside and outside venues and metal shuttered shops hardly helps to dispel concerns about alcohol-related violence. People may be deterred not only from offending but from frequenting the area in question.

A second concern with crime prevention mechanisms is that they may make people less likely to take direct involvement in reporting crime.

CCTV again provides a potentially useful example. Williams (2004) states that people may be less likely to report offences if they believe that images will have been caught on camera. People may view CCTV not as 'big brother' but as 'big father' 'solving all their problems' (ibid.: 282). This disengagement is difficult to measure. Some crime prevention measures may have this effect whilst others may increase community involvement. A potential example of the latter was a project in London to improve street lighting. The results appeared to be staggering: in the area with improved lighting, assaults, car crime and threatening incidents fell by 75 per cent in the six weeks after the lighting was improved (Painter 1988). The author attributed this in part to an increased level of informal surveillance and a correspondingly higher chance that offenders would be identified. This though is largely conjecture (Crawford 1998) and other studies have suggested that lighting improvements, like CCTV, do not have a major effect on crime though they do help reduce the public's fear of victimisation (Atkins et al. 1991; Ramsay 1991a).

One of the greatest concerns with crime reduction strategies relates to civil liberties. There is a danger that some forms of situational crime prevention can be exclusionary in character. This concern is particularly acute with regards to CCTV (Crawford 1998; Norris and Armstrong 1999; Wilson and Sutton 2003). Research by Williams and Johnstone (2000) provides evidence that CCTV is used to move on individuals who have not offended but who do not appear to have a 'respectable' reason for being in a public place. The young were particularly vulnerable. Wilson and Sutton (2003) point out the dangers of concentrating solely on the crime prevention potential of CCTV. They argue (ibid.: 6) that we need to 'ensure that CCTV is used in ways that observe the need for public space to be open and inclusive, as well as safe and secure'. Despite the fact that such measures may have popular appeal, research has shown that crime control can lead to social control. It is therefore paramount that a check is kept on such technology or, more specifically, the uses to which it is being put and by whom.

Policing

As the discussion above makes clear the police have an important role to play in preventing crime before it occurs. This section looks at broader strategies for policing areas where alcohol-related crime is prevalent. The distinction between this section and the preceding one is somewhat artificial. As the police are involved in both activities it may have been sensible to have dealt with the police's role together. One of the difficulties that face those researching the police is determining their exact function. Researchers have studied what the police do in practice (see later) but this does not exactly define their role as an organisation.

Potential roles can conflict. Should the police function be concerned with maintaining order or with ensuring that all criminals are prosecuted? One of these functions would legitimate the police taking no further action against an offender provided order was maintained, the other would not.

A secondary concern is who exactly has what could be termed a 'policing' function. If one narrowed the enquiry to the police themselves one would ignore such individuals as private security officers, store detectives, stewards at sports events and, crucially for the purposes of this book, door stewards in licensed premises. Hobbs *et al.* (2002) show how important door stewards are in this context. Manchester city centre attracts an average of 75,000 people on Friday and Saturday nights. These individuals are 'policed' by almost 1,000 door stewards and about 30 police officers. It is not surprising then that the police are fully aware of the need to work in conjunction with door staff in order to effectively deal with alcohol-related crime (Maguire and Nettleton 2003). The following discussion will focus on the 'official' police, although interesting work has been done recently on how door stewards operate (Hobbs *et al.* 2002, 2003).

The police in England and Wales: function and powers

Police officers in England and Wales operate with considerable discretion. Individual officers are not under an obligation to arrest anyone committing an offence (indeed enforcing a mandatory-arrest policy for all offences would be impossible in practice due to the sheer range of conduct that can be categorised as criminal). Instead officers operate in the words of one commentator as 'street level politicians' (Muir 1977), making on-the-spot decisions as to how best to deal with particular incidents. This may or may not involve using a power to arrest.

Similarly, the fact that an offence exists does not mean that an individual will be charged. The police through a mixture of necessity and choice have to select when it is appropriate to use the criminal law; Lord Scarman (1982: 104) famously described the 'art of suiting action to particular circumstances' as 'the policeman's daily task'. The nature of policing is unusual in that often the most far-reaching decisions – whether or not to arrest an individual – are not taken by those senior in the organisation but by the most junior officers who respond to the majority of incidents (Wilson 1968). What this means in practice is that many who offend are not formally dealt with by the criminal justice system and that this decision is usually taken by officers on the ground (for a fuller discussion see Dingwall and Harding 1998).

There are a range of offences concerning drunkenness which could be used by the police before an intoxicated individual potentially commits another offence. These offences often give the police considerable latitude. For example, '[any] person who in any public place is guilty, while drunk, of disorderly behaviour' is guilty of an offence (s.91(1) Criminal Justice Act 1967). Even if an officer does not adjudge someone to have been disorderly section 12 of the Licensing Act 1872 provides that it is an offence to be 'found drunk in any highway or other public place, whether a building or not, or on any licensed premises'.

The official criminal statistics do not collate the data relating to offences of drunkenness on a national basis for such offences are judged to be too minor in character. However Deehan (1999) provides the data between 1985 and 1995. In 1985, 49,176 people were convicted of offences of drunkenness in England and Wales but this figure had fallen to 19,789 by 1995. The drop is marked but becomes slightly less so when the figures for those who were convicted are combined with those who received an official police caution (for more on cautions see Dingwall and Harding 1998): in 1985 the combined figure was 75,324 and in 1995 it was 42,598. Nonetheless the decrease remains striking.

When one combines the number convicted with the number cautioned for drunkenness offences, the aggregate total initially rose between 1986 and 1988 (when it peaked at 92,822) before falling year on year to the 1995 figure. What we do not know is whether this fall is due to a fall in the number of offences of drunkenness occurring. Not only are drunkenness offences not recorded by the official statistics but they are not surveyed in the British Crime Survey. The decrease could equally be explained, either in whole or in part, by a change in policing strategies or priorities. What is absolutely certain is that many, and probably the vast majority, of individuals who have technically committed a drunkenness offence have not been convicted or cautioned for it.

Another option would be to prosecute those who ply people who are drunk with alcohol. If anything this option is probably used even less. One wonders how many thousands of people could be prosecuted for the following offence on any given night:

1. A person commits an offence if, on relevant premises, he knowingly obtains or attempts to obtain alcohol for consumption on those premises by a person who is drunk. (Licensing Act 2003, s.142)

Section 141 of the same Act also makes it an offence either to knowingly sell or attempt to sell alcohol to a person who is drunk or to knowingly allow alcohol to be sold to a drunken person. Again this offence would appear to be seldom enforced.

Under-enforcement of the criminal law is not inherently problematic; one should not assume that any benefit automatically accrues from prosecution. It may be far better from a public policy perspective for the police to proceed only in situations where drunken individuals are being especially disorderly or pose a serious danger to themselves. Similarly prosecuting an intoxicated individual who buys an intoxicated friend a drink would appear to be a waste of public resources in many cases.

However, some have argued that a robust policy of prosecuting more minor offences associated with drunkenness would act as a useful crime prevention measure (Rashbaum 2002b). This could either be because such a policy would act as a useful deterrent to excessive drinking or because early arrest would stop a proportion of individuals from going on to commit more serious offences. This line of reasoning is implicit in so-called Zero Tolerance Policing strategies that have been in political vogue of late.

Zero Tolerance Policing

Zero Tolerance Policing only has a limited history in the UK (Hopkins Burke 2002), despite the considerable media and political attention that it has attracted (see further Newburn 2002; Watson and Burleigh 2000). Other countries as diverse as Ireland (O'Donnell and O'Sullivan 2002) and Brazil (Wacquant 2003) have also adopted such a strategy. Its roots can be traced to a number of influential publications in the US (most notably Wilson and Kelling 1982, but see also Kelling and Coles 1997; Skogan 1990). These writers' theories of crime influenced policing in parts of the US, though it should be said that the influence was far from universal. Many parts of the country never adopted the policy. Zero Tolerance Policing has always been controversial both in principle and in practice.

There is debate as to what exactly is meant by Zero Tolerance Policing (Knox 2001). The pioneering publications rested on a premise that vigorously policing minor forms of public deviance – or as Bayley and Shearing (1996: 589) put it 'stopping the disorderly, unruly, and disturbing behaviour of people in public places' – both reassures the public at large and reduces the number of more serious offences committed. One activity which such a strategy frequently targets is drinking in public (Rashbaum 2002b). Advocates on both sides of the Atlantic have claimed that such a policy has led directly to a reduction in crime rates (Bratton 1997; Fagan and Davies 2001).

In opposition the current government were keen advocates of Zero Tolerance strategies. Jack Straw, then the Shadow Home Secretary, visited New York, home of the most famous scheme, and was highly impressed with the apparent success of Police Chief Bratton's Zero Tolerance strategy. On his return he claimed that Labour would 'reclaim the streets' from the 'aggressive begging of winos, addicts and squeegee merchants' (quoted in Anderson and Mann 1997: 256) whilst parks would be reclaimed 'from drunks and drug users' (quoted in Bowling 1999: 533). The Labour Party appeared to be fully committed to introducing a national Zero Tolerance policy if elected (Labour Party 1997).

Despite this, Zero Tolerance has not become a widespread policy since Labour gained office. In the British context it has been particularly identified with schemes in Cleveland, Strathclyde and the King's Cross area of London. The Conservative opposition have since advocated Zero Tolerance in relation to drugs policy (Newburn 2003) and in the 2004 election for the London mayor. In a recent key-note speech the Conservative leader Michael Howard (2004) made clear his support for Zero Tolerance Policing:

> As Ray [Mallon] has shown in Middlesbrough, and Rudi Giuliani showed in New York, by challenging disorder you begin to claim ground back from the yobs and hoodlums controlling our cities. You demonstrate that there is a line people cannot cross – and as police confidence rises in challenging unacceptable behaviour, so public confidence rises in the police. By challenging so-called small crime head-on, you push back the burglars, car thieves and drug dealers responsible for so much of the crime in Britain today.

Given the Labour Party's earlier enthusiasm it is not easy to see why Zero Tolerance was not expanded as part of a policy of wide-ranging policing reforms. It may be that, in the run up to the election, endorsing Zero Tolerance was seen to be politically expedient. It is also the case that, since Jack Straw's visit to New York, doubt has been cast on the apparent success of Zero Tolerance strategies (Bowling 1999; Greene 1999; Innes 1999; Karmen 2000; Manning 2001). Not only do critics point out that other factors could legitimately explain all or part of the reduction in reported crime in specific locations (e.g. Bowling 1999 cites changes in the pattern of drug use in New York) but falls in the crime rate in areas which operate a Zero Tolerance policy have tended to coincide with falls in other areas which do not operate such a strategy (see also Rashbaum 2002a). Innes uses the British example of Cleveland to illustrate the point:

> Whilst recorded crime has fallen in Cleveland, between June 1996 and June 1997 recorded crime fell by over 10 per cent in the surrounding police forces of Durham, Northumbria, North Yorkshire, West Yorkshire and South Yorkshire. The drop in crime in areas such as Cleveland where [Zero Tolerance Policing] has been introduced are not extraordinary, there are deeper and wider structural adjustments at work. (1999: 404)

Perhaps we should not be surprised. Research has suggested that mandatory arrest policies have fared little better when they have been employed in the context of specific crimes. Two brief examples may be cited in this context. The first relates to the compulsory arrest of perpetrators of domestic violence. This was advocated by those who wished first to send out a signal that such behaviour was not acceptable in contemporary society and second by those who believed that such a policy may act as a deterrent. Sherman (1992) found that such a policy could actually increase the chance of further victimisation, although he later modified this position by stating that mandatory arrest could reduce future victimisation, but only if the police dealt with arrestees in a non-aggressive manner (Sherman 1997).

The second example relates to the compulsory arrest of drink drivers in Australia. After assessing the policy Homel concluded that:

> There simply is no convincing evidence that the routine nostrums of the law and order lobby, such as increasing police numbers, putting more officers 'back on the beat', beefing up the number of patrols, or intensifying the surveillance of chronic or repeat offenders, will yield the benefits in increased public safety, which are claimed. (1994: 32)

Why should such strategies meet with limited success? One factor that may impede the success of Zero Tolerance is the danger that such a policy will bring the police into direct conflict with marginalised sections of the community, in turn increasing hostility and the risk of subsequent offending. Many commentators have highlighted the discriminatory nature of Zero Tolerance schemes. In the Brazilian context Wacquant (2003) has argued that Zero Tolerance does little more than penalise poverty whilst the following account by a British journalist provides a useful account of Zero Tolerance in operation in New York and highlights vividly the detrimental effect Zero Tolerance could have on police-community relationships:

> Suddenly [the officer] sees something. A young man, bundled against the cold, is leaning over some iron railings. He has glimpsed the man swigging from an open bottle of beer – an offence in New York. The man will have to appear in court but will probably get nothing worse than a ticking off or a small fine. 'These are the cases you feel bad about but we have a policy of Zero Tolerance in the park', [the officer] says. (Hannaford 2002)

Certainly Zero Tolerance Policing runs counter to the traditional approach taken in the UK (Buchan 2002; Hopkins Burke 2002). Rather than operating a policy of selective under-enforcement, Zero Tolerance supposedly reduces the discretion that an individual officer has in responding effectively to an incident. According to Innes, Zero Tolerance strategies alter the nature of policing by highlighting its coercive nature:

> The legitimacy and effectiveness of the English approach to policing has been held to reside in the veiled nature of the available coercion, it was 'an iron fist in a velvet glove'. The production of order by the police was for the most part accomplished through a discrete blend of charismatic and legal authority that functioned as an adjunct to the office of constable, the imposition of coercive force was a last resort. Under the rhetoric of [Zero Tolerance Policing], the disguised nature of the coercive enforcement functions of policing are foregone, the police function becomes that of an 'iron fist in an iron glove'. (1999: 398)

The 'iron fist in an iron glove' has also occasionally been misused. In New York, the scheme lost much legitimacy after a Haitian security guard, Abner Louima, was tortured and a West African street vendor, Amadou Diallo, murdered by the city's Street Crimes Unit.

Problem oriented policing

An alternative strategy to Zero Tolerance is what has been referred to as Problem Oriented Policing. This strategy, most commonly associated with Goldstein (1977, 1979, 1990) challenges the widely-held presumption that police officers predominantly act as law enforcers (Lumb 1996). Instead Problem Oriented strategies recognise that the police are a service that responds to a wide variety of incidents, many of which are non-criminal in character. Academic research demonstrates that a focus on the police as law enforcers is misleading. In a study of 1,944 incidents that the police attended in a research division, Hough (1985) found that only 36 per cent involved crimes. This proportion is higher than that found by most researchers. In a comparison of policing studies in the UK and the US, Bayley (1996: 31) concluded that studies consistently show that only 25 per cent of calls to the police relate to crime (the distinction is not quite as clear as this; as Mawby (2000: 107) notes many of the events which are not classified as crimes are potential crimes).

Advocates of Problem Oriented Policing recognise that the popular image of the police officer as law enforcer is both misleading and potentially damaging. It is damaging in that, if the image of police as law enforcers persists (for a discussion of the cultural issues involved see Cope 2004), policing could become an unrewarding career. This is due to the fact that all too often the same officers are responding to the same kind of incidents involving the same people without action being taken at a fundamental level to address the underlying cause. Officers can feel frustrated that their work appears ineffectual whilst, at the same time, the public can start to believe that the police are not doing a satisfactory job because they have unrealistic expectations.

Problem Oriented Policing demands that forces carefully study what incidents officers are called to deal with and then develop as detailed a picture as possible about the most prevalent and important problems in their area. As Cope (2004: 201) comments '[policing] is increasingly relying on intelligence to target, prioritise and focus interventions'. Strategies can then be devised to effectively deal with these problems. The strategy may or may not involve the police acting as law enforcers but the central aim will be to target the underlying cause of the problem.

Herein lies the fundamental difference between a Problem Oriented strategy and a Zero Tolerance strategy. The former seeks to move beyond the law enforcement role towards resolving the underlying issue – although law enforcement may be part of that strategy. The latter does not move beyond the law enforcement role as it believes that the rigorous enforcement of minor offences is a universally effective way of reducing more serious forms of offending. This is a crucial distinction. Proponents of the Zero Tolerance model effectively disregard the deeper causes of crime in the belief that these do not impact on an effective policing strategy (Hopkins Burke 2002). Critics argue that the two cannot be divorced – a policing strategy which ignores the underlying causes of crime will not ultimately be successful (Matthews 1992) even if it may have short-term success (Hopkins Burke 2002).

The Australian Institute of Criminology (2004) lists the following as the ten key elements of Problem Oriented Policing:

- Ensuring that the problem is the basic unit of police work rather than a crime, a case, calls, or incidents. A problem is something that concerns or causes harm to citizens, not just the police.

- Addressing problems means more than quick fixes: it means dealing with conditions that create problems.

- Individual police and their organisations must routinely and systematically analyse problems before trying to solve them. The analysis of problems must be thorough even though it may not need to be complicated.

- Problems must be described precisely and accurately. Problems often aren't what they first appear to be.

- Problems must be understood in context. Different participants are affected in different ways by a problem and have different ideas about what should be done.

- The way the problem is currently being handled must be understood and the limits of effectiveness must be openly acknowledged in order to come up with a better response.

- Initially, any and all possible responses to a problem should be considered so as not to cut short potentially effective responses. Suggested responses should follow from what is learned during the analysis.

- The police must pro-actively try to solve problems rather than just react to the harmful consequences of problems.

- Individual police officers require the freedom to make or participate in important decisions. At the same time, police must be accountable for their decision-making.

- The effectiveness of new responses must be evaluated so these results can be shared with other police and so the entire organisation can systematically learn what does and does not work.

An example of this in action is provided by the following project which was set up specifically to deal with the problem of alcohol-related crime in Cardiff. It has been suggested (Doherty and Roche 2003; Shepherd 1994) that a more inclusive approach to policing would be more effective than reactive strategies when it comes to dealing with intoxicated offending.

The Tackling Alcohol-related Street Crime (TASC) Project

A pertinent example of a Problem Oriented approach can be seen in the Tackling Alcohol-related Street Crime (TASC) project that was launched in Cardiff in July 2000. The extent of alcohol-related violence and disorder in central Cardiff was discussed in Chapter 2. It was clear from the data that there was a significant problem with regard to both violence and disorder that was concentrated geographically on a number of 'hot spots' (Maguire and Nettleton 2003: 44–45). The strategy that was adopted clearly fulfils many of the criteria that the Australian Institute of Criminology (2004) identify with Problem Oriented Policing. Essentially the TASC project involved eight specific strategies that were designed to deal effectively with the problem (Maguire and Nettleton 2003: 13):

- Focussed dialogue between the police and members of the licensed trade.

- Measures aimed at improving the quality and behaviour of door staff.

- Attempts to influence licensing policy and practice.

- Measures aimed at publicising the problem of alcohol-related violent crime.

- Targeted policing operations directed at crime and disorder 'hot spots'.

- A cognitive behavioural programme for repeat offenders (COV-AID).

- A training programme for bar staff (Servewise).

- A programme of education about alcohol for school-age children.

- Support for victims of alcohol-related assaults attending hospital.

One thing which is immediately apparent is the range of people and organisations involved in the project. Central to TASC was the involvement of licensees in the city centre and the training of door staff. To this end, a forum of licensees was set up prior to the project starting in 2000. This forum was described in the scheme's evaluation as arguably 'the most significant development' (ibid.: 13). Although initial interest was limited, 100 licensees are currently members of the forum (ibid.: 14). A number of tangible benefits arose out of meetings between licensees and the police. Two examples relate to licensees being briefed prior to a potentially fractious soccer match about known 'trouble makers' and licensees agreeing only to sell beer in unbreakable glasses during major rugby matches (ibid.: 15). Other examples of the police liaising with other bodies include their collaboration with the County Council to train and register door stewards (ibid.: 18).

A range of other bodies were also involved. The Probation service implemented the cognitive behavioural programme, COV-AID (Control of Violence in Angry Impulsive Drinkers), in conjunction with psychologists from Cardiff University (ibid.: 27) whilst the University of Wales Institute ran the 'Servewise' course for bar and hospitality staff (ibid.: 28). Schools were involved in the educational aspect of the scheme, although the materials were devised by the police (ibid.: 30). Finally, a nurse in the Accident and Emergency Department of the local hospital was charged with contacting assault victims after they had been treated with the aims of offering them more support, persuading the victim to report the offence and obtaining additional information about the incident which would benefit the researchers (ibid.: 30).

The disparity of organisations and people involved resulted in a number of logistical and administrative difficulties. Some of these were associated with setting the project up and, once operational, have gone or at least receded. To take one such problem by way of example, the initial hostility to the scheme amongst licensees apparently had its genesis in a fundamental dispute over whether particular premises where violent incidents occurred should be 'named and shamed' in the local press (ibid.: 14). Licensees, who felt that this could be both misleading and unfair, became more accepting of the project once this practice stopped. Other problems remain more entrenched. Door staff, for example, still view the police with suspicion despite some positive feedback about the new training course (ibid.: 22; although with a sample of 12 we should be wary of reading too much into this). Generally the evaluation of the project notes that '[some partners] did not show the desired speed or enthusiasm in assisting planned reforms' (ibid.: 32). The County Council along with regional and national managers of large pub chains were singled out for particular criticism (ibid.: 32).

Ultimately the scheme will be judged on whether it was successful in reducing alcohol-related violence and disorder in central Cardiff. The results were mixed. Dealing first with alcohol-related violence, Maguire and Nettleton concluded that:

> Over the 18-month evaluation period when the TASC project was in operation, there was a decrease in the numbers of violent incidents known to have occurred in the targeted area. The first year of full implementation saw a fall of four per cent and the next six months saw little change. This reduction took place despite a significant rise in licensed premise [sic] capacity in the area, and despite increases in recorded incidents of violence against the person elsewhere in South Wales. The best estimate is that in its first year of operation, the impact of TASC was to reduce the expected level of violent incidents by eight per cent (i.e. by about 100 incidents). (2003: 59)

Incidents of disorder though rose during the first year by 49 per cent (ibid.: 49, Table 4.1). What appears to explain the discrepancy is the location of the incidents. The project appears to have been far more successful at dealing with incidents inside licensed premises – where the majority of violent incidents take place – than at reducing crime which takes place on the street, where the majority of disorderly incidents take place. Certain strategies (increased police targeting of problematic premises, liaison with managers and training door staff) were highlighted as being especially effective at reducing violence (ibid.: 60).

As violence is presumably of greater concern than incidents of disorder, TASC was undoubtedly a successful project which will no doubt be carefully studied elsewhere. Regrettably the substantial increase in disorder may make the public feel more at risk from alcohol-related crime, especially as the evaluation attributes much of the rise to disorder on the city's main street (ibid.: 51). There was a rise of 99 per cent in the number of incidents of disorder in the first year that the project was in operation in this location (ibid.: 51; the data also shows a rise of 42 per cent in the number of violent incidents on that street in the first year). Maguire and Nettleton attribute these rises to the number of new licenses granted to premises on the street and note that the TASC team specifically objected to these licenses being granted (ibid.: 51).

It is ironic that the success of TASC appears to have been marred by a factor beyond their control and one which they both identified and brought to the attention of the authorities. There is a considerable body of research both in the UK (Bromley and Nelson 2002; Costanza *et al.* 2001; Nelson *et al.* 2001) and elsewhere (Cochrane *et al.* 1999; Gorman *et al.* 2001; Lipton and Grueneweld 2002; Speer *et al.* 1998; Zhu *et al.* 2004) which has suggested that there is a clear link between the density of licensed premises and violence. In one American study, Scribner *et al.* (1995) found a statistically significant link between reported assaults and density of licensed premises in 74 cities in Los Angeles County. They calculated that a 1 per cent increase in the density of licensed premises was associated with a 0.62 per cent increase in the rate of violent offences.

Alcohol Disorder Zones: encouraging a collaborative approach?

The government is proposing to introduce a new method of dealing with areas where there is a problem of intoxicated crime and disorder. It draws heavily on concepts central to Problem Oriented Policing. Alcohol Disorder Zones would cover areas where there was alcohol-related disorder caused in part by the licensed premises in that area (Department for Culture, Media and Sport *et al.* 2005: para 2.2). Establishments would be given time to take agreed steps to reduce the problem – the government proposes a minimum period of eight weeks – but, if the steps are not taken, the premises would be required to contribute not only to the policing costs but to the other local costs associated with alcohol-related disorder. The scheme would come into operation where 'there was strong evidence of alcohol related disorder having reached clearly unacceptable levels' (ibid.: para 2.3). Designating areas as zones would be the last resort:

> Zones would only be designated after the licensed premises in an area had been warned of the possibility and been given both a period of time to tackle the problems of alcohol fuelled disorder in the area and notice of the actions which would be required in order for a zone not to be designated in this way. Our objective is that the issues creating disorder should be resolved through an agreed action plan without a zone having to be designated. (ibid.: para 2.5)

Even if a zone was designated, the premises would be given instructions as to the steps that they would have to take to get the designation – and the financial contribution – lifted (ibid.: para 2.5). The government recognises that there are a number of difficult issues that would have to be resolved before the scheme could come into operation.

A few of the most pertinent issues can be briefly identified. Firstly, how should the responsibilities for preventing an area being designated an Alcohol Disorder Zone and the costs if an area is so designated be apportioned between the premises in that area? Options include a flat rate for all of the premises or a differential rate that takes account say of the capacity of the premises or the rate banding used for licensing fees (ibid.: para 2.9). Another consideration is should off-licenses be included? Finally should payment of the fees be enforced by the licensing system so that a premises which failed to meet its financial commitment would automatically lose its license? The government favours this approach (ibid.: para 2.14).

The problems of classifying policing strategies

Although it was important to distinguish between Zero Tolerance and Problem Oriented approaches in the earlier discussion, it can be difficult to classify particular strategies in practice. Often a strategy that appears closer to one model will be sold to the media in a manner which appears closer to the other. This is vividly illustrated by the 'nationwide police blitz' on 'alcohol-fuelled violence' that ran in parts of England and Wales during the summer of 2004 (Home Office 2004a). The rhetoric was itself misleading: the scheme was nationwide only in so far as it targeted 92 areas situated between North Cumbria and Cornwall and the Isles of Scilly. The scheme only operated in certain areas within each force. These areas were limited in number. The Metropolitan Police with 10 areas had the most whereas other forces sometimes only had one area participating (e.g. Bedfordshire, Cambridgeshire and Cheshire).

After one month the Home Office was claiming to the press that the scheme had met with 'large-scale success' (ibid.). Quite how they arrived at this conclusion is unclear. The tactics that were employed were various. Police along with partners from other agencies visited more than 14,000 licensed premises and found that 5 per cent had committed an offence. Bearing in mind the kind of offences that can be committed by licensees it is perhaps somewhat surprising that 95 per cent of them had committed no offence whatsoever. Sting operations were also carried out on 646 licensed premises and it was found that 51 per cent of on-licenses and 29 per cent of off-licenses were prepared to sell alcohol to underaged people. As the Association for Chief Police Officers' spokesman said, this was the most disturbing aspect of the interim report (ibid.). Finally the police issued 1,869 fixed penalty notices and confiscated alcohol from 1,764 under-18s and from 25 adults who were drinking in a 'designated area'. Given the concentration of police in these areas it is perhaps unsurprising that a comparatively high number of fixed penalty notices were issued.

All of the rhetoric is consistent with a Zero Tolerance approach. The report talks of a 'nationwide police blitz' and a 'police enforcement campaign', the Home Secretary of a 'co-ordinated police blitz' and a determination 'to tackle the problem head-on with tough enforcement action' whilst the ACPO spokesman highlights the 'determination of the police service to robustly enforce the licensing laws' and to 'bring the full weight of the law on licensees who act in an irresponsible manner' (ibid.). And yet, on closer inspection, aspects of the 'blitz' appear far more akin to a Problem Oriented approach.

First, there is a recognised problem – 'alcohol-fuelled violence'. The strategy then attempts to address three activities which are perceived to be causes of this problem: the activities of irresponsible licensees, the consumption of alcohol in public, and underage drinking. Another aspect of the campaign which is closer to a Problem Oriented model relates to the involvement of people other than the police. The Home Secretary states that he intends to work alongside the alcohol industry 'to tackle irresponsible selling' whilst the sting operations were carried out not only by the police but by Trading Standards Departments. One wonders whether this co-operation with the alcohol trade will be jeopardised if the government act on a proposal contained in the Alcohol Harm Reduction Strategy (Prime Minister's Strategy Unit 2004: 71) which seeks a 'voluntary' 'financial contribution' from the drinks industry towards the cost associated with 'the harms caused by excessive drinking'. Ominously, at least for the alcohol industry, is the veiled threat that if this does not prove successful 'the Government will assess the case for additional steps, including possibly legislation' (ibid.).

What we appear to have is an example of a Problem Oriented Policing strategy which involves an element of strict enforcement by the police but which has been sold effectively as an example of Zero Tolerance Policing. This again highlights the fact that crime reduction measures often defy easy categorisation.

Conclusion

It would be difficult to accuse the government of doing nothing to address alcohol-related crime. There is a clear recognition that it represents a major problem in society and that dramatic steps need to be taken to reduce its prevalence. A number of different crime prevention and policing strategies have been used and, on the face of it, appear to have met with some success. However, evaluation is inherently problematic. To take one example, the government have invested very considerable amounts of money in CCTV (Koch 1998; Welsh and Farrington 2002). Other countries have done the same (Wilson and Sutton 2003). The introduction of some of these cameras, such as the ones in central Glasgow, coincided with significant falls in the crime rate (Scottish Office 1999b). However all too often crime has also fallen in areas where the measure was not in use making it difficult to attribute the drop in crime to the new crime prevention measure. This is a general concern but has been noted in particular with regard to CCTV and Zero Tolerance Policing (Innes 1999). This is not to say that such measures never work, there are examples in the literature of crime prevention strategies that have met with considerable success (e.g. the TASC project appears to have significantly reduced alcohol-related violence in central Cardiff; Maguire and Nettleton 2003), rather it is a warning as to the difficulties of assessing whether particular strategies are effective in reducing crime.

The government appear to be keen on adopting a holistic approach to the problem. The Home Secretary has made it clear that a number of different agencies are to be involved in the 'blitz' on alcohol-related crime and that he wants to work in partnership with the drinks industry (Home Office 2004a). Maguire and Nettleton (2003) believed that the involvement of licensees in the TASC project was central to its success so it is important that a genuine partnership between the drinks industry and the police can be established. One problem that emerged in the Cardiff study was that many licensed premises, particularly in city centre 'hot spots', are part of national chains and that individual licensees cannot stop what the police see as irresponsible drink promotions. Regional and national managers were singled out in the evaluation as hindering the success of the project (ibid.: 32). It will be interesting to see whether a national strategy, particularly with the government's threat of legislation if the drink's industry fail to comply (Home Office 2004b), will prove more successful.

To some extent the government's policy recognises reality. Dealing with alcohol-related crime falls on a huge number of agencies both within and outside the formal criminal justice system. The involvement of the Prime Minister's Strategy Unit (2003) is welcome for it demonstrates this and vividly itemises the cost to society. Similarly, the Home Office's recognition that there is a problem, that it should not be tolerated but that a number of strategies need to be employed to counter it is gratifying.

Despite this, a number of important concerns remain. At the beginning of the chapter it was said that crime reduction and policing are inherently political activities. Crime concerns voters and alcohol-related crime appears to concern the public (Simmons *et al.* 2003). Fear of crime is an important issue as it can substantially impair people's quality of life (Zedner 2003) and it is right for politicians to address it. This can be done in a number of ways. One could, for example, show that the fear is illogical. One could adopt policies that will, hopefully, reduce the incidence of that type of crime. Alternatively one could introduce a raft of reactionary measures either in the belief that these will work or in an attempt to convince the public that you are serious in your commitment to tackle crime. To make matters worse, there can be a conflict between reducing crime and reducing the fear of crime (Williams 2004). Crime prevention measures may simultaneously reduce crime but increase the fear of crime.

It is, therefore, somewhat inevitable that the politics of crime prevention and policing require a degree of sleight of hand. Politicians may need to 'talk tough' whilst introducing measures that could be criticised as being unduly lenient. There is a danger that this can lead to brinkmanship between the major political parties as they try and jostle each other to be seen as the 'party of law and order'. We have, for example, seen both Labour and Conservative politicians endorse Zero Tolerance Policing; although, once elected, the Labour Party did not seek to make it mandatory across the country. Instead they have tried alternative strategies, arguably with more success. If the British Crime Survey is to be believed, and everybody bar Michael Howard (2004) believes it is the most accurate picture of crime available, crime has continued to fall throughout their period of office.

Politics though may determine policy as much as empirical success. The most extensive evaluation (Welsh and Farrington 2002: 27) of the measure which accounts for more than three quarters of crime prevention expenditure concluded, on the basis of pooling data from nine studies which met strict methodological criteria, that there was no evidence that CCTV had led to a reduction in crime in city centre locations. Despite this, it is still used and new schemes are still set up. There is undoubtedly a residual belief that CCTV is a valuable crime prevention tool – and some schemes have met with considerable success – but there are also vested interests which may partly explain its attraction (Williams *et al.* 2000).

Finally, there are ethical issues which have to be addressed. Even if it could be proved that certain measures were effective in terms of crime reduction they may legitimately be rejected on other grounds. In the introduction the example of prohibition was given. We may legitimately say that this would be a disproportionate response, although some would disagree. However, measures such as banning drinking in public places and Zero Tolerance Policing, which often go together, also discriminate against certain groups. These groups are often comprised of marginalised individuals who have little ability to influence political decision-making. They are also individuals who are vulnerable to becoming scapegoats for popular concerns about disorder. Some drinkers clearly cause significant harm. Most do not. The challenge is to introduce measures which stop the harm without unnecessarily restricting the freedom of the majority.

Chapter 5

Intoxication and criminal responsibility

Unlike the previous chapter, which looked at interventions designed to stop alcohol-related offending before it happens, this chapter considers how the criminal law responds to those who offend whilst intoxicated. To see why this is a problematic, and hence contentious, issue we need first to consider some basic principles of criminal liability.

The law usually requires the prosecution to prove that the defendant either intended to cause the harm or was reckless about causing it. If he was drunk at the time this could be difficult to prove and, if the prosecution fail to prove beyond reasonable doubt either that the defendant intended to cause the prohibited harm or was reckless about causing it, then one would think that the defendant should be entitled to an acquittal. Many would find this outcome unacceptable. The drunken defendant is usually to blame for putting himself in that state and many would say that he should be held to account for any harm he causes as a result.

There is, therefore, a conflict between an understandable desire to protect the public from harm and certain general precursors to criminal liability (Tolmie 1999). Most legal systems would find it unacceptable to punish someone who neither intended to cause harm nor could foresee the risk that such harm might materialise. On the other hand most parliaments and judges would balk at the possibility of letting people evade liability because they had of their own volition got so drunk that they had no idea what they were doing. It is not just judges and politicians who share this view. In Canada acquitting those who caused serious harm to others on the basis of their intoxication led to such a degree of public outrage that the law had to be hastily reformed (see later).

The most obvious and fundamental question will be the primary concern of this chapter: if someone is intoxicated at the time of the offence, should this factor be taken into account in determining his criminal liability? The discussion, as a result, focusses deliberately on the general question of attributing criminal liability.

An alternative approach would be to deal with the problems caused by alcohol in a piecemeal fashion and determine whether specific offences are required to deal with particular harms. It is not proposed to go through all of the offences that could fall within this category as it varies from jurisdiction to jurisdiction, extensive coverage is available elsewhere and, in practice, many of these specific offences raise evidential rather than substantive legal problems. This is not to denigrate the importance of these offences; if anyone is in any doubt of their importance they should spend a day in any magistrates' court. Our enquiry is thus broader and more intrinsic: how should the general criminal law respond to drunken offending?

Before we consider this there are three issues that merit brief consideration: first, the degree of intoxication that is required; second, the question of whether the intoxication was voluntary or involuntary; and, finally, the relationship between intoxication and other criminal law defences.

The degree of intoxication required

Despite the findings of the empirical studies discussed in Chapter 2, the criminal law is only concerned with the most extreme forms of intoxication (Lynch 1982). Although alcohol use may be a common feature in many cases, it is not often the case that someone was so drunk that his actions were wholly involuntary. The criminal law usually requires what common law jurisdictions refer to as *mens rea* on the part of the accused. This means that the prosecution have to prove that the defendant had the particular state of mind specified by parliament or the courts for that offence. The prosecution might, for example, have to prove that the defendant intended the prohibited conduct. If they fail in this task, the defendant is entitled to an acquittal. However, only rarely is it the case that an intoxicated defendant was so intoxicated that he was unable to have any appreciation of what he was doing.

It is clear that the degree of intoxication must be very high if it is to have any relevance to the accused's liability for the offence. The courts in England and Wales have though shown confusion in relation to the direction that should be given to the jury in appropriate cases. The direction that used to be given to the jury in cases where evidence of intoxication could be considered (see later) was to determine whether the defendant had formed the specific intent for the offence (*R v Sheehan* [1975] 1 WLR 739; followed in *R v McKinley* [1994] Crim LR 944 and *R* v *Bennett* [1995] Crim LR 877). However, in *R* v *McKnight* (2000) (*The Times* 5/5/2000) the Court of Appeal upheld a direction asking the jury to consider whether the defendant was incapable of forming the intent as opposed to whether the defendant had formed the required intent. It is important that this issue is clarified and it is suggested that the direction in *Sheehan* is preferable.

As the threshold is appropriately high, intoxication is usually only of practical relevance at the sentencing stage (see the next chapter). However, every jurisdiction has had cases where a defendant has claimed that he was so intoxicated that he was unable to form the necessary *mens rea* for the offence in question. This has forced the courts to examine some of the most fundamental tenets of attributing criminal liability, although the evidence in most of these leading cases suggests that in any event the degree of intoxication would have been insufficient to avail the defendant (e.g. *HM Advocate* v *Savage* 1923 JC 49; *DPP* v *Beard* [1920] AC 479; *DPP* v *Majewski* [1977] AC 443).

Voluntary and involuntary intoxication

Intoxication can either be voluntary or involuntary; an example of the latter is where a person's drink is 'spiked' with alcohol by someone else. 'Involuntary' intoxication is a convenient and widely used phrase in criminal law but its use is not without problems. This is because case law has restricted it to situations where the defendant did not realise that he or she was drinking alcohol. It does not cover other situations where arguably the intoxication was involuntary; perhaps most notably if the offender was addicted to alcohol. Nonetheless, with this caveat in place and with the absence of a satisfactory alternative, the phrase involuntary intoxication will be used where necessary in this chapter. The criminal law distinguishes between voluntary and involuntary intoxication on the basis that the latter carries no degree of culpability and accordingly should attract no criminal liability (see further Horder 1993; Smith and Wilson 1993; Sullivan 1994; Wilson 1995). As this position appears universal (*Ross* v *HM Advocate* 1991 SLT 564; *R* v *Kingston* [1994] 3 All ER 353; *S* v *Johnson* 1969 (1) SA 201) and principled, the rest of the chapter is concerned with the more common occurrence of voluntary intoxication and any subsequent reference to intoxication in this chapter should be taken to mean voluntary intoxication.

It should be noted again that the degree of intoxication is paramount. In *Kingston* it was held that the defendant could be held criminally liable. Even though the intoxication was involuntary in that it was administered without his knowledge by a third party, the degree of intoxication was not sufficient for him to be unable to form the required *mens rea* for the offence.

Intoxication and other defences

Second, intoxication can also become an issue when the defendant raises a defence to a charge. He may, for example, plead self defence on the basis that he mistakenly believed that he was about to be attacked and this mistake was due to the fact that he had been drinking (e.g. in the English case of *R* v *O'Connor* [1991] Crim LR 135). How the law responds to such a claim is clearly an important question and one that has generated a considerable amount of case law and academic comment. The response has often not been wholly consistent (compare, for example, *R* v *Richardson* [1999] 1 Cr.App.R.392 and *Jaggard* v *Dickenson* [1981] QB 527 with *R* v *Fotheringham* (1988) 88 Cr.App.R.206).

Primarily for reasons of space, the chapter will concern itself with the fundamental issue of attributing criminal liability to intoxicated individuals, although, in places some mention will be made to the relationship between intoxication and defences such as insanity and diminished responsibility.

The four models of criminal liability

The remainder of this chapter will evaluate in turn the four main approaches to intoxication and criminal liability that can be observed in western legal systems. These can be grouped as follows: 1. Intoxication is irrelevant in all cases; 2. Intoxication may be relevant in cases of 'specific' intent but not those of 'basic' intent; 3. Intoxication may be relevant in cases of 'basic' intent and in cases of 'specific' intent; 4. Intoxication may be relevant in cases of 'basic' intent and in cases of 'specific' intent but in combination with an offence of causing harm whilst intoxicated. These categories can also be used to describe stages of development. England and Wales, for example, is currently in the second category yet this is only due to a gradual transition from the first category during the nineteenth century, whilst Canada has shifted categories more than once.

1. Intoxication is irrelevant in all cases

This position represents the original position found in most common law countries (McAuley 1997; McCord 1992; Singh 1933). Today it still represents the law in Scotland and would appear to represent the stance taken in the Netherlands. The following case graphically illustrates both the simplicity and the consequences of such a position. When John Savage cut the throat of Jemima Grierson there were defence witnesses who were prepared to testify that Savage was drunk on the night in question. The Scottish High Court of Justiciary found this evidence to be totally irrelevant (*HM Advocate* v *Savage* (1923) JC 49). Despite it being a murder case, and despite the fact that the offence then carried a mandatory death penalty, Lord Justice Clerk stated that:

> To say that a man, who takes drink and while under its influence commits a crime, is to be excused from the penalty of the crime merely because he made himself drunk would of course be a most perilous doctrine. And it is not the law of Scotland. The man himself is responsible for getting drunk, and the mere fact that he has taken drink, and while under its influence committed a crime, is not sufficient to excuse him from the consequences of his crime. (p. 50)

Even if the jury were to believe the defence witnesses' account, Savage would have been unsuccessful in arguing that his intoxication should reduce the charge from murder to culpable homicide (roughly analogous to the English crime of manslaughter). What is striking about the case to an outsider (at least in terms of my legal education!) is the dogmatic way in which the issue was settled at trial with scant reference to the principles of criminal law. Since then the issue has been considered only periodically by the Scottish courts and has been subject to relatively little academic attention.

Given the practical importance of the topic this may appear strange but Scotland is a small jurisdiction and can hardly be expected to generate the same volume of case law as a larger jurisdiction. This factor helps explain both the relative dearth of authority and the fact that High Court of Justiciary cases are cited as authority more frequently than courts of first instance elsewhere as there are a correspondingly small number of criminal appeals. Moreover, Scots law is not as dependent on precedent as certain other jurisdictions. It has a somewhat unique hybrid status somewhere between a common law system and a civil law system. What is more difficult to explain is the apparently cursory way in which the judgment dealt with the issues of criminal law principle. Writing generally about Scots criminal law, McCall Smith and Sheldon (1997: v) have argued that several important cases in the 1990s have shown 'a breadth of analysis, and a reliance on authority and doctrine not perhaps so evident in the case law prior to that time'. This trend is attributed to the approach taken by recent Lord Justice-Generals and runs counter to the traditionally pragmatic 'genius' of the Scots criminal law (see generally Farmer 1996). To date though this form of doctrinal analysis has not been applied to the question of whether intoxication should be taken into account in determining criminal liability.

The recent reaffirmation of the first paradigm

More recent case law continues to demonstrate pragmatism rather than principle. Intoxication was considered again by a Full Bench of the High

Court of Justiciary in *Brennan* v *HM Advocate* 1977 SLT 152 (for analysis see McClory 2001). In essence the judgment reaffirmed the ruling in *Savage* in light of developments south of the border (which equate to the second approach discussed below) and two Scottish judgments (*HM Advocate* v *Campbell* 1920 2 SLT 317, *Kennedy* v *HM Advocate* 1945 SLT 11) which suggested that this new English approach was also being followed in Scotland. Any relaxing of the traditional position that self-induced intoxication afforded no defence in Scots law was emphatically rejected. What is interesting is the way in which the court arrived at this conclusion by re-emphasising the distinctiveness of Scots criminal law, both specifically with regard to murder (p. 156) and, more generally, by rejecting any distinction between crimes of 'basic' intent and crimes of 'specific' intent (pp. 155–156) which formed the basis of the new English approach.

In *Brennan* the defence put forward two possible ways in which intoxication could, in their opinion, be relevant to determining criminal liability. The facts were not in dispute. Brennan had stabbed his father to death after drinking between 20 and 25 pints of beer and taking a quantity of LSD. The first ground of appeal was that a temporary impairment of someone's mental faculties may be sufficient to amount to the defence of insanity in Scots law, even if this impairment was due to self-induced intoxication. The court were quick to dismiss this submission. Noting that Hume's influential *Commentaries* were clear that 'the law of Scotland views this wilful distemper with a quite different eye from the other, which is a visitation of Providence' (1797: 45) they concluded that:

[Insanity] in our law requires proof of total alienation of reason in relation to the act charged as the result of mental illness, mental disease or defect or unsoundness of mind and does not comprehend the malfunctioning of the mind of transitory effect, as the result of deliberate and self-induced intoxication. (p. 154)

As the High Court of Justiciary quoted so extensively from Hume, it is worth considering the many justifications he advances in support of this distinction. Crudely they can be classified as a mixture of the philosophical and the pragmatic. On philosophical grounds, Hume starts by asserting that an intoxicated offender should not be afforded a defence as his conduct was 'wilful' (p. 45) and that mitigation cannot be justified by conduct which 'itself shews [sic] a disregard of order and decency' (p. 45).

At a practical level, Hume notes the difficulties both of distinguishing between different degrees of intoxication and of ascertaining whether an individual was genuinely intoxicated at the time of the offence (p. 45). There is no doubt that factual questions about the veracity of the defendant's claim and establishing the degree of intoxication are inherently difficult but one can obviously debate whether these evidential difficulties justify removing the possibility of a defence in all cases, including those where the jury would have no problem in concluding that the defendant was intoxicated at the time of the offence and that the degree of intoxication was such that some defence should be available. As we will see later, more recent comparative research shows that juries only rarely allow a defendant to rely on intoxication in countries where the law allows it to be taken into account (Orchard 1993; Skene 1983; Smith 1981) raising questions about just how difficult it is for juries to make this determination.

Hume's next justification – namely that a reversal of the law would compromise public safety by allowing a possible defence to those who drank in order to gain the necessary courage to offend – has been recognised as an exception to the general rule in those countries which do allow intoxication to be taken into account, either for all offences or for some. The final justification offered by Hume, and one which continues to have an enduring appeal both to the Scottish courts (*Brennan* v *HM Advocate* 1977 SLT 152: p. 153 and p. 158) and those elsewhere, is a general policy argument based on public safety. Arguments that 'it is indispensable to guard the safety of the peaceable and decent' from the 'dissolute and worthless' (p. 45) remain popular today. But whether public protection does actually require such an approach to be taken seems questionable in light of the restricted number of individuals who could claim to have been so intoxicated that they could form no *mens rea*.

Rejecting the second paradigm

The second, and more substantial, ground of appeal was based on developments outside Scotland, most notably in England and Wales (see *DPP v Beard* [1920] AC 479), since the time of Hume's work. It was argued on Brennan's behalf that the trial judge should have given the jury the option of returning a verdict of culpable homicide as there was evidence that the appellant was so drunk that he could not have formed the necessary 'specific' intent for murder. This was based on the decisions in *HM Advocate v Campbell* 1920 2 SLT 317 and *Kennedy v HM Advocate* 1945 SLT 11 where the courts held that Scots law was identical to English law in so far as self-induced intoxication could negate the required intention to kill or cause serious injury. *Brennan* rejected this view on the basis that the *mens rea* requirement for murder under Scots law is wider than under English law:

> In England the crime involves 'malice aforethought', a technical expression which requires proof of either the specific intention to

kill or to do serious injury. In the law of Scotland, however, the crime of murder is constituted by any willful act causing the destruction of life, whether intended to kill or displaying such wicked recklessness as to imply a disposition depraved enough to be regardless of the consequences. Our definition of murder includes the taking of human life by a person who has an intent to kill or to do serious injury, or whose act is shown to have been wickedly reckless as to the consequence. (p. 156)

And, as the *mens rea* may be satisfied by wicked recklessness:

[It] is extremely difficult to understand how actings may lose the quality of such recklessness because the actor was in an intoxicated state brought about by his own deliberate and conscious purpose. (p. 157)

The court, therefore, relies upon the specific mental state required for murder in Scotland to justify its conclusion in the case. Two issues arising from the case merit further comment, the first relating specifically to the law of murder and the second to the scope of the judgment with regard to other offences.

In the context of murder, the High Court of Justiciary argued that the courts in England and Wales and the courts in Scotland had both attempted to find ways of mitigating the mandatory death penalty in murder cases (see also Sellers 1978). In Scotland the courts developed the concept of diminished responsibility (which can be traced back as far as *HM Advocate* v *Dingwall* (1867) 5 Irv. 466) long before the concept was recognised elsewhere. A successful plea of diminished responsibility reduced the charge to culpable homicide, thereby evading the mandatory sentence. The English approach, which will be considered shortly, allowed a verdict of manslaughter to be returned where self-induced intoxication had rendered the accused unable to form the 'specific' intent for murder (*DPP* v *Beard* [1920] AC 479). What is important to realise is that, despite the common purpose highlighted in the judgment (p. 155), the different approaches could lead to dramatically different results. We have already seen how Savage was unable to escape a murder conviction on the grounds of his alleged intoxication. If the same incident had happened south of the border, it would have been open to the jury to find him guilty of manslaughter on the basis of his intoxication. By adopting different strategies, the courts were in effect determining that different categories of offender should be spared the death penalty for murder. The Scottish courts were more restrictive than their English counterparts – a position which remains, despite the abolition of the death penalty, to this day.

The second issue, which is of obvious practical importance, relates to the scope of the ruling in *Brennan*. Does it apply to other offences or is it limited to murder? This is not immediately apparent as the court largely bases its decision on the different requirements for murder in English and Scots law. However, many of the policy arguments cited by the court would appear to be equally applicable to other offences (or, at the very least, to other offences of violence). The High Court of Justiciary also took the opportunity to state that the distinction between crimes of 'basic' intent and crimes of 'specific' intent does not form part of the law of Scotland (pp. 155–156) and commented that the English approach had 'rightly been recognised as illogical' (p. 155). Given the court's robust endorsement of Hume's justifications along with their hostility to the English approach, it would appear sensible to conclude that *Brennan* is not restricted to murder cases, and any other appeal on the basis of a distinction between crimes of 'basic' and crimes of 'specific' intent would be unlikely to succeed.

Further evidence that *Brennan* should have this wider application can be found in *Ross* v *HM Advocate* 1991 SLT 564, a case dealing with involuntary intoxication. Lord Justice-General Hope distinguished this scenario from cases of self-induced intoxication, stating that in self-induced intoxication cases there is a policy exception to the general rule that an absence of *mens rea* entitles the accused to an acquittal and that '[in] *all* such cases the accused must be assumed to have intended the natural consequences of his act' (p. 566, italics added). Similarly, Lord McClusky saw *Brennan* as 'an extremely careful judgment which did not stray beyond dealing with the particular kind of case under consideration, the case of the criminal responsibility of a person who voluntarily and deliberately consumes known intoxicants' (p. 577). There is certainly no indication that he felt that *Brennan* was limited in scope to murder (see further Chalmers 2001).

Nevertheless, widening the scope of *Brennan* to offences other than murder is conceptually problematic. Even if one accepts that getting intoxicated is 'wickedly reckless' rather than merely 'reckless' for the purposes of murder, there are a number of offences which specify a particular intention in Scots law. As Jones and Christie observe:

When the courts insist upon a particular *mens rea* (such as intention to ravish) in the definition of a common law crime they do so because it is that particular mental element which renders the accused more blameworthy than when that element is absent. A refusal to regard as relevant any claim that the accused lacked the requisite *mens rea* appears to defeat the purpose of including the specific mental element in the definition of the crime. (1992: 160)

As the next section demonstrates, it was this recognition that certain offences require a 'specific' intent and that intoxication, whether self-induced or not, can stop someone from forming that intent, that led the law in England and Wales, and in certain other jurisdictions, to follow a different course from the law in Scotland.

2. Intoxication may be relevant in crimes of 'specific' intent

The current position in England and Wales is the archetypal example of this approach. It has been followed at various times by other common law jurisdictions and is still the most common position found in the US. The Irish Court of Criminal Appeal also endorsed the position in 2004 (*DPP* v *Reilly* (unreported); Dillon 2004; Spencer 2005).

Strictly speaking intoxication in itself is never a defence in English law. As in Scotland, the courts have not been prepared to accept that intoxication can give rise to a defence of insanity unless the defendant's drinking had resulted in a 'disease of the mind' recognised under the famous, dated, but still applicable *M'Naghten* (1843) 10 Cl & Fin 200 rules. The difference between insanity and intoxication in the absence of a 'disease of the mind' was articulated by Stephen J. when he directed the jury in *Davis* (1881) 14 Cox CC 563:

> [Drunkenness] is one thing and diseases to which drunkenness leads are different things; and if a man by drunkenness brings on a state of disease which causes such a degree of madness, even for a time, which would have relieved him from responsibility if it had been caused in any other way, then he would not be criminally responsible. (p. 564)

Whilst this could afford a defence to someone suffering from a condition such as delirium tremens or alcoholic dementia, the consequences of a special verdict remain uncertain and potentially significant. In murder cases only, the Scots law concept of diminished responsibility was introduced in England and Wales in the Homicide Act 1957. However the scope was again limited, in this case it applied:

> [If the person] was suffering from such abnormality of mind (whether arising from a condition of arrested or retarded development of mind or any inherent causes or induced by disease or injury) as substantially impaired his mental responsibility for his acts and omissions in doing or being a party to the killing. (s.2(1))

Case law has shown the limited circumstances when a defendant who was intoxicated at the time of the offence can successfully plead diminished responsibility. In *Tandy* [1989] 1 All ER 267 the court held that diminished responsibility would be an available defence either where the defendant's alcoholism was such that he was totally unable to resist the impulse to drink or where the defendant's alcoholism had led to brain injury which had resulted in either gross impairment of judgment or emotional response. This can be contrasted with *O'Connell* [1997] Crim LR 683 where it was argued, with the support of expert evidence, that the defendant's perceptions at the time of the killing may have been adversely affected by a combination of alcohol and a sleeping drug. Even if this had been the case, the Court of Appeal held that the defence of diminished responsibility was not available as the state could not amount to a 'disease or injury' due to its transitory nature.

In summary, intoxication cannot amount to a defence in England and Wales, however, if the defendant's drinking has led to a 'disease of the mind' sufficient for the *M'Naghten* test for insanity or, in murder cases, falls within the test for diminished responsibility in *Tandy*, then the resulting medical condition can give rise to a defence of insanity or diminished responsibility (see further Tolmie 2001). Whilst this is identical to the Scottish position (see the earlier discussion of *Brennan* v *HM Advocate* 1977 SLT 152) the similarity ends here because, unlike Scots law, English law does allow the jury to take account of intoxication in cases where a 'specific' intent is required. When dealing with 'specific' intent cases, intoxication is not technically a defence. Instead, intoxication is considered to be relevant evidence from which the jury may, or may not, conclude that the defendant did not have the necessary intent for the offence. The next section considers the development of this approach.

The development of the English position

The case of *DPP* v *Beard* [1920] AC 479 provides a useful summary of the historical development of the law in this area in the nineteenth century in England and Wales (pp. 494–504). The earlier case law cited by Lord Birkenhead demonstrates a gradual shift away from a position where intoxication could never be of any relevance in determining criminal liability to a position where it could be of relevance with respect to certain offences which required a 'specific' intent on the part of the accused (see McAuley 1997; McCord 1992; Singh 1933). Until the beginning of the nineteenth century the position was clear. As in Scotland, early writers maintained that intoxication was irrelevant in determining criminal liability: Hale (1736: 32) commenting that a 'person committing homicide shall not be punished simply for the crime of homicide, but shall suffer for his drunkenness'. Though this meant that 'the formal cause of his punishment is rather the drunkenness than the crime committed in it' (p. 32) the practical consequences were identical.

Similar conclusions were reached, though without the same articulated rationale, by Hawkins (1716: s.6), Coke upon Littleton (1832: 247a) and Blackstone (1769). This early approach can be witnessed in the early case of *Reniger* v *Fogassa* (1552) 1 Plowd. 1 where the prisoner's drunkenness was deemed to be of no relevance because it was occasioned 'by his own act and folly'.

There then followed a move away from this extreme position in the nineteenth century until the landmark judgment in *R* v *Doherty* (1887) 16 Cox C.C. 306 where it was stated by Stephen J. that 'when the crime is such that the intention of the party committing it is one of its constituent elements, [the jury] may look at the fact that a man was in drink in considering whether he formed the intention necessary to constitute that crime' (p. 308). However mere drunkenness was not enough: the accused 'must have been so drunk as to be incapable of knowing what he was doing' (*R* v *Stopford* (1870) 11 Cox C.C. 643) or, in other words, would not have been able to form any 'specific' intent required (see also *R* v *Monkhouse* (1849) 4 Cox C.C. 55). As Lord Birkenhead noted in *Beard* (p. 495) this shift was both gradual and difficult to attribute to any one particular judgment. The shift was never fully justified on the basis of criminal law principle. Rather it seemed to emerge as a purely pragmatic mechanism for mitigating the mandatory punishment for murder. Inconsistency clearly occurred in this transitional period, with far reaching consequences for those adversely affected. Indeed the judge in the first reported case where intoxication was allowed to be taken into account (*R* v *Grindley* (1819) unreported, cited in *Beard* at p. 495) apparently changed his mind in subsequent cases (see *R* v *Carroll* (1835) 7 C & P 145).

After reviewing the nineteenth century authorities, Lord Birkenhead summarised the state of the law as follows:

[Where] a specific intent is an essential element in the offence, evidence of a state of drunkenness rendering the accused incapable of forming such an intent should be taken into consideration in order to determine whether he had in fact formed the intent necessary to constitute the particular crime. If he was so drunk that he was incapable of forming the intent required he could not be convicted of a crime which was committed only if the intent was proved. (p. 499)

As a survey of the existing authorities, the judgment retains considerable value. The statement above represents an accurate summary of the position by 1920. The Lord Chancellor saw his task as determining the current law from the early authorities. As such his approach is avowedly historical and he himself claimed that he was not engaged in a normative assessment of what the law should be: '[the] reasoning may be sound or unsound . . . [but] the law is plain beyond all question' (ibid.: p. 500). Unfortunately, after attempting to clarify the existing law, Lord Birkenhead did then engage in a normative assessment of the law. This took the form of questioning the distinction between crimes of 'basic' intent and crimes of 'specific' intent. He said:

> I do not think that the proposition of law deduced from these earlier cases is an exceptional rule applicable only to cases in which it is necessary to prove a specific intent in order to constitute the graver crime – e.g. wounding with intent to do grevious bodily harm or with intent to kill. It is true that in such cases the specific intent must be proved to constitute the particular crime, but this is, on ultimate analysis, only in accordance with the ordinary law applicable to crime, for, speaking generally (and apart from certain special offences), a person cannot be convicted of a crime unless the *mens* was *rea*. (ibid.: p. 504)

This is an argument of principle, but it is an argument of principle in favour of the third approach – that of allowing intoxication to be of relevance with respect to both crimes of 'specific' intent and crimes of 'basic' intent. It is not an argument in favour of the second approach which, earlier in the judgment, he took to represent the law. His argument ironically pre-empts the justifications that were later used to depart from the second approach in some other common law jurisdictions. Commentators at the time (Stroud 1920) noted that it would be a radical departure from the common law position if the courts took this wider statement to represent the law in England and Wales. *Beard* could have plunged the law into a period of great uncertainty as it is inherently contradictory. This did not happen as the courts did not appear to notice the glaring inconsistency for over half a century. Ironically its lack of clarity has perhaps given the case a greater belated international importance than it merits for parts of it have been cited with approval both by courts wishing to retain the second approach and by courts wishing to reject it!

Majewski: reinforcing the second approach

Prior to the House of Lords' judgment in *DPP* v *Majewski* [1977] AC 443, courts in England, Wales and Northern Ireland were of the opinion that, despite the view Lord Birkenhead expressed above, *Beard* established that self-induced intoxication was only potentially of relevance to those cases involving a requirement for a 'specific' intent. It followed that self-induced intoxication was irrelevant to crimes of 'basic' intent. This was the view expressed by the House of Lords in two appeals from Northern Ireland (*Attorney-General for Northern Ireland* v *Gallagher* [1963]

AC 349; *Bratty* v *Attorney-General for Northern Ireland* [1963] AC 386). At the same time, however, there was mounting academic criticism of this approach on the basis that it lacked philosophical coherence and, as will be documented later, this criticism was recognised and acted upon in some other jurisdictions by a move to the third approach. As many of these concerns continue to be aired they will be discussed after the judgments in *Majewski* are analysed.

Procedural problems of an almost farcical nature (documented by the Court of Appeal: pp. 449–451) blighted the early history of the case. The facts, involving a violent outburst in a pub where Majewski attacked a number of people after consuming a combination of alcohol and drugs, were, as the Court of Appeal recognised, so commonplace that they do not require further elaboration. It is though worth noting that two of the Law Lords did not believe that Majewski was sufficiently intoxicated that he could not have formed the necessary intent for the offences in question (see Lord Simon of Glaisdale: p. 480; Lord Russell of Killowen: p. 498). This meant that, even if the House of Lords had determined the law differently, Majewski's appeal would in all probability have failed on the facts.

In the Court of Appeal, Majewski's lawyer argued that *Beard* had been misunderstood by the judiciary for the past 55 years. This was, in the words of the court, 'bold and persuasive advocacy' (p. 451) but, due to the fact that the legal position appeared both 'well-established' and 'strong', the Court of Appeal were taken aback when counsel for the Crown said that he could not support Majewski's convictions. The Court of Appeal then invited the Director of Public Prosecutions to take over the role of the Crown and present the case for the prosecution. Were it not for the Director of Public Prosecutions' involvement, the legal position post-*Beard* would have been highly uncertain; the Court of Appeal decision in *Majewski* would appear to have conflicted with the case law leading up to *Beard* and with the comments in the two House of Lords' judgments from Northern Ireland. And, whilst the Court of Appeal is usually bound to follow the House of Lords, technically these two recent decisions of the House were only of a highly persuasive value in the present case (p. 454).

It was submitted on behalf of Majewski that, properly understood, Lord Birkenhead's comments in *Beard* were correct as a matter of principle. With the exception of certain offences which require no intent whatsoever on the part of the accused – the so-called offences of 'strict' liability – it was an accepted principle of criminal liability that the prosecution had to prove a guilty intent on the part of the accused for all other offences (*R* v *Tolson* (1889) 23 QBD 168; *R* v *Morgan* [1976] AC 182). Case law had established that the offences Majewski had been charged with, assault occasioning actual bodily harm and assaulting a police officer in the execution of his duty, required proof of intent (*Fagan* v *Metropolitan Police Commissioner* [1969] 1 QB 439) and it was therefore necessary to leave evidence of intoxication to the jury as this could be relevant to the issue of whether Majewski had that intent. It was submitted that Lord Birkenhead's reasoning was logical and should be taken to represent the applicable law.

Surprising as it may seem, counsel for the Director of Public Prosecutions conceded that 'if the law about the relevance of self-induced intoxication to criminal responsibility was logical, no distinction should be drawn between specific intent and any other kind of intent' (p. 455). However, the law on this topic, he maintained, had developed pragmatically. He referred to the development of the law in the nineteenth century as a policy to 'relax the strict common law' (p. 456) either where the punishment was perceived as disproportionate or where there would be a degree of popular sympathy for the accused. He also noted that in the period in question, despite a great deal of reforming zeal, parliament had never considered whether self-induced intoxication should become a general defence in criminal law.

The Court of Appeal dismissed Majewski's appeal against conviction. Lord Justice Lawton felt satisfied that the historical context was so central to Lord Birkenhead in *Beard* that self-induced intoxication could only be of relevance to crimes of 'specific' intent (p. 456). However, the Court of Appeal allowed an appeal to the House of Lords as the case involved a point of law of general public importance.

The House again dismissed the appeal, maintaining the distinction between crimes of 'basic' intent and crimes of 'specific' intent. Their Lordships again devoted considerable attention to the historical development of how the law responded to self-induced intoxication but what is of more interest for present purposes are their attempts to justify this distinction on the basis of public policy and criminal law principle. Several considerations are readily discernible. The most notable is their Lordship's belief that such a distinction was necessary in order to protect the public. Extending the rule would, in their opinion, have clearly jeopardised public safety. A typically robust expression of this view is provided by Lord Simon of Glaisdale:

> One of the prime purposes of the criminal law, with its penal sanctions, is the protection from certain proscribed conduct of persons who are pursuing their lawful lives. Unprovoked violence has, from time immemorial, been a significant part of such proscribed conduct. To accede to the argument on behalf of the appellant would leave the citizen legally unprotected from unprovoked violence where such violence was the consequence of drink or drugs having obliterated the capacity of the perpetrator to know what he was doing or what were its consequences. (p. 476)

Popular conceptions of justice also featured heavily in their reasoning. Lord Edmund-Davies, in stating that '[the] universal object of a system of law is obvious – the establishment and maintainance of order', felt that this was so widely accepted that it would explain 'the sense of outrage which would naturally be felt ... were [Majewski] to go free' (p. 495). Lord Salmon similarly argued that widening the situations where self-induced intoxication could be relevant 'would rightly bring the law into contempt' (p. 484). Even if the distinction was illogical, this was a price that their Lordships would be willing to pay in order to protect the public. Lord Russell of Killowen expressed his opinion that '[logic] in criminal law must not be allowed to run away with common sense, particularly when the preservation of the Queen's Peace is in question' (p. 498, see also Lord Salmon: p. 484).

This suggestion that English common law is 'founded on common sense and experience rather than strict logic' (Lord Salmon, p. 482) shows that pragmatic ingenuity is far from being a uniquely Scottish trait. Nonetheless it would be unfair to dismiss *Majewski* as no more than a policy judgment. Whilst a great deal of emphasis was undoubtedly placed on the need to offer adequate public protection, attention was also given by at least some of the Law Lords as to how this could be achieved without distorting the fundamental principles of criminal liability. Lord Edmund-Davies in particular analysed and rejected claims that the distinction between crimes of 'basic' intent and crimes of 'specific' intent lacked both consistency and any ethical foundation. Central to his reasoning was his belief that getting voluntarily intoxicated was sufficiently blameworthy to merit punishment on the grounds of recklessness (p. 496). Crimes could be classified as ones of 'basic' intent in his view if the *mens rea* could be satisfied by recklessness. In arriving at this conclusion, he drew support from the views of Stroud who wrote that:

[Drunkenness] is not incompatible with *mens rea*, in the sense of ordinary culpable intentionality, because mere recklessness is sufficient to satisfy the definition of *mens rea*, and drunkenness is itself an act of recklessness. The law therefore establishes a conclusive presumption against the admission of proof of intoxication for the purposes of disproving *mens rea* in ordinary crimes. Where this principle applies, it does not make 'drunkenness itself' a crime, but the drunkenness is itself an integral part of the crime, as forming, together with the other unlawful conduct charged against the defendant, a complex act of criminal recklessness. This explanation affords at once a justification of the rule of law, and a reason for its inapplicability when drunkenness is pleaded by way of showing absence of full intent, or of some exceptional form of *mens rea* essential to a particular crime, according to its definition. (1914: 115)

The other Law Lords spent less time attempting to justify the distinction. Instead their primary concern was to come up with a satisfactory test for classifying different offences in terms of 'basic' and 'specific' intent. Each of these tests has been subsequently criticised (Smith 1976). Lord Edmund-Davies, as we have seen, saw the availability of recklessness as a sufficient criterion for making the determination (see Macdonald 1986). Lord Elwyn Jones, with whom Lord Kilbrandon agreed, put forward an alternative strategy based on the test recently adopted in the House of Lords by Lord Simon in the case of *R* v *Morgan* [1976] AC 182. Using this test, crimes of 'basic' intent were:

> [Those] crimes whose definition expresses (or more often implies) a *mens rea* which does not go beyond the *actus reus*. The *actus reus* generally consists of an act and some consequence. The consequence may be very closely connected with the act or more remotely connected with it: but with a crime of basic intent the *mens rea* does not extend beyond the act and its consequence, however remote, as defined in the *actus reus*. (p. 216)

Finally, Lord Simon expressly adopted the test formulated by Fauteux J. in the Canadian case of *George* (1960) 128 C.C.C. 289 namely:

> In considering the question of *mens rea*, a distinction is to be made between (i) intention as applied to acts considered in relation to their purposes and (ii) intention as applied to acts apart from their purposes. A general intent attending the commission of an act is, in some cases, the only intent required to constitute the crime while, in others, there must be, in addition to that general intent, a specific intent attending the purpose for the commission of the act. (p. 301)

This, ironically, could conflict with the earlier test he adopted in *Morgan* and which was followed by Lord Elwyn Jones and Lord Kilbrandon in *Majewski*. Despite internal contradiction and widespread criticism, the position post-*Majewski* can be summarised with ease. Their Lordships maintained the distinction between crimes of 'basic' and 'specific' intent that remains at the heart of the second approach. At a practical level case law has established which offences are treated as ones of 'specific' intent (e.g. murder and theft) and which are classified as 'basic' intent (e.g. rape and criminal damage).

There remains little practical uncertainty, although a determination has to be made each time a new offence is created. For most, but not all, offences of 'specific' intent there is a corresponding (and lesser) offence of 'basic' intent for which the intoxicated offender can be convicted. In practice this potential reduction in charge acts as a compromise: the offender will deservedly be punished but not to the extent of his sober counterpart (Clarkson 1978). It should also be said that, despite periodic suggestions (Law Commission 1993), parliament has not considered reforming the law in this area (see Draft Offences Against the Person Bill 1998, clause 19). There is also evidence that most practitioners find the system workable and do not support radical change (Law Commission 1995). But this should not disguise the fact that most academic commentators find the approach deeply unsatisfactory at a conceptual level.

Criticising Majewski

The approach in *Majewski* has remained the subject of consistent and considerable academic criticism (e.g. Beaumont 1976; Cavender 1989; Farrier 1976; Smith 1976, 1987; Smith and Hogan 1992; Virgo 1993). Those whose early writings were dismissed by the House of Lords launched the initial assault. Glanville Williams, to take a notable example, trenchantly criticised the way in which offences were classified into those of 'basic' intent and those of 'specific' intent post-*Majewski* (1983: 472–473; for similar concerns see Ward 1986; White 1989). Classification was determined, in Williams' opinion, largely on the basis of linguistic distinctions which, in practice, were meaningless. He demonstrated this by considering how the courts have interpreted the word 'killing' in murder cases:

> When we talk of killing ... a person, we may conceptualise or verbalise the event in either of two ways. We may take killing ... to mean doing an act (striking etc.) that causes death ... where the act and its consequence are treated as two separate events; or we may have a composite notion of 'doing an act of killing' ... where the result is included in the notion of the act. The choice is only a question of words, but it is a choice with legal implications under the rule in *Majewski*. Traditionally, murder is thought of as a 'killing', and that is how it is legally described. But, the judges' scheme being to have a rule that will let the drunkard off the graver charge only, they decide to think of murder for this particular purpose as 'an act done with intent to cause death (and succeeding in that purpose)' rather than as an act of self-contained 'intentional killing' ... This is one of many examples that could be given of judges making a meaningless distinction of language yield legal results. (1983: 472)

It is clear that the list of offences which are categorised under the headings of 'basic' and 'specific' intent are arbitrary and do not always satisfy the tests articulated for classification purposes in *Majewski*. Murder provides a useful example. It is clear from the case law that murder has been categorised as a crime of 'specific' intent (*DPP v Beard* [1920] AC 479). In *Majewski*, Lord Elwyn Jones and Lord Kilbrandon adopted the test for 'basic' intent given by Lord Simon in *R v Morgan* [1976] AC 182. Yet, applying this test would seem to suggest that murder should not be a crime of 'specific' intent but of 'basic' intent; the *actus reus* is killing and there is no need to prove any *mens rea* beyond this (Smith 1976: 377). Lord Simon used a different and potentially conflicting test in *Majewski*. The distinction which he found useful in the judgment of Fauteux J. in *George* (1960) 128 C.C.C. 289 was between 1. intention as applied to acts considered in relation to their purposes and 2. intention as applied to acts apart from their purposes. According to Smith there is no real purposive element in the *mens rea* of murder so again the offence should have been classified as an offence of 'basic' intent. Not only are the tests potentially inconsistent but they do not appear to have been followed consistently (Quigley 1987b).

J. C. Smith (1976) noted a further significant ramification of *Majewski*. Qualifications now have to be read into every criminal law statute specifying a *mens rea* requirement for a 'basic' intent offence. This is because, following *Majewski*, the prosecution are under no obligation to prove any intention or foresight if the offence is one of 'basic' intent and the defendant seeks to rely on voluntary intoxication regardless of what the statute itself may provide. By way of example he cites the word 'maliciously' and says that the following caveat would have to be added: 'except where the accused was intoxicated through the voluntary taking of drink or drugs' (ibid.: 376). And, whilst he notes correctly that qualifications are already read into statutes so as to accommodate general defences such as self defence, this is different in that the qualification being read in is unfavourable to the accused.

The underlying presumption

Underlying the second (and to an even greater effect the first) approach is a presumption of some magnitude. In effect the second approach creates a presumption of 'basic' intent as it is assumed that proof of intoxication is proof of 'basic' intent (Healy 1994: 518). This, in turn, eliminates a key element from the definition of the offence. In cases of extreme intoxication, the prosecution do not have to prove that the defendant had the required *mens rea* for a 'basic' intent offence. Indeed claiming intoxication for 'basic' intent offences is not an irrelevance as might be supposed but actually is *detrimental*: in effect the defendant concedes *mens rea*.

An alternative approach would, at least, allow a claim of intoxication to be a neutral factor. In *Richardson* [1999] 1 Cr.App.R.392 the court held that the evidence of intoxication was to be ignored and the jury were to be asked to answer a hypothetical question: would the accused have had the *mens rea* if he had not been intoxicated?

As the jury would presumably conclude in the ordinary course of events that the defendant would have foreseen the natural and probable consequences of his acts if he had not been intoxicated then only rarely will this approach benefit the defendant. Nonetheless, there may be cases where there were factors other than intoxication which should be taken into account to explain the defendant's mistake. If *Richardson* were to be followed, the jury would be allowed to consider these factors. On the facts, the decision in *Richardson* seems odd. The convictions in the case were quashed by the Court of Appeal despite the apparent absence of any explanation for their conduct other than their drunkenness. There are grounds for believing that *Richardson* may not be good law. The case was primarily concerned with a drunken, and hence mistaken, belief in consent. As the mistake was caused by intoxication the case is inconsistent with authorities such as *Fotheringham* (1988) 88 Cr.App.R.206 which stated that a mistaken belief in consent could not be considered in a rape case if the mistake was due to intoxication.

Yet, even if the approach in *Richardson* is adopted there are still fundamental questions about the extent to which the second approach is compatible with the presumption of innocence, an issue of even greater importance in the British context since the Human Rights Act 1998 came into force. Evidence which suggests that the defendant did not have the necessary *mens rea* is being withheld from the jury.

Defending Majewski

Not all writers have found the *Majewski* approach indefensible (e.g. Colvin 1981; Dashwood 1977). In an important, and often overlooked, article Gardner (1994) has robustly criticised some of the assumptions made by other writers, though he concedes that the post-*Majewski* position is far from satisfactory (ibid.: 284, fn.26). Gardner takes issue with the subjective stance that advertence should be a requirement for recklessness. Drawing on examples from case law, he shows how English law is prepared to attribute liability for recklessness where the defendant fails to think about what he is doing and his failure to do so is reckless and where the defendant mistakenly believes that he is not satisfying the *actus reus* of an offence but the mistaken belief is blameworthy. He continues:

> [Inadvertence] or mistake as a result of voluntary intoxication must be the archetypal cases of blameworthy inadvertence or blame-worthy mistake. These deficient states are known to all as the potential result of intoxication by alcohol or dangerous drugs, and there is a clearly recognised moral stigma upon engendering them in this way. So in recognising intoxication as a basis of inculpation, *Majewski* may be seen as, far from a doctrinal pariah, very much part of this tradition. (ibid.: 282–283)

This is, in many ways, an argument that goes beyond *Majewski* for it relates to a far wider debate about the overall direction that the criminal law is, and should, be taking. Gardner provides a counter-balance to the subjectivism which underlies many of the criticisms made of *Majewski*. His article correctly maintains that subjectivism is but one route the criminal law can take and that those advocating such a position need to argue for it properly, both because the existing criminal law is more complex than is sometimes assumed and because unqualified subjectivism may conflict with popular notions of blameworthiness. Since Gardner's article was written, there has been a further significant retreat from objectivism (*R* v *G* [2004] 1 AC 1034 overturned *R* v *Caldwell* [1982] AC 341, the leading authority on objective recklessness) in the criminal law. In *R* v *Stephenson* [1979] QB 695, Lord Justice Lane remarked that:

> There is no doubt that the subjective definition of 'recklessness' does produce difficulties. One of them which is particularly likely to occur in practice is the person who by self-induced intoxication by drink or drugs deprives himself of the ability to foresee the risks involved in his actions. Assuming that by reason of his intoxication he is not proved to have foreseen the relevant risk, can he be said to have been 'reckless'? Plainly not, unless cases of self-induced intoxication are an exception to the general rule. (p. 704)

Whilst *G* clearly endorsed a subjective approach to recklessness, it also stated, albeit in passing, that self-induced intoxication was an exception to the general principle:

> [It] is not clearly blameworthy to do something involving a risk of injury to another if (for reasons other than self-induced intoxication: *R* [sic] v *Majewski* [1977] AC 443) one genuinely does not perceive the risk. Such a person may fairly be accused of stupidity or lack of imagination, but neither of those failings should expose him to conviction of serious crime or the risk of punishment. (p. 1055, *per* Lord Bingham of Cornhill)

Despite a robust, general subjectivism, therefore, the House of Lords maintained that voluntary intoxication was not only an exception to the general rule but the only exception to the general rule. If *G* was striking because of the strident manner in which their lordships overturned *Caldwell*, it was equally striking how readily the House followed *Majewski*.

3. Intoxication may be relevant in crimes of 'basic' and crimes of 'specific' intent

The third approach is commonly associated with Australasia, but that is too sweeping and therefore misleading. Not all of the states in Australia have adopted it; it never applied in the Northern Territory, Queensland, Tasmania and Western Australia and it no longer applies in New South Wales or the Australian Capital Territory. Additionally, there are questions about the extent to which it still applies in New Zealand (see the comments in *Roulston* [1976] 2 NZLR 644: pp. 652–653 and in *Hart* [1986] 2 NZLR 408: p. 413). It is no longer the law in South Africa as the landmark decision in *S v Chretien* 1981 (1) SA 1097 has been superceded by the Criminal Law Amendment Act 1 of 1988. Canada has also moved away from this approach, albeit in part, following widespread public anger after a series of controversial acquittals.

The primary explanation as to why some jurisdictions have moved to this position is a belief that the distinction between crimes of 'basic' intent and crimes of 'specific' intent upon which the second approach rests cannot be supported as a matter of principle. The New Zealand Court of Appeal sums this up succinctly:

> The alternative [to the third approach] is to say that when drunkenness is raised in defence there is some special exception to the Crown's general duty to prove the elements of the charge. We know of no sufficient authority for that, nor any principle which justifies it. (*Kamipeli* [1975] 2 NZLR 610: p. 616)

Allied to this is the following objection, here expressed in the Canadian Supreme Court:

> It simply cannot be automatically inferred that there would be an objective foresight that the consequences of voluntary intoxication would lead to the commission of the offence . . . Nor is it likely that someone can really intend to get so intoxicated that they would reach a state of insanity or automatism. (*R v Daviault* [1994] 3 SCR 63: p. 91)

These views were often far from universally shared by the judiciary in the jurisdictions in question. In *R v O'Connor* (1980) 146 CLR 64 (see Fairall 1980; Orchard 1980), the leading Australian case, the High Court split with four judges ruling in favour of this wider approach and three adopting the position in *Majewski*. It may have been a victory for the third approach but it was a victory by the slenderest of margins.

For the purposes of this chapter, it is instructive to study the reasons why the majority of the Australian High Court decided not to follow

Majewski and allowed evidence of intoxication to be taken into account by a jury in a crime of 'basic' intent. As the jury had acquitted O'Connor of two crimes of 'specific' intent – stealing and wounding with intent to resist arrest – presumably because they felt that his intoxication meant that he could not have formed the required *mens rea*, the Court of Criminal Appeal discharged him of the 'basic' intent offence of wounding. The question for the High Court was simply whether the Court of Appeal had been correct to abandon the crime of 'specific' intent/crime of 'basic' intent distinction. Right at the start a fundamental difference can be observed from the approach taken by the House of Lords. In Australia, the Lord Chief Justice saw this as a question of principle not public policy:

> That the society needs protection against violence by such persons can readily be conceded. But so it does in relation to armed robbery and, indeed, to housebreaking which is not infrequently accompanied by violence to the person. So it does in relation to many crimes of so-called specific intent. The question, it seems to me, which is posed for this Court is whether it is consonant with the common law to make such an exception in the case of self-induced intoxication as has been held to be the case by the House of Lords. (p. 87)

The High Court of Australia is not bound by House of Lords' judgments, though, because of a shared common law background, they are treated as highly influential (see *Cullen* v *Trappell* (1980) 146 CLR 1). So, whilst there was no question of the High Court being bound by *Majewski*, the Australian judges all subjected it to careful scrutiny. The manner with which the Lord Chief Justice dealt with the English case law is interesting. *Majewski* was flawed both on the grounds of principle *and* because it misinterpreted *Beard*, a case which accorded with the Lord Chief Justice's understanding of criminal law principle. Criminal law principle was therefore used to support the validity of one House of Lord's judgment and to discredit another.

It will be recalled that *Majewski* interpreted Lord Birkenhead's summary of the common law on intoxication in *Beard* to mean that evidence of intoxication could only be relevant if the offence was one of 'specific' intent, notwithstanding an apparently contradictory passage in Lord Birkenhead's judgment. Lord Chief Justice Barwick, on the other hand, understood Lord Birkenhead's judgment in *Beard* thus:

> [Far] from erecting a distinction between so-called basic intent (an expression not then current) and specific intent, it seems to me that his Lordship was pointing out that the cases to which he had had occasion to refer did not really represent a departure from but were in truth no more than illustrative of fundamental principle, i.e. that

a person could not be convicted of a crime unless the mens was rea.
(p. 84)

It was this fundamental principle that was key to the majority in
O'Connor and which encapsulates the reasoning behind the third
approach. Such a position does not mean that a suitably culpable
individual should escape responsibility for his actions but demands that
the mechanism employed to attribute responsibility accords with Criminal Law principle. The Lord Chief Justice accepted that someone who
voluntarily became so intoxicated that he could not form an intent to act
was sufficiently blameworthy to 'be visited with severe consequences'
but could not see any grounds 'for presuming his acts to be voluntary
and relevantly intentional' (p. 87). Creating a suitable offence, however,
was a task for parliament and not for the courts.

O'Connor continues to divide Australian opinion. New South Wales
reformed their law after a drunk individual shot and killed a sleeping
child (Gough 2000). The case did not actually involve intoxication and
criminal responsibility directly but, as the sentence imposed was
perceived as unduly lenient, the case acted as a lightning conductor for
popular concerns about the adequacy of the legal response to drunken
acts of violence. This has not been the only case that has caused concern.
Another high profile incident involved an unprovoked, drunken attack
on two women by a Canberra Raiders rugby player. He was acquitted
on the grounds that he was so intoxicated that he could not have formed
the required *mens rea* (*SC Small v Noa Kurimalawi* (1997) unreported). *The
Australian* reported the incident under the heading 'When drunkenness
means disorderly law' (28/10/97) whilst the *Herald Sun* were equally
damning in their headline: 'Time to change drunk defence' (both
headlines from Gough 2000).

These incidents led to a variety of responses at state level. New South
Wales has reintroduced a 'basic' intent/'specific' intent distinction
following the case of *R v Paxman* unreported 21/6/95 (New South Wales
District Court). So too has the Australian Capital Territory (Criminal
Code 2002, s.33). Victoria has retained the *O'Connor* approach after two
Law Reform Commission reports (1986, 1999) stridently defended it.
South Australia also continues to follow *O'Connor* after two private
member's bills failed to gather sufficient support (Gough 2000), although
a procedural limitation on the circumstances in which a defendant can
appeal on the grounds of intoxication was introduced in s.269 (1) of the
Criminal Law Consolodation (Intoxication) Amendment Act 1999. Finally, Tasmania – a code state which was not bound to follow *O'Connor* –
appears to be following such a course after the *Attorney-General's
Reference No.1 of 1996* [1998] TASSC 12 (see Bradfield 1999). The academic
consensus is that *O'Connor* has not had any adverse effect on public
safety (Orchard 1993; Skene 1983; Smith 1981). There is a view that

arguing intoxication can actually be a dangerous tactic. Prior to their recent reform, the Chief Justice in New South Wales commented that:

> It is true that, as a matter of law, intoxication can go to questions of intent. The great risk for trial counsel who rely on intoxication, however, is that a jury will regard the consumption of alcohol, not as an excuse for what occurred, but simply as an explanation of how it might come about that an otherwise apparently decent person would kill somebody. Reliance on alcohol, therefore, is tactically dangerous. (*Ainsworth* (1994) 76 A Crim R 127 at 676)

The Canadian experience

Whilst *O'Connor* has generally survived high profile incidents of drunken offending, the reaction to *R v Daviault* [1994] 3 S.C.R. 63 in Canada resulted in rapid legislative reform.

Prior to this judgment, Canadian law adopted the English position. In *Leary v The Queen* [1978] 1 S.C.R. 79 it was held that evidence of intoxication could be taken into account in determining whether the defendant had the relevant *mens rea* for offences requiring a 'specific' intent. The case generated considerable academic criticism (e.g. Mewett and Manning 1985; Quigley 1987a; Schabas 1984). If the offence was one of 'basic' intent such evidence was deemed to be irrelevant. There was far less judicial consensus in the later case of *R v Bernard* [1988] 2 S.C.R. 833 (for comment see Healy 1990; Quigley and Manson 1989). Although the appeal was dismissed, three judges out of seven (Dickson C.J., Lamer and La Forest J.J.) proposed abolishing the distinction between crimes of 'basic' and crimes of 'specific' intent. Four judges favoured retention (McIntyre, Beetz, Wilson and L'Heureux-Dubé J.J.). In itself this was an important shift from *Leary* but what was more important was the court's view on whether this approach was constitutional. Two of the judges who favoured retaining the distinction, McIntyre and Beetz J.J., argued that the approach did not breach the constitution if the prosecution proved intoxication as a substitute form of *mens rea* for a 'basic' intent offence. Unsurprisingly, the three judges who wanted to abolish the distinction claimed that the traditional approach was unconstitutional as it relieved the Crown of its duty to prove the defendant had the *mens rea* required for the offence charged. What was key in *Bernard* was that the remaining two judges who favoured retaining the distinction, Wilson and L'Heureux-Dubé, suggested that the approach might nonetheless be unconstitutional. In *Bernard* there was insufficient evidence to suggest that his intoxication was sufficiently extreme. That, however, was far from the case in *Daviault*.

Daviault, a chronic alcoholic, had sexually assaulted a 65 year old disabled woman after they had been drinking brandy together. He claimed to have no recollection of the incident. At his trial an expert witness testified that the amount of alcohol consumed by the defendant would have either killed or put the average person into a coma. The trial judge accepted that Daviault could have been in a state akin to automatism and accepted defence counsel's argument that this should entitle him to an acquittal. The Quebec Court of Appeal substituted a conviction and Daviault appealed to the Canadian Supreme Court.

It is unnecessary to analyse the Supreme Court judgment in any depth as many of the arguments have already been addressed in relation to *O'Connor* and the academic critique of *Majewski*. As in *O'Connor*, a majority, though in this case a more pronounced one, held that evidence of intoxication could be considered in determining whether the defendant had the required *mens rea* in cases requiring either a 'specific' or a 'basic' intent (a full consideration of the judgment is provided by Grant 1996; Healy 1994). The Supreme Court's terms of reference primarily related to whether the existing law breached Daviault's rights under the Canadian Charter of Rights and Freedoms – a point of comparative interest given that the Human Rights Act 1998 gives defendants the right to challenge existing law with reference to the European Convention of Human Rights. In particular, it was argued that the existing law conflicted with s.7 which provides that no-one should be deprived of their liberty 'except in accordance with the principles of fundamental justice' and s.11(d) which states that any person charged with an offence has the right 'to be presumed innocent until proven guilty'.

Despite Healey's claim (1994: 544) that the parties argued the case on a different basis to the Supreme Court's judgment, some of the most telling aspects of the judgment relate to matters of principle. Foremost amongst these is the claim made by the majority that intoxication, even if it is self-induced, can lead to a state of 'moral innocence'. As Healy comments:

> The effect of this conclusion is to equate moral innocence with the formal mathematical logic of criminal liability: that is, if intoxication is the reason why the prosecution cannot prove all of the inculpatory elements in the definition of guilt, the remainder is moral innocence. But what sort of moral innocence is this, especially as it would appear at first blush to contradict the view that there is some significant quotient of fault, blameworthiness and guilt in criminal acts committed in a state of self-induced intoxication? (ibid.: 547)

Healy presents two possible interpretations of the phrase 'moral innocence' and highlights the significant differences between them:

> Does [moral innocence] refer to the absence of a necessary element of fault, by reason of intoxication, in the commission of an act? Or

does it refer more broadly to the absence of moral blameworthiness for harm done while in an intoxicated state? The difference between these two is that the latter leaves open the possibility of attributing blame for conduct that is not accompanied by an element of fault in the commission of an act. It leaves open the option to say that a person who does harm while in a state of self-induced intoxication is nonetheless liable for the harm done. (ibid.: 548)

The Canadian media expressed outrage at the judgment. *The Vancouver Sun* (5/10/94) led with 'Criminal Defence of Drunkenness an Offence to Reason' (taken from Grant 1996). Against a tide of concern, particularly as other defendants were acquitted on the basis of intoxication in sexual cases, the Canadian government moved quickly and decisively to reverse aspects of *Daviault* (Hogg and Bushell 1997). For reasons that will become apparent, however, it is too simplistic to say that the legislative changes simply reverted Canadian law back to the second approach.

The preamble to the legislation (Chapter 32 1995) which reformed the Criminal Code demonstrate that parliament shared popular concerns with the Supreme Court's ruling. Parliament recognised a 'close association' between violence and intoxication and was 'concerned that self-induced intoxication may be used socially and legally to excuse violence, particularly violence against women and children'. Despite the empirical evidence in earlier chapters, 'the potential effects of alcohol . . . on human behaviour are well known to Canadians' and the government shared 'with Canadians the moral view that people who, while in a state of self-induced intoxication, violate the physical integrity of others are blameworthy in relation to their harmful conduct and should be held criminally accountable for it'. What is perhaps most telling is that the first two factors noted in the preamble relate to concerns about violence in Canada and the rights of women and children under the Canadian Charter of Rights and Freedoms to equal protection and benefit of the law. *Daviault* was seen to have afforded a defence to men who drank and assaulted women and children. It was this underlying concern which informed the following amendment to the Criminal Code:

33.1 1. It is not a defence to an offence referred to in subsection 3. that the accused, by reason of self-induced intoxication, lacked the general intent or the voluntariness required to commit the offence, where the accused departed markedly from the standard of care as described in subsection 2.

2. For the purposes of this section, a person departs markedly from the standard of reasonable care generally recognised in Canadian society and is thereby criminally at fault where the person, while in a state of self-induced intoxication that renders the person unaware of, or incapable of consciously controlling, their behav-

iour, voluntarily or involuntarily interferes or threatens to interfere with the bodily integrity of another person.

3. This section applies in respect of an offence under this Act or any other Act of Parliament that includes as an element an assault or any other interference or threat of interference by a person with the bodily integrity of another person.

As can be seen this does not amount to a complete U-turn as the section only applies to offences of violence. It would appear that Daviault still represents the law with regard to non-violent offences. This leaves Canadian law in a complicated position. If the offence is a violent offence, evidence of intoxication cannot be considered if the offence requires only a 'basic' intent. The position here is identical to the second approach. If, however, the offence is not an offence of violence, evidence of intoxication can be considered even if the offence only requires a 'basic' intent.

At first glance this might appear to be ludicrously inconsistent yet the position is not totally indefensible. One could argue that in offences of violence public policy demands are such that the rights of potential victims should be given a higher priority than in cases involving property and that a different approach to the effects of intoxication on criminal liability can therefore be justified. However, this approach ultimately rests on a fiction: at a basic level how can the prosecution prove all of the aspects required to ensure a fair trial if they cannot show that the defendant had the required *mens rea* (Macmillan-Brown 1995)? This has been recognised by some state Supreme Courts which have held that the reforms are unconstitutional (e.g. *R* v *Brenton* (1999) 180 D.L.R. (4th) 314) although others have held that these reforms could be justified on constitutional grounds (e.g. *R* v *Vickberg* [1988] BCJ 1034).

There has not been an avalanche of cases in any of the jurisdictions to suggest that adopting the third approach would seriously jeopardise public safety (Orchard 1993; Skene 1983; Smith 1981). *Majewski* overstates the need for public protection. However, it is equally clear that a very limited number of high profile acquittals can lead to a popular sense that justice is not being done, a point not lost on the court in *Majewski* (see Lord Edmund-Davies: p. 495 and Lord Salmon: p. 484). There is though a danger that one forgets principle in the desire to allay popular anxiety. Healy (1994: 532) asks the correct question: '[even] if an open defence would yield only one acquittal of a serious offence, is that outcome desirable or even tolerable?'. The fourth approach addresses this concern. It rests on the assumption that someone who causes harm whilst intoxicated does deserve punishment, but that the response should be principled.

4. Intoxication may be relevant in cases of 'basic' intent and in cases of 'specific' intent but in combination with an offence of causing harm whilst intoxicated

It is often forgotten how much support there has been for this approach. A proposal along similar lines was suggested by the English Law Commission in a Consultation Paper in 1993 (Law Commission 1993; Virgo 1993). The Commission claimed that the position in *Majewski* was untenable for a number of reasons. First, it was argued that there were 'no agreed criterion for classifying an offence as of specific or basic intent' (para 3.4) and highlighted the variety of approaches taken by the Lords themselves. This echoed the earlier view of the Criminal Law Revision Committee in 1980 (Criminal Law Revision Committee 1980: para 258). The second objection to the existing position was that it was justified on the grounds of public protection, yet the *Majewski* distinction meant that the public were supposedly protected from some offences and not others (para 3.9). This is compounded by the fact that the seriousness of the offending conduct is not a determinant of categorisation (para 3.10). Finally, the Law Commission believed that the *Majewski* approach led to many practical difficulties at the trial stage (paras 3.17–3.23). These concerns related to exactly what evidence the jury could take account of. The Law Commission, not surprisingly, argued that the current position could not be maintained:

> Only if there is no alternative ought practical problems of this sort be met by a rule that is difficult to expound, and is admitted to be illogical by the judges who formulated it. If there is a better, more rational way of achieving the same policy objectives, it would be unduly cautious to retain the present law merely because it is firmly entrenched and familiar. Even some members of the House of Lords in *Majewski* recognised that the common law principle they were laying down might not be the ideal solution to the problem, but was the best that could be done without legislation. (para 4.4)

Instead the Commission considered a number of options including codifying the rule in *Majewski* (paras 4.8–4.10), applying *Majewski* to recklessness only (paras 4.11–4.19), reverting to the first approach and stating that voluntary intoxication should be irrelevant for any offence (paras 4.36–4.46) and moving to the third approach by abolishing the *Majewski* distinction (paras 5.8–5.25). Given their earlier anxieties, it is perhaps hardly surprising that the Law Commission rejected the option of codifying *Majewski* and, on grounds of principle, did not advocate returning to the first approach. One might have thought, given their general approach, that the Commission would have been sympathetic to the third approach however they had real concerns that such a move would 're-open the concern ... that both public safety and respect for the law would suffer' if such a course were adopted (para 5.25).

The Commission advocated abandoning the *Majewski* approach and replacing it with a new offence (paras 6.30–6.88) which will be considered shortly. A useful feature of the consultation paper is that it documents the fact that widespread support for this approach existed (para 6.2). In the intervening years this has often been overlooked. Not only was a similar approach recommended by a Committee on Mentally Abnormal Offenders (1975) it was also supported by a minority of the Criminal Law Revision Committee (1980). The minority in question comprised of the two most distinguished academic lawyers of their generation, Professor Glanville Williams and Professor John Smith. Other members of the academic community who shared their view were cited (Ashworth 1975; Fingarette 1974; Quigley 1987a; and see also Schabas 1984). The approach was mentioned as a possibility by Lord Elwyn-Jones and Lord Edmund-Davies in *Majewski* (p. 475 and p. 496), by Barwick C.J., Stephen J. and Murphy J. in *O'Connor* (p. 87, p. 103 and p. 113) and by Justice Cory and Justice Sopinka in *Daviault* (p. 100 and p. 131), though with varying degrees of enthusiasm. Nonetheless, this suggests that some of those intimately associated with the second and third approaches may have believed that a more appropriate course could be taken but, as such an approach would necessitate legislative intervention, they were forced in effect to choose the most palatable alternative on the menu.

The Law Commission cite two reasons for having such an offence. The first is categorised intriguingly as an argument of 'prudence or social protection' (para 6.6). Quite why it is an argument of prudence is unclear. Instead it would appear to be a simple argument based on the notion that 'whatever protection' criminal law affords the public should not depend on whether the offender was sober at the time of the offence (para 6.7). The Consultation Paper remains non-committal about the extent to which the criminal law does provide such a function. The argument instead being that public protection concerns dictate that the law does not discriminate between harm caused whilst intoxicated and harm caused whilst sober. Their second argument relates to culpability: 'a person who chooses to become intoxicated cannot legitimately complain if he is punished for the criminal harm into which that intoxication leads him' (para 6.9). Above all, the creation of a new offence would lead to greater transparency:

> A new offence can implement directly and overtly the policy considerations ... by laying down clear rules in the light of that policy. That will enable the policy-making operation to be recognised for what it is, and thus the various elements of the policy to be rationally discussed, and to be reflected in the detailed terms of

the new offence; rather than, as at present under the *Majewski* approach, for those elements of policy to be hidden amongst rules that, misleadingly, purport to be only an application of technical legal doctrine. (para 6.11)

The proposed new offence was summarised thus:

The offence would be committed by a person who, while deliberately intoxicated, caused the harm proscribed by any of the listed offences set out in subparagraph (b) below. (para 7.5(a))

'Deliberate intoxication' was considered at length in the Consultation Paper (paras 6.48–6.61). Consideration was also given as to which offences should come within the list (paras 6.34–6.41). The list seems rather too inclusive given that one of the justifications for having an offence was protecting the public from 'dangerous and unlawful' acts (para 6.7): as well as homicide and other serious offences against the person, the list included criminal damage (para 6.41). To quote Leader-Elliott (1994: 151–152) '[it] lumps together individuals who should be convicted of the most serious offences of violence with others who are, at worst, civilly liable for negligence'.

The need to restrict offences of this nature is highlighted by an offence found in s.154(1) of the Criminal Code of the Northern Territory in Australia. The section, which is far wider in scope than the English proposal, states that:

Any person who does or makes an act or omission that causes serious danger, actual or potential, to the lives, health or safety of the public or to any member of it in circumstances where an ordinary person similarly circumstanced would have clearly foreseen such danger and not have done or made that act or omission is guilty of a crime and is liable to imprisonment for 5 years.

It is clear that the section is designed at least in part to punish those who cause harm whilst intoxicated. Subsection (5) stipulates that voluntary intoxication is not a relevant consideration when determining what the ordinary person similarly circumstanced would have clearly foreseen. And, for the purposes of sentencing, intoxication is seen to be a highly aggravating factor. Subsection (4) states that, if the offender was intoxicated at the time of the act or omission, he or she is liable for an additional period of four years' imprisonment.

Leader-Elliott (1994: 157) correctly points out the dangers inherent in such a provision. Because it is framed so widely, the offence would have to be enforced selectively. If the law has to be applied in a discriminatory manner then it could operate unfairly with the consequence that it discredits those charged with enforcing it. It would also appear to have been particularly ineffective if the desire was to reduce offending by intoxicated individuals. Taking account of population, citizens of the Northern Territory are proportionately far more likely to be admitted to hospital for an 'alcohol-related' assault than anywhere else in Australia (Cain 2002). The Northern Territory offence though is far wider in scope than the offence proposed by the Law Commission. Clearly the manner in which such an offence is drafted is important and potentially contentious. This concern is not, however, unique to this offence and experience in other jurisdictions suggest that such concerns can be overstated.

The Law Commission's abandonment of the fourth approach

Given the force of the Law Commission's critique of the *Majewski* approach, the *volte face* that followed was little short of remarkable (Gough 1996; Horder 1995; Paton 1995). It is clear that many of those who responded to the Consultation Paper did not share the Law Commission's enthusiasm for a new offence of causing harm whilst intoxicated, but it is equally clear that the objections to the proposed offence (or at least those cited) were all of a practical nature. They did not relate primarily to the ambit of the actual offence. The concerns were apparently shared by respondents such as the Criminal Bar Association and JUSTICE, who wished to abolish *Majewski*, and those such as the Law Society and the judges of the Queen's Bench Division, who favoured its retention (Law Commission 1995: para 5.9). Those who had diverse views therefore united to defeat the proposal. It is striking that these practical concerns were more important to the Law Commission than the underlying rationale for having such an offence in the first place. The 'cogent' (para 5.10) reasons given by the respondents who rejected the idea of a new offence were summarised as follows:

- Defendants (however unrealistically) would see the offence as a chance to be convicted of a lesser offence with the consequence that there would be an increase both in the number of trials and their length (para 5.10);

- The offence would also necessitate expert evidence which would again elongate trials (para 5.11);

- The police would have to spend additional time investigating the defendant's consumption of alcohol prior to the offence (para 5.12);

- Finally, the prosecution would not know whether to include the new offence as an alternative offence on the indictment (para 5.13).

Given that many of these objections would appear to be just as applicable to the third approach, it is regrettable that the Commission did not consider whether these practical problems existed elsewhere. Most of those jurisdictions do not appear to have been overwhelmed by practical difficulties. Where reform has occurred the rationale appears to have been broadly philosophical: there was a widespread belief that an intoxicated offender who caused harm and escaped conviction did not receive his just deserts. This is the very attraction of the fourth approach. The offender receives a sentence proportionate to his culpable behaviour *provided the offence can be framed appropriately.*

It is also ironic, given the practical nature of these concerns, that the Crown Prosecution Service broadly supported the new offence (para 5.15). However, they had a number of qualifications relating to causation (para 5.16) and sentencing (para 5.17), which were felt by the Law Commission to be so far-reaching that they would defeat the whole purpose of the offence (para 5.14). There has been no subsequent interest in the approach in the UK. The 1995 report proposes codifying the present law (para 6.6) and suggests using the availability of recklessness as the mechanism for distinguishing between crimes of 'basic' and 'specific' intent (para 6.6). This, the Commission notes, *may* (para 6.7, italics in original) represent the existing law.

Conclusion

This chapter has focussed on the most commonly found common law approaches to attributing criminal liability to those who were intoxicated when they offended. Despite the different approaches that have developed, it is all too easy to forget that on many things there is agreement. Those who are involuntarily intoxicated are not held criminally liable. Similarly, all jurisdictions require a very extreme degree of intoxication – sufficient to negate any *mens rea* – if it is to be of any relevance in cases where the consumption was voluntary. And, if the person formed the intention to commit the offence and then drank in order to gain the courage to commit it, all of the approaches we have considered would deem the intoxication irrelevant. The disagreement, therefore, relates to a very narrow subset of cases involving intoxication: those where the defendant voluntarily got so intoxicated that he could not form the required *mens rea* for the offence in question according to the standard rules of attributing criminal responsibility and had not formed that intention prior to getting intoxicated. The degree of intoxication required is such that the issue only arises in a few cases each year (Mitchell 1988; Shiner 1990). These cases necessitate a response but it has to be remembered that in practical terms there is much agreement in a comparative context. The majority of intoxicated offenders will be dealt with identically in all common law jurisdictions when it comes to determining their criminal liability.

In the introductory section it was argued that the diversity of approaches could largely be explained on the basis of an omnipresent conflict between the public policy argument that those who offend whilst drunk should be punished in order to protect the public and the general principles of criminal law which usually dictate both that the defendant satisfies the *mens rea* requirement for the offence and the *actus reus* requirement that his action was voluntary. Someone who does not intend to cause harm nor is, in the usual sense of the word, reckless in causing it is not generally deemed deserving of punishment (although there are exceptions). There is, however, a sense that intoxicated offenders are different. If the intoxication is voluntary then they put themselves in that reduced capacity – they are not blameless. The central question remains though: should the individual be held criminally liable for the offence in question and, if so, on what basis?

The first approach, typified by the Scottish approach, is unashamedly pragmatic. The courts have robustly taken the stance that such an individual should be held criminally liable. Their rationale is primarily based on the perceived need for public protection – a perfectly justifiable aim. However, as the Scottish courts have themselves recognised, this approach does not square easily with the principles of Criminal Law. In an attempt to address this, the courts have adapted the concept of recklessness by holding that the act of getting intoxicated is inherently wickedly reckless. The problems with this approach are that, firstly, it uses the term recklessness in a more general sense than is usual for it is a recklessness in getting sufficiently intoxicated rather than in causing a particular foreseeable harm. Secondly, there is a problem of degree. Even if one accepts the court's reasoning so far, has the individual been wickedly reckless (as is required for murder under Scots law) or merely reckless? Finally, there is the important issue of how one reconciles this rule with those offences where recklessness will not suffice. A strict application of principle might suggest that intoxication should be relevant in cases requiring an intention, however the High Court of Justiciary appears in little doubt that the rule is of general application. There may be strong grounds for punishing individuals who cause harm whilst intoxicated but the abrogation of principle in the Scottish approach has little to commend it.

The second approach, commonly associated with England and Wales, has also been widely attacked on the basis that it lacks principle. There is a danger that the voluminous and often sophisticated critiques of *Majewski* can miss a rather simple point, namely whether a distinction between crimes of 'basic' and crimes of 'specific' intent can be justified at all as opposed to which of the various tests for categorising offences is preferable. As Healy notes (1994: 541) the approach 'rests on a fiction that intoxication can negate some mental states but not others'.

This flaw was recognised in those jurisdictions which moved to the third approach outlined above. The essence of this position is that the distinction between crimes of 'basic' and 'specific' intent cannot be justified as a matter of principle and that, save in those rare cases where no *mens rea* is required, evidence of intoxication can be considered in order to establish whether the defendant had the required *mens rea*, whether that be intention or recklessness. It is easy to portray this as a victory for principle over common sense, but the point was well made in *O'Connor* and in *Daviault* that other mechanisms could be employed to protect the public from drunken violence.

There are good reasons to remain sceptical of claims that public protection requires holding those who were so intoxicated that they could form no *mens rea* criminally liable. Research (Orchard 1993; Skene 1983; Smith 1981) suggests that there has been no significant increase in drunken offending since *O'Connor*, a view which makes sense given the very limited number of offenders who could claim convincingly to have been unable to form any *mens rea*. There is also a large body of criminological research which suggests that criminal justice strategies which have been designed primarily to protect the public have met with little success. There is though another compelling reason why such individuals should be held criminally liable. It relates not to public protection but to culpability. Quite simply those who get so intoxicated that they cause serious harm deserve to be punished. If they are not punished, the public rightly feel that justice has not been achieved. This argument depends upon which theory of punishment is adopted and will therefore be explored in more detail in the next chapter. The Canadian reaction to *Daviault* has been unfortunate. Having recognised a justifiable popular concern that a culpable individual had escaped punishment, the Canadian government reverted to an untenable position rather than take the opportunity to frame a law which would adequately reflect the culpability of an individual like Daviault.

This is the attraction of the fourth approach: having a separate offence for those very rare cases when the defendant was unable to form the *mens rea* for the ordinary offence. If framed carefully, this would reflect the degree of culpability of the defendant more honestly whilst, at the same time, ensure that the law does not fall into disrepute. This is not quite the radical proposal it seems. A number of distinguished writers have suggested it before (though others have strongly opposed it). It was cited as a possible avenue for reform in *Majewski, O'Connor* and *Daviault*. Nor is it quite as radical as sometimes feared. Such an offence already exists in a number of civil law jurisdictions. Of course important issues remain but it is suggested that the practical objections to the original Law Commission (1993) proposal are not insurmountable given experience elsewhere.

The most difficult issue would in all probability relate to sentencing the offence, as the disagreement on this issue between the Law

Commission and the Crown Prosecution Service demonstrates. However, this is part of a far wider issue. How does one determine the appropriate sentence for intoxicated offenders? The problem is therefore not confined to the fourth approach but one which should concern all legal systems regardless of the approach that they take to attributing substantive criminal liability. This crucial, and often overlooked, issue is fully considered in the next chapter.

Chapter 6

Sentencing issues

Whichever of the approaches the substantive criminal law adopts, few individuals will be sufficiently intoxicated to have been unable to form any intention whatsoever. As a result, in all but a few exceptional cases, the fact that an individual has been drinking is not relevant to determining whether or not he can be found guilty of the offence. The only issue that the court has to determine is the appropriate sentence. Bearing this in mind, it is surprising how little attention has been paid to the impact intoxication should have on sentencing. Before the sentence is imposed, it is often made known to the court that the offender had been drinking prior to committing the offence (Rumgay 1998; Shapland 1981). Presumably this is done in the expectation that sentencers will judge the offender more favourably and apply a lesser sentence. However, it is far from clear that this is the case. In England and Wales, intoxication would appear to have no effect on sentence in most cases, reduce the sentence in some and, albeit very rarely, increase it in others (Wasik 1999). This variation makes the need for analysis even greater.

Part of the problem is that there are strong arguments why intoxication should act as mitigation, but equally, there are strong reasons why it should be treated either as a neutral factor or as an aggravating factor.

When a defence lawyer puts forward evidence of intoxication and asks the court to look favourably at this, the underlying assumption is that the intoxication reduces the offender's culpability. The argument assumes that someone who stabs someone whilst sober is more blameworthy than someone who did the act whilst intoxicated. In the latter case it may be suggested that the individual would not have committed the offence unless he or she had been drinking. Although we know that it is problematic to make such a causal connection, many would subscribe to the view that whilst someone who offends whilst intoxicated is blameworthy and deserves punishment the presence of alcohol makes the person less blameworthy and therefore deserving of less punishment than someone who offended whilst sober.

Some though would maintain that intoxication should make no difference at all to the sentence imposed. In a recent reform of sentencing law, New Zealand stated categorically that intoxication was not to be treated as a mitigating factor (Sentencing Act 2002, s.9(3)). Parliament wished to make it clear that intoxicated offending was as serious as offending whilst sober (the act would appear to be silent on whether intoxication could be treated as an aggravating factor). The United States Federal Sentencing Guidelines take a similar view (Hanly 2003). Similarly, when Potas (1994) asked sentencers in New South Wales the effect that intoxication should have on sentence, the vast majority said that it should not affect sentence one way or the other, although, when presented with actual case studies, a wide disparity of opinion emerged (see later). Arguments that could be put forward to support such a position include the need for society to send out a message that irresponsible drinking will not be tolerated, the hope that such a stance will act as a general deterrent and the belief that an intoxicated offender is as culpable as a sober offender (provided the intoxication was voluntary).

Finally, there is a school of thought that the presence of alcohol does not lessen the seriousness of the offence but makes it more serious. Recently the Sentencing Guidelines Council (2004) took this position in England and Wales. Committing an offence 'while under the influence of alcohol or drugs' (para 1.22) made the offender more culpable in their opinion. According to s.172 of the Criminal Justice Act 2003 all courts must have regard to the relevant guidelines.

In certain situations the belief that intoxication is to be treated as an aggravating factor is recognised by the substantive law; causing death by dangerous driving whilst under the influence of alcohol or drugs carries a greater sentence than causing death by dangerous driving. Most people would agree with this in the context of driving as everyone should know of the dangers associated with drink driving. The Sentencing Guidelines Council though argue that this approach should have a general application. Again, several arguments can be advanced in support of this position. First, one could say that it is right that society sends out a particularly strong message that drunken violence is no longer acceptable. This might be especially persuasive in the context of domestic violence. Second, some would argue that this approach is necessary to act as a deterrent to others. Finally, some would argue that the presence of alcohol in itself aggravates. This would, for example, be the position in Islamic states. It is interesting that the guidelines from the Council (ibid.) and the advice from the Sentencing Advisory Panel (2004: para 52) on which they are based do not justify the approach. It is taken as a given fact.

This chapter will attempt to explain why this apparent inconsistency should come as no great surprise. With reference both to British and international experience, the chapter will illustrate how a divergence of opinions about the proper purposes of sentencing has often resulted in compromise. In an attempt not to undermine judicial independence, legislation is often framed in such a general fashion that individual sentencers retain almost complete freedom to sentence as they see fit. However, it will also be shown that even when legislation attempts to introduce a uniformity of approach, sentencing is a problematic activity. In England and Wales, the Criminal Justice Act 1991, which adopted a comparatively clear mechanism for determining sentence, soon ran into trouble. The overriding aim of the chapter is to make some tentative suggestions about how those who offend whilst intoxicated should be sentenced with regard both to comparative experience and to the general aims of punishment.

Justifying punishment

It is useful at this juncture to consider some of the most common justifications for punishment as this provides a useful analytical tool for considering different ways of dealing with offenders who were intoxicated when they offended later in this chapter. Such an exercise is also inherently beneficial. The fact that those who offend should be punished is often taken for granted. Yet the reasons why this should be the case deserve scrutiny as punishment by necessity involves the state doing something unpleasant to an individual, be it confining him in a prison cell or depriving him of his financial assets.

Although some writers (see Bianchi and van Swaaningen 1986; Christie 1977, 1981) aver that punishment cannot be justified and that more constructive alternatives should be sought, most commentators believe that punishment forms a role in regulating society but do not necessarily agree on how it can be justified. These differences of opinion are not only of academic interest as they can have far-reaching practical ramifications.

The two primary justifications for punishment are retribution and utilitarianism (for a general introduction to penal theory see Hudson 2003 and the readings in von Hirsch and Ashworth 1998). Both have long and, to our contemporary sensibilities, at times barbaric histories. Equally both have at times led to enlightened penal reform. It is important to point out that, as this is an introductory section, what follows represents something of an oversimplification; there is insufficient space to provide a full analysis of either philosophy. Instead, I intend to outline the features which will have a direct bearing on our subsequent discussion.

Retribution

Retribution is based on two comparatively simple notions: an offender deserves punishment and that punishment should be proportionate to the offender's culpability (Bagaric 2000a; von Hirsch 1986). Retributivists do not have to believe that punishment needs to serve any future benefit to society: it does not need to deter others, it does not need to rehabilitate the offender and it does not need to physically incapacitate the offender to stop him re-offending. Quite simply punishment is deserved. As the chapter will show, the apparent logic of retributivism can disguise the fact that retributivists are faced with complex calculations if their justification is to have any validity. Most notably, how do you calculate an individual's culpability? And, once that has been done, how does one calculate a proportionate penal response? The next section will consider whether retributivists should take account of intoxication in calculating an offender's culpability and hence his proportionate sentence.

How should retributivism deal with intoxication?

Should intoxication generally act as mitigation?

So, how should a retributive sentencing framework take account of intoxication? For intoxication to act as mitigation, one would have to find a way of saying that intoxication reduced the offender's culpability and hence should lead to a lesser proportionate sentence. One argument that could be made would be that the intoxication was uncharacteristic. An example of such a plea comes from Rumgay's observation of court practice:

> These offences were clearly committed under the influence of drink and my client can remember very little of the events. He has been shown statements and evidence to the effect that it was he who did these things and no-one else and therefore he accepts that this must be so. This particular behaviour is out of all character to him. (1998: 154)

A distinction is drawn on the basis that past experience makes the individual more morally culpable because he or she knows that it is possible that such conduct will follow the consumption of alcohol. This distinction though is problematic. Imagine X is a frequent drinker who is frequently intoxicated. On one occasion when he was intoxicated he assaulted someone. Can we say that this one incident is sufficient to raise his moral culpability if he gets intoxicated again on numerous occasions before assaulting someone else four years later? If X was a rational being he may calculate that, although he had been violent once in the past, the likelihood of violence occurring again is sufficiently remote that he can get intoxicated with impunity. However morally unacceptable we may find such a calculation, statistically it would appear correct. Of course, if the harm is serious that has to be weighed against the probability of it occurring. Most drivers who are above the drink drive limit do not cause injury or kill but nonetheless when an accident occurs the harm is so severe that it is not unreasonable to restrict the drinking habits of those who drive. So, if X causes criminal injury to another, it does not seem morally unreasonable to say that he should modify his behaviour in future so as to reduce the likelihood of repetition even if this may be statistically unlikely. Similarly, it does not seem unreasonable to say that if he continues to get intoxicated and then re-offends we should have less sympathy for him than we did the first time around.

The influence that an individual's previous criminal experience should have on his culpability for a subsequent incident has long troubled those interested in penal theory. It has been a particular issue for retributivists (von Hirsch 2002). In order to work out a proportionate sentence, retributivists have to work out what factors impact on an offender's culpability other than the magnitude of the harm caused. As von Hirsch comments:

> The issue of prior criminality is critical to a desert-based theory of sentencing, because it influences the structure of the penalty scale so much. If prior record is irrelevant, then penalties can be ranked unidimensionally to reflect the comparative seriousness of offenders' current crimes. If it is relevant, a two-dimensional grid is required, in which penalties are ordered to reflect not only the gravity of the current act but the extent of the criminal record as well. It then becomes essential to decide how much weight the record should carry. Should the emphasis remain on the current crime, or should it shift primarily to record? (1986: 77–78)

Most (e.g. von Hirsch 1986), but not all (e.g. Fletcher 1978), retributivists accept that previous convictions are of some, limited relevance but believe that the effect of previous convictions on sentence needs to be severely curtailed. There is therefore a marked reluctance amongst retributivists to increase sentences incrementally each time an individual re-offends on the basis of escalating culpability. This is driven by the belief that this would give undue weight to the offender's prior convictions and would downplay the actual harm caused by the current offence. In extreme cases the sentence imposed could bear little relation to the harm caused. It would also raise the possibility that someone who committed a comparatively minor offence could receive a greater sentence than someone who committed a more serious offence on the basis of his previous record.

One solution that has been adopted is that, rather than increasing culpability for having a lengthy criminal record, credit should be given to those who have no, or few, past convictions (Wasik and von Hirsch 1994). It could be argued that such individuals are less culpable than those who had offended before. According to von Hirsch:

> [Tolerance] is granted on the grounds that some sympathy is due human beings for their fallibility and their exposure to pressures and temptations – and some respect is owed their capacity, as moral agents, to reflect on the censure of others. The temporary nature of the tolerance – the fact that it diminishes (and eventually wholly withdrawn) with repetitions – is critical. This assures that, ultimately, people are held fully accountable for their misdeeds, as any conception of desert requires. (1986: 85)

Applying this reasoning, the first time intoxicated offender could deservedly receive a lesser sentence than an individual who had previously offended whilst intoxicated. However the converse could not be tolerated: after a certain number of offences, the offender would have lost all mitigation but the continuation of a pattern of offending would not in itself be aggravating. This reasoning is consistent with the approach taken by the New South Wales Court of Criminal Appeal in *Coleman* (1990) 47 A Crim R 306. Because of his prior convictions, Coleman had lost the right to claim mitigation on the basis that the offence was out of character but, at the same time, his prior record would not legitimate the imposition of a lengthier sentence than normal.

Retribution and the problem drinker

A survey of sentencing cases demonstrates that the courts are generally vague on whether intoxication should have a bearing on sentence but are unequivocal that an offender who recognises that he has a drinking problem and seeks help for it will be treated favourably (see later). *Howells* [1999] 1 WLR 307 confirmed this in the context of a retributively based framework. During the course of her research, Rumgay (1998) found a number of instances when it was claimed that the offender had taken steps to address his problem drinking. The following plea was typical:

> He feels his alcohol problem is now under control and is aware that this must continue if his relationship is to survive. Drinking and offending are not acceptable to his partner. He has a strong incentive to prevent the problem from re-emerging. (ibid.: 155)

The offender's culpability is arguably enhanced in such cases both because of a willingness to take appropriate steps to avoid repetition and because his intoxication did not have the usual degree of voluntariness. The fact that the offender was an addict in itself may not suffice. It could be argued that credit can only be given when the offender takes the additional step of addressing his addiction. In such a case he could be said to be doing something additional and positive that should be favourably reflected when it comes to imposing a sentence. Conversely, one could argue that the sentence should depend upon his culpability *at the time of the offence*. If one were to adopt this stance then credit would not be given for action taken after the commission of the offence. There is a logic to this position, but one can cite other situations were creditworthy activity after the offence, for example helping the authorities or pleading guilty, are recognised in mitigation. One task for retributivists is to determine the period over which culpability should be measured.

The other issue of interest relates to the choice of sentence. In some cases only one form of punishment might be a proportionate response. For example, only a lengthy custodial term would be commensurate with a serious offence of violence. In other cases however one could argue that different forms of punishment would be equally onerous – say different types of community sentence – and that the sentencer should therefore be free to choose whichever is most appropriate for the offender. If one form of punishment would allow the offender to get the help that he needs to address a drinking problem then this could legitimately be prioritised above another form of punishment provided it remained a proportionate response to the offender's culpability (von Hirsch 1993: 60). Equally, if a custodial sentence is seen as the proportionate response to his offending, there is nothing objectionable in offering him assistance to deal with his alcohol-related problems once he is in prison.

Utilitarianism

In contrast to retribution, utilitarian justifications for punishment focus on the future benefit that punishment will bring. According to classical utilitarian philosophy, harm cannot be justified unless it will lead to a greater good (see generally Scarre 1996). So, to take two examples, a lengthy term of imprisonment would be justified if it protected the public from further serious criminal victimisation by the offender or an intensive rehabilitation programme would be justified if it successfully stopped the offender from re-offending by addressing the root cause of his criminal activity (Bagaric 2000b).

Many traditional justifications for punishment are utilitarian in character. Rehabilitation, deterrence and incapacitation all fall within this category. In each case their overall aim is identical – to stop future offending – but their methods are different. Rehabilitation seeks to modify the offender's behaviour by addressing the root cause of his offending. Deterrence aims to make either the particular offender or the public at large desist from engaging in similar criminal conduct by making the penalty on being caught sufficiently unattractive. Finally, incapacitation physically removes the possibility of the offender re-offending, usually in a contemporary context by imprisoning him.

Once again, utilitarians have to address some problematic issues. To justify a particular punishment from a utilitarian perspective one needs to be able to show that a greater good was achieved. In other words one has to show that the sentence did rehabilitate, or deter, or incapacitate. But how do we know that the individual would not have stopped offending anyway? One cannot automatically assume that a future decision not to offend is directly attributable to the use of a particular penal measure. This is one of the issues that we will revisit when we consider the effectiveness of programmes designed to rehabilitate offenders with drinking problems.

Retributivists have a further objection. To a retributivist punishment has to be proportionate to the offender's culpability. Two offenders with equal culpability should therefore receive identical sentences. However, as utilitarianism operates on a different basis, this premise does not necessarily follow if one is punishing in order to deter, rehabilitate or incapacitate. Two offenders with equal culpability might be seen to pose a different degree of future threat or have different rehabilitative needs which could justify different sentences. Again this is an issue we will revisit later.

Utilitarianism and intoxication

As we have noted already, different justifications for punishment come under the general umbrella of utilitarianism. Whilst they all justify the harm of punishment on the basis that it will prevent a greater future harm, each justification aims to prevent the harm caused by future offending in a different way. It is convenient to discuss the relationship between intoxication and deterrence, public protection and rehabilitation in turn although we need to recognise that the courts do not always distinguish between these aims satisfactorily. This is particularly apparent when the judiciary talk generally about public protection as the public can be protected in a number of ways. Usually public protection would appear to be synonymous with incapacitating the offender but, in a wider sense, the public would also be protected if the offender was successfully deterred or rehabilitated.

Intoxication and deterrence

> We need ... to ensure that the system of offences and penalties
> works so as to discourage unacceptable alcohol-fuelled behaviour
> (Department for Culture, Media and Sport 2005: para 4.2).

It is obvious from the case law that the courts have often been concerned
that allowing credit to be given for intoxication would be detrimental to
society. This is seen both in the context of attributing criminal liability
when an offender was intoxicated at the time and in the context of
sentencing. What though do the courts mean when they say that it
would be 'detrimental to society'? Specifically, do the judiciary believe
that withholding credit from those who offend whilst intoxicated acts as
a deterrent?

At the sentencing stage, it could be argued that a general stance of not
allowing intoxication to count as mitigation is consistent with a belief
that if it was treated as mitigation there would be little disincentive for
others not to get dangerously intoxicated. This view has not been
expressly articulated by sentencers. On the contrary, in cases such as
Kirkland (1975) unreported (cited in Wasik 2001: 62) and *Bradley* (1980) 2
Cr.App.R.(S.) 12 the Court of Appeal gives no specific reason why
intoxication should not be treated as a mitigating factor. As a consequence, one cannot say whether it is because the judges believed that
such offenders were as culpable as those who committed identical crimes
whilst sober and therefore deserved the same sentence on retributive
grounds or whether it was because the court wished to send out a
message to others that no credit would be given for intoxication in the
belief that this would act as a deterrent. One could also argue that in the
reported cases where intoxication did act as mitigation – either where the
offence was perceived to be a 'drunken frolic' (*Abrahams* (1980) 2
Cr.App.R.(S.) 10) or out of character (*Spence* (1982) 4 Cr.App.R.(S.) 175;
Young (1973) unreported) – the court had come to the conclusion that
repetition by the offender was not a major concern.

We can therefore say that the reported case law is consistent with a
belief in deterrence, even if the courts do not expressly justify their
sentences on this ground. What we cannot say is that the courts did
sentence on the basis of deterrence. There is a further complication. The
Court of Appeal have, in other contexts, demonstrated that they do not
always distinguish between different sentencing objectives satisfactorily.
A remarkable example comes from the case of *Cunningham* (1993) 14
Cr.App.R.(S.) 444. In this case the Court had to interpret a section of the
Criminal Justice Act 1991 which quite clearly required them to determine
the proportionate sentence on the basis of retribution. Instead they took
the opportunity to introduce deterrence to the equation, despite clear
legislative intent to the contrary, stating that the sentence had to be

proportionate both as a punishment and as a deterrent. This 'flagrant misreading of the statute' (Ashworth 2000: 87) demonstrates either a blatant refusal to interpret a statute or an inability to appreciate that basing a sentence on both retributive and deterrent grounds would almost inevitably lead to compromise as the two grounds operate from different philosophical standpoints. This judicial reinstatement of deterrence in spite of clear legislative provisions to the contrary has happened elsewhere. In New South Wales, the court in *DPP* v *El Karhani* (1990) 21 NSWLR 370 stated that the failure of sentencing legislation to endorse deterrence as an aim was merely a 'legislative slip' (p. 378).

What *Cunningham* does demonstrate is an enduring belief in the importance of deterrence by the Court of Appeal. This has now been given statutory approval in the Criminal Justice Act 2003 where s.142(1) states that sentencers must have regard to the deterrent effect of a sentence in all cases. Deterrence is now a matter that the courts *must* take into account when sentencing those who offend whilst intoxicated (but in combination with the other objectives listed in the section). Are there any grounds to suggest that sentencing may successfully deter either the individual offender or other potential offenders from offending in the future?

General conclusions of deterrence research

Criminological research has generally shown that punishment severity has little impact on crime rates (see Bagaric 2001; Home Office 2001a; Lewis 1986; von Hirsch et al. 1999). Equally, it appears to be the case that the likelihood of apprehension and some level of punishment appears to have some deterrent effect (Canadian Sentencing Commission 1987; Farrington et al. 1994; Langan and Farrington 1998; Nagin and Paternoster 1991). Crime rose when the police went on strike in Liverpool and in Melbourne and when the Danish police were interred by the Nazis (Bagaric 2001).

Given the intuitive appeal of deterrence, why does the severity of punishment appear to make so little difference to crime rates? Implicit in any theory of deterrence is an assumption that offenders, or perhaps more accurately potential offenders, operate rationally. That is to say that they carefully balance the anticipated benefits of offending against the likelihood of being caught and punished in a particular manner. Yet how rational is most offending? We already know that a high proportion of offenders have been drinking which may well impact on their ability to weigh up the probable consequences of offending. But even without this factor, how many potential criminals actually know the likelihood of getting caught and, if they are convicted, the likely penalty? Surveys of the public consistently show that people underestimate the sentences that are imposed by the courts (Home Office 2001a; Hough and Roberts 2002).

There is, therefore, empirical evidence that sentencing on the basis of deterrence has met with limited success and, despite the fact that deterrence has a definite intuitive appeal, there are clear reasons why the theoretical basis is flawed: even if offending is a rational activity, and that is a major assumption, most offenders lack the requisite information to make an informed choice. It is difficult not to agree with Beyleveld's (1979) conclusion that we do not have the required empirical base to structure sentencing policy around deterrence.

Intoxication and public protection

The discussion in the previous chapter illustrated how the substantive criminal law regarding intoxication had been informed by a sense that to absolve those who offended whilst intoxicated from criminal liability would jeopardise public safety. In *Majewski* [1977] AC 443, the leading English case, the House of Lords maintained that '[to] accede to the argument on behalf of [Majewski] would leave the citizen legally unprotected from unprovoked violence where such violence was the consequence of drink' (Lord Simon of Glaisdale: p. 476). Similarly, in Scotland, allowing an offender to avoid criminal liability on the basis of intoxication has been described as a 'perilous doctrine' (*HM Advocate* v *Savage* (1923) JC 49: p. 50).

Even in those jurisdictions where intoxication may be relevant in determining *mens rea* in all cases, it is accepted that the public need protection from drunken violence (see *R* v *O'Connor* (1980) 146 CLR 64 at 87). The difference in *O'Connor* is that the Australian High Court saw that society needed protecting from a variety of other offenders and questioned whether an exception to the general principles of attributing criminal liability could be justified on this basis. The issue was therefore whether an exceptional case for abandoning principle could be justified on the grounds of public protection in cases involving intoxicated offenders. From a utilitarian perspective this would require clear evidence that the future benefit (public protection) would outweigh the harm caused by abandoning the general principles of criminal liability. Subsequent Australian research has suggested that the High Court was right not to be persuaded that abandoning the *Majewski* distinction would lead to an increase in drunken violence (Orchard 1993; Skene 1983; Smith 1981).

Prison may be seen as the most obvious way of protecting the public from intoxicated offenders but it is worth remembering that there are other less invasive measures that can be used to the same end. Three possible requirements of a community order are especially relevant in this context. First, a prohibited activity order requires an offender not to participate in an activity specified in the order either on day(s) so specified or during a defined period (Criminal Justice Act 2003, s.203(1)).

Second, a curfew requirement could be imposed which states that the offender has to remain at a specified place for periods specified in the order (Criminal Justice Act 2003, s.204(1)). Finally, an exclusion order prohibits an offender from entering a specified place for the period specified in the order (Criminal Justice Act 2003, s.205(1)). These measures, either alone or in combination, could be used to restrict the drinking habits of someone who posed a danger to the public whilst intoxicated without recourse to the prison system.

The exclusion order is, in effect, a wider version of the power courts already have to exclude individuals from licensed premises. Section 1 of the Licensed Premises (Exclusion of Certain Persons) Act 1980 allows the court to make an order prohibiting an individual who committed an offence in a licensed premises from entering those premises or any other specified premises if the offence involved the use or threat of violence. Such an order is made either in addition to a discharge (Licensed Premises (Exclusion of Certain Persons) Act 1980, s.1(2)) and has effect for a period of between three months and two years (ibid., s.1(3)). Breaching the order is an offence under s.2 of the Act and the offence is punishable with a fine not exceeding £200 and/or imprisonment for one month.

For such an order to be made, the court has to be of the opinion that the offender posed at least a nuisance and a possible danger to the public in licensed premises. Thus it was held to be inappropriate in R v Grady (1990) 12 Cr.App.R.(S.) 152 where the offender, who admitted pushing and punching a landlady during an argument, was a mature women of previous good character. If such an order is made the courts are wary of making them too restrictive, although, on the facts, the Court of Appeal upheld an order banning the offender from entering 165 specified licensed premises in the Borough of Crewe and Nantwich in Arrowsmith [2003] 2 Cr.App.R.(S.) 301.

The realisation by the court in R v Arrowsmith of the dangers of restricting an offender's freedom too much demonstrates that, in effect, the courts are attempting to protect public safety without placing too onerous a restriction on the offender's freedom. Yet herein lies an apparent contradiction. Following the reasoning in Grady such an order is only appropriate if the offender poses a general nuisance to the public in licensed premises. If the offender satisfies this test, then it is difficult to argue that the general nuisance that he poses is restricted to a few particular premises. If the exclusion order is to have its desired effect then it has to be used only in appropriate cases but, if such a case is identified, then its coverage should not be unduly restricted. This then raises the crucial question present in much of the discussion about measures designed to protect the public: how does one identify an individual who poses a danger to the public? With regard to exclusion orders, the stakes may not be as high as with imprisonment but we still need to address this issue if we are proposing to restrict an offender's freedom of movement, not least because the offence that he committed may have been minor and he may even have been discharged for it. Some comfort may be derived from the fact that the power is not used frequently (Ashworth 2000: 303).

As well as the problems of measuring whether such measures do in fact offer public protection (Zimring and Hawkins 1995), there are moral issues that need to be addressed. Given that one is usually dealing with imprisonment, I have summarised the situation elsewhere in the following terms:

> [You are] imprisoning an offender ... on the basis of an offence which, at best, he has not yet committed and, at worst, would never have committed if at liberty. (Dingwall 1998: 177)

To a retributivist this is unacceptable as you are sentencing not on the basis of the current offence but on the basis of a perceived future risk. The sentence imposed could therefore be disproportionate to the actual offence committed (von Hirsch 1986). However, the Criminal Justice Act 2003 is alert to this possibility for it states that the restrictions on liberty imposed by the order must be commensurate with the seriousness of the offence (s.148(2)(b)). At least in principle, public protection is restrained by retributive considerations.

The government have also recently announced that they plan to introduce a new order called the Drinking Banning Order (Department for Culture, Media and Sport et al. 2005: para 4.6). This order will allow individuals aged 16 or over who are responsible for 'alcohol related' disorder to be excluded from the area in which they committed their offences. The order could be triggered in a number of ways: for example, the court might be required to consider it following a third or subsequent conviction for this type of offence or the police or a Local Authority could apply to the court following the issue of a similar number of alcohol-related fixed penalty notices (ibid.: para 4.6).

There are still some issues that the government have to determine. First, should such an order have minimum or maximum terms? Second, should the order be limited to the area in which the offender had previously offended or should it be extended so as to stop displacement to neighbouring areas? Finally, should the order only apply during certain times, for example 6pm–6am, or should the courts be given discretion to decide in each particular case?

Intoxication and rehabilitation

There is a long history of measures being adopted with the aim of rehabilitating those whose offending was believed to be linked to drinking. The early history of the Probation Service in England and

Wales is closely linked to the church and the temperance movement. The Church of England Temperance Society started using Police Court Missionaries in 1875 (Bochel 1981: 6). Their role became more formal with the enactment of the Summary Jurisdiction Act 1879, which allowed magistrates to conditionally discharge a person convicted of a trivial offence on condition that the offender be of good character. If not, the offender could be recalled for sentence.

The background of those employed to work with offenders in the early days shows the clear link with organised religious movements who believed in temperance; the missionaries came from the Church of England Temperance Society, the Church Army, the Federation of Local Free Church Councils, the Roman Catholic Westminster Education Fund, the National Temperance Association and the Reformatory and Refuge Union (ibid.: 40). That alcohol was perceived to be a cause of crime at the time, is highlighted by the Criminal Justice Act 1914 which made specific regard to abstaining from intoxicating liquor when it gave the courts additional powers to determine conditions attached to discharging offenders in this way. The system continued until 1938 when the Home Office employed those who had worked as probation officers and the missions directed their attention to running hostels for those on probation.

With specific regard to offenders with drinking problems, the Habitual Drunkards Act 1879 allowed for the voluntary treatment of habitual drunken offenders instead of the more usual forms of punishment (see Chapter 1). The Inebriates Act 1898 removed the requirement of voluntariness – if certain specified criteria were met then the offender could be compulsorily detained for up to three years in State or Certified Inebriate Reformatories. Although two State Reformatories and thirteen Inebriate Reformatories were established all of them had closed by 1921 (Thom 1999: 96–97). Since then, despite support from certain quarters, there has been no general political acceptance that such offenders should receive treatment against their wishes. Thom remarks that:

> The use of compulsory treatment to deal with the problem of the homeless, habitual drunk had been demanded by some sectors of the populace since the nineteenth century and was to be brought up again in committees and policy discussions into the 1970s. But it never gained serious credence at policy level, possibly because the increasingly powerful medical lobby argued against compulsory incarceration as an effective response to the problem. Over the course of the 1960s, at least within professional and policy circles, the emphasis became more firmly fixed on a treatment model, rather than a penal model as the appropriate response. (ibid.: 88)

With this aim in mind, official policy was to encourage the establishment of hostels to provide help for homeless, discharged offenders (Home

Office 1966). The Home Office was impressed by the work being done in certain hostels, most notably St. Luke's House in London (ibid.: 9–10). They envisaged a system comprised of hostels, which would provide help for alcoholics and smaller 'group centres' which would be allied to psychiatric hospitals and would provide intensive support and treatment for 'very disturbed or deteriorated' alcoholics (ibid.: 10).

The help offered 'had its roots partly in traditional nineteenth-century approaches to rehabilitation, partly in the group therapy and self-help approaches which had been introduced into alcoholism treatment in the 1950s and partly in emerging social work techniques' (Thom 1999: 92). The warden of St. Luke's House (a Cambridge Law graduate) admitted that most of the employees had no relevant qualifications nor were there standard guidelines for running a hostel (ibid.: 93). According to those Thom interviewed, the workers, who typically came from privileged backgrounds, felt an 'immense sense of excitement' occasioned by working in a pioneer field (ibid.: 95).

At any one time different sentencing justifications tend to dominate official thinking (Fox 1999). After a period of confidence in what could be achieved with offenders, rehabilitation came under serious scrutiny for a period of time. Confidence in the potential to rehabilitate was at its lowest in the mid-1970s. In a seminal paper published in 1974, Martinson, after a comprehensive analysis of a large number of rehabilitative programmes, came to the infamous conclusion that 'nothing works'. The United States National Research Council (1978) found that there were no significant differences in recidivism rates between offenders who had received different types of punishment, again challenging the effectiveness of those measures designed specifically to rehabilitate.

This empirical challenge came at the same time that practical difficulties surfaced which undermined the effectiveness of many rehabilitative schemes. A useful illustration is provided by the experiment with detoxification units in the mid 1970s. The Home Office (1971) had stated a clear intention to respond to public drunkenness by setting up units which were 'demonstrably medical and social work facilities with a clearly therapeutic purpose' (ibid.: 191). Those found drunk by the police could be taken to a centre instead of being arrested. Initially three experimental facilities were planned. One failed to materialise, but the one in Leeds and the one in Manchester were both highly unsuccessful. The experiment failed for a number of reasons, including limited funding, confusion over departmental responsibility, lack of clarity over the aims of detoxification centres and that 'by 1970 some of the passion had gone out of the alcohol field' (Thom 1999: 102). The 'heady times' had been replaced by a realisation that rehabilitation was difficult to achieve.

Towards 'what works?'

Over time research has demonstrated that some dispositions are more successful than others in terms of reducing reconviction rates (Martinson himself retracted his earlier conclusion, 1979). Bagaric remains especially optimistic about the potential to rehabilitate:

[There] is some evidence that [rehabilitation] will work for a small proportion of offenders and ... there is no firm evidence showing that it cannot work for the majority of offenders. (2001: 155)

Whatever optimism there is may be guarded, but nonetheless the emergence of data which suggests that some measures are demonstrably more effective has shifted the terms of the debate: the question has become 'what works?' (McGuire 1995).

This shift in the debate highlights a key methodological issue. How do you measure success? It has become increasingly recognised that the use of reconviction rates can be misleading. For example, there is a temptation to say that if an offender does not reoffend then the programme has been a success. Yet we do not know if the offender would have reoffended if he had been dealt with in another way or, indeed, if he had not been punished at all. Similarly, one has to avoid the conclusion that a programme automatically failed if an offender does reoffend. How do we know that he would not have reoffended sooner or committed a more serious offence if he was dealt with in a different manner? Then there is the obvious point that the offender may be reoffending but may not have been reconvicted for any offence. In short there are formidable methodological hurdles that have to be overcome in assessing whether a particular way of dealing with an offender successfully rehabilitates. However, there are those who argue that offering rehabilitative programmes for those who misuse alcohol could successfully reduce crime rates (Deehan 2001; Jernigan and Mosher 2001; Saunders 1998; Wright 1993). It has also been argued that lack of success has often been due to issues such as insufficient funding and inadequate planning rather than any underlying defect with rehabilitation (Giesbrecht and Nesbitt 2001).

Traditionally rehabilitative measures have been closely associated with community penalties and, in particular, with the work of the Probation Service (though much valuable work is undertaken in the prison system and by other official and voluntary agencies; Wright 1993). One of Britain's leading experts on community penalties, Sue Rex, argues that these are 'propitious times' for community penalties:

In addition to the proliferation of new orders, we have seen the establishment of a National Probation Service for England and

Wales. And we are in the heyday of the 'What Works' movement. The Joint Prisons/Probation Accreditation Panel has been tasked with approving a core curriculum of demonstrably effective programmes for offenders. In pursuit of the goal of reduced recidivism, a range of evaluated 'Pathfinder' projects have been funded under the Crime Reduction Programme – the resettlement of prisoners, the acquisition of basic skills and community service – as well as cognitive-behavioural programmes more traditionally associated with reducing offending. This initiative undoubtedly gives considerable impetus to probation work. (2002: 139–140)

This all suggests a clear governmental believe that rehabilitative work is beneficial. The Criminal Justice Act 2003 introduced one new measure specifically designed to help those with alcohol-related problems. Termed the alcohol treatment requirement (s.177(1)(j)), it is further defined in s.212(1) of the Act and requires the offender:

[To] submit during a period specified in the order to treatment by or under the direction of a specified person having the necessary qualifications or experience with a view to the reduction or elimination of the offender's dependency on alcohol.

There are several criteria that have to be fulfilled before such a requirement can be made. Section 212(2) states that the court has to be satisfied that (a) the offender is dependent on alcohol; (b) that his dependency is such as requires and may be susceptible to treatment; and (c) that arrangements have been or can be made for the treatment to be specified in the order. The offender has to be willing to comply with the requirements of the order (s.212(3)) however, as the alternative may be more severe, so one could debate the extent to which an offender operates from a position of genuine choice.

This is a novel departure (though a requirement to treatment for alcohol dependency could previously have been made as part of a probation order: Powers of the Criminal Courts Act 1973, Schedule 1A). Other jurisdictions have had special provisions for a considerable period of time. For example, Tasmania's treatment orders date back to the Alcohol and Drug Dependency Act 1968. One has to wonder what importance there is in giving the requirement this new status.

It may have the benefit of raising awareness amongst sentencers. One of the questions Potas (1994) asked in his study of sentencers in New South Wales suggests that how this information is disseminated is important. When asked if there was a sufficient range and number of rehabilitation resources or programmes available for treating alcoholic offenders in their area, only one in three of his sample replied 'yes' (ibid.: 77). A high proportion of judges (45 per cent) stated that they did not know, which can perhaps be explained by the greater experience magistrates have of offenders with alcohol problems but is worrying nonetheless. Obviously this research took place in another jurisdiction but it has also been suggested (Norton 1998) that magistrates in England and Wales would benefit from better training about the availability of alcohol programmes for offenders.

If this issue has been addressed another one also merits attention. Some parts of the country may be better served than others when it comes to being able to offer the necessary treatment, especially if residential treatment is required. This is a particular concern in rural areas (Davies 1999) where there are practical difficulties in running schemes due to greater geographical distances and lower population density. As an alcohol treatment requirement can only be made if arrangements can be made for the necessary treatment (Criminal Justice Act 2003, s.212(2)(c)) there is the potential that offenders in a rural area may be denied this form of treatment. This raises the possibility that justice will depend to some extent on geography.

If the facilities are available, how successful will they be? There are some grounds for optimism. Some programmes run by the Probation Service have impacted positively on reconviction rates. One offending behaviour programme which the National Probation Service is rightly proud of is the Drink Impaired Drivers programme. This was first accredited in 2001. A study of reconviction rates after two years showed that 14 per cent of those who had taken part in the programme had been reconvicted as opposed to 21 per cent sentenced to other disposals (National Probation Service 2003). However, it is dangerous to draw a direct parallel. The types of offender are different; those who drink and drive may not be 'dependent on alcohol', a requirement for those who will be subject to alcohol treatment requirements. One cannot assume that the apparent success of one measure will be mirrored in another. Equally though, one cannot draw the conclusion that the alcohol treatment requirement will be any less successful. It will simply have to be judged on its own terms.

From principle to practice

It should be clear from the above discussion that the choice of sentencing rationale is important. Different objectives could, and indeed frequently should, lead to different sentences being imposed in practice. Similarly how sentencers respond to particular factors, such as intoxication, should differ depending on the philosophical basis that is being used to determine sentence. In practice though sentencers have frequently operated in a criminal justice system which does not prioritise potentially conflicting aims. As a consequence what available evidence there is suggests that intoxication is dealt with in something of a haphazard manner by sentencers, depending on their personal sentencing philosophy and with consequent issues about consistency and fairness.

British governments have traditionally left sentencing policy to the senior judiciary in the belief that this was necessary to preserve judicial independence (see Munro 1992). The senior judiciary, however, believed that sentencing was something of an art form and should therefore be left to the individual judge or magistrate who would have a unique knowledge of both the crime and the offender. This lack of central direction by government and the senior judiciary meant that different sentencers could quite legitimately follow different sentencing directions. Some sentencers might have felt that a sentence should be justified on its rehabilitative effect, for example, whilst others would be guided by the need to deter others who might be minded to engage in similar forms of criminal activity. At the same time, each approach was equally valid. What sentencers needed, and lacked, was guidance from senior judges about how to approach sentencing in cases involving intoxication.

Early guidance by the courts

Given the frequency with which sentencers had to deal with claims that offending behaviour was caused at least in part by uncharacteristic intoxication (Rumgay 1998; Shapland 1981), it is something of a surprise how little information there is of how sentencers treated intoxication at the time. As Wasik (1999: 724) notes, alcohol is mentioned in passing in many reported sentencing cases from the Court of Appeal in England and Wales but a judgment concerned wholly with the issue is lacking.

What limited evidence there is from the Court of Appeal suggests that, in itself, intoxication was generally treated as irrelevant. Fallon (1975: 103) cites three cases (*Enright* [1962] Crim LR 712; *Fagan and Fagan* [1962] Crim LR 495; *Hugman* [1967] Crim LR 248) which would support such a conclusion. Thomas (1979: 209) also cites a number of Court of Appeal decisions from the 1970s which support the view that sentencers did not view intoxication favourably. In one of the cases Lord Justice Lawton concluded that '[the] courts do not normally take drunkenness into account as a mitigating factor for criminal offences' (*Kirkland* (1975) unreported, cited in Wasik 2001: 62).

This view was endorsed in *Bradley* (1980) 2 Cr.App.R.(S.) 12. The offender had punched a police officer in the face as the officer was in the process of arresting him. Later he assaulted one of the officer's colleagues in a police detention room. Taking account of both the gravity of the offences and of the offender's previous good character, the judge sentenced Bradley to six months' imprisonment. Bradley appealed on the basis that consideration should also have been given to the fact that he was drunk at the time of the assaults. The Lord Chief Justice stated that:

[The] day is long past when somebody can come along and say 'I know I have committed these offences, but I was full of drink'. If the drink is induced by himself, then there is no answer at all. (p. 13)

One might be tempted to think that a statement of this nature by the Lord Chief Justice, the judge who presides over the criminal division of the Court of Appeal, would have settled the matter. Such sentiments have been expressed again more recently (*Attorney General's Reference No.79 of 1999* [2000] 2 Cr.App.R.(S.) 124; *R* v *Parkhouse* [1999] 2 Cr.App.R.(S.) 208). However, there are examples from the law reports of instances where intoxication was treated, either expressly or by implication, as a mitigating factor.

The first examples relate to minor property offences. In *Abrahams* (1980) 2 Cr.App.R.(S.) 10, ironically the case preceding *Bradley* in the law reports, the theft of a plastic dinghy had 'the characteristics of a drunken frolic, rather than . . . a premeditated crime of dishonesty' (p. 11). Lord Justice Cumming Bruce appears to have placed weight on the fact that, although the alcohol had been voluntarily consumed, the effects of that type of alcohol may not have been foreseeable to the defendant:

He had drunk a good deal of scrumpy, which sometimes, to the uninitiated, has a greater effect in stimulating irresponsible activity than the drinker immediately expects. (p. 11)

This is of interest for the English courts have been clear that a lack of awareness about the strength of the alcohol consumed is irrelevant in determining substantive criminal liability: the consumption remains voluntary (*R* v *Allen* [1988] Crim LR 698). *Abrahams* suggests that, despite this, it might legitimately be treated as a mitigating factor when it comes to sentencing.

Caution is clearly required in analysing what are rare and short Court of Appeal decisions. It is possible that the judges involved were engaged in some complicated unarticulated theoretical appraisal which allowed them to differentiate between the scenarios. Equally, they may have felt that such petty matters should not have come to court and preferred to label them as 'drunken frolics' rather than a 'premeditated crime' to make the point.

Less easy to explain on this basis are a couple of serious sexual cases which appear to be at odds with *Kirkland* and *Bradley*. In both cases alcohol was cited as a relevant factor in reducing the sentence. In *Spence* (1982) 4 Cr.App.R.(S.) 175 intoxication was mentioned as one factor why a six year sentence for rape was disproportionate. No reason why intoxication was relevant in this context was given. Perhaps it is noteworthy that the other factor that the court deemed relevant was previous good character (p. 176). This combination of good character and alcohol was also cited in the earlier case of *Young* (1973) unreported. This is consistent with Thomas's (1979) opinion that intoxication has no independent mitigating effect but may add some minor additional weight to other recognised mitigating factors. It is unfortunate though that in these cases the Court of Appeal referred to both factors whilst in cases such as *Bradley* only good character was seen as relevant. This does not necessarily mean that defendants were being treated in a discriminatory manner – the aggregate reduction in sentence could have been identical – but it has the unfortunate effect of suggesting that there was a disparity of approach.

This inconsistency has been noted in other commonwealth jurisdictions. Potas (1994) found a similar pattern in a survey of Australian practice. In most cases intoxication had no bearing on sentence whereas it could also on occasion act as a mitigating factor. There were also rare examples where it was treated as an aggravating factor. He cites the following passage from the New South Wales Court of Criminal Appeal in *Coleman* (1990) 47 A Crim R 306 to illustrate the way in which the courts believed that adopting a uniform position would not be appropriate:

> Only one matter of general principle was debated, and that was the extent to which the appellant was entitled to have his intoxication at the time of this offence taken into account in mitigation. The degree of deliberation shown by an offender is usually a matter to be taken into account; such intoxication would therefore be relevant in determining the degree of deliberation involved in the offender's breach of the law. In some circumstances, it may aggravate the crime because of the recklessness with which the offender became intoxicated; in other circumstances, it may mitigate the crime because the offender has by reason of that intoxication acted out of character. (p. 327)

Again one can see that the combination of previous good character and intoxication could result in a lesser sentence being imposed. In the case itself, which involved a serious sexual assault, the offender's prior record meant that he was not entitled to a sentence discount as the offence was not out of character. A similar requirement that the offence was uncharacteristic was noted at the time in Canada (Ruby 1980) and in New Zealand (Hall 1987).

If the courts were generally unsympathetic to those who offended whilst intoxicated, they were prepared to look favourably on offenders who recognised that they had an alcohol problem and showed a willingness to address it (Gilyeat 1994; Thomas 1979). It is clear, however, that the offender had to be prepared both to admit to his addiction and to have done something to address it. The courts were not sympathetic to addiction in itself. This was shown most forcefully in the case of *Lawrence* (1988) 10 Cr.App.R.(S.) 463 where the Court of Appeal stated that the 'sooner and more firmly' people are disabused of the notion that addiction counts as mitigation the better. Similar positions have been taken in the US and in Ireland (Hanly 2003).

In the last section the retributive concern that rehabilitative schemes could lead to a disproportionate amount of punishment being imposed was raised. The Court of Appeal were obviously mindful of this danger and held that sentencers should not impose disproportionate sentences so that those with alcohol problems could receive additional treatment (*Roote* (1980) 2 Cr.App.R.(S.) 368; *Bassett* (1985) 7 Cr.App.R.(S.) 75).

Empirical evidence for disparity

Given the lack of direction from appellate courts, it is instructive to see how sentencers in the lower courts saw intoxication, especially as Walker and Padfield (1996: 51) claim that the Court of Appeal were stricter on the issue. As part of a national study into alcohol misuse and violence, a study was undertaken by the Australian Institute of Criminology to assess how sentencers in New South Wales viewed intoxication at the sentencing stage (Potas 1994). Three hypothetical cases were designed – a pub brawl, a serious incident of domestic violence and an armed robbery – and the respondents were asked a series of questions relating to sentencing the offences. The questions covered a range of issues so as not to place undue influence on the fact that the offenders were intoxicated at the time that they offended. The sample comprised of 80 magistrates (a response rate of 63.5 per cent) and 37 District Court judges (a response rate of 66.1 per cent). For the purposes of this chapter, the following two cases will be used by way of example:

Case 1: 'Peter Smith had been at home baby-sitting his 10-year old sister. He knew his mates would be at a pub. At about 9 p.m. he decided to join them and left his sister locked in the house. His mates were intoxicated when he arrived at the pub and he also soon became intoxicated. He was known to become argumentative and aggressive when drunk. When one of his mates made a crude joke about his sister, Smith broke the top of a 'stubbie' [small beer] bottle and attacked him. As a result Smith lacerated his mate's cheek, before he could be restrained by others.' (ibid.: 72)

Case 2: 'The victim, Debbie Tanner, had obtained an Apprehended Violence Order against her husband John. There was a history of domestic violence. He was required to leave the matrimonial home and not contact her for 12 months. About three months later, the offender, who had been drinking, entered the victim's home in her absence, with the intention of talking to her. When she arrived home she found him drinking her Scotch. An altercation ensued and he violently assaulted her. The offender was affected by alcohol at the time of the offence. He left the scene when interrupted by a neighbour.' (ibid.: 72)

The results demonstrate just how much disagreement there was between the participants in the study.

Table 6.1 Percentage of respondents who regarded intoxication as aggravating or mitigating in each scenario (adapted from Potas 1994: p. 73)

	Case 1	*Case 2*
Highly mitigating	0.0	0.9
Mitigating	9.4	4.3
Slightly mitigating	26.5	30.8
Neutral	29.1	23.9
Slightly aggravating	14.5	20.5
Aggravating	17.1	17.1
Highly aggravating	3.4	2.6

Potas (1994: 74) concluded that there is 'no clear policy or consensus as to whether alcohol intoxication is mitigating, aggravating or a neutral factor' in the two scenarios above. What is also striking, given the general stance of the appellate courts outlined in the section above, is that, far from being a rare occurrence, many sentencers do regard intoxication as an aggravating factor when it comes to sentencing (35.0 per cent in Case 1 and 40.2 per cent in Case 2). To what extent this is unique to New South Wales and to what extent this manifests itself in sentencing practice are moot points. The results do though suggest that the discussion should not just be framed in terms of whether intoxication should be treated neutrally or as a mitigating factor at the sentencing stage.

Another interesting conclusion from Potas's study is that, despite a broadly consistent pattern emerging, the magistrates in the study were more likely to select one of the aggravating categories whilst judges were more likely to select one of the mitigating categories. He puts forward (ibid.: 76) the possible explanation that magistrates may be 'hardened' as much of their work involves drink driving offences. It would also be interesting to know to what extent both magistrates and judges' views were influenced by the predominant culture in the courts in which they operated.

The sample were also asked a more general question namely '[as] a general principle should alcohol intoxicated offenders be treated differently?'. A clear majority ('about six out of 10 respondents'; ibid.: 78) stated that alcohol intoxicated offenders should not be treated differently whilst about one in four of the sample stated that they would treat such offenders more leniently. One judge said that he would treat an intoxicated offender more severely, as did one in eight magistrates. When asked a stark question as opposed to being given case scenarios to deal with, a higher proportion of the sample treated intoxication as a neutral factor. Similarly, a far smaller proportion stated that it should be treated as an aggravating factor although, again, magistrates were more likely than judges to come to this conclusion. One of the magistrates who viewed intoxication as an aggravating factor added the following observation:

> Alcohol plays a role in as much as and probably more than 90 per cent of the crimes dealt with by me. Over 20 years as a practitioner and judicial officer I have seen nothing to change this percentage. (ibid.: 78)

Potas concluded that the wide disparity of approach should lead to judicial and magisterial reflection on the impact intoxication should have on sentence with a view to improving consistency of approach (ibid.: 80). The degree of disparity of opinion uncovered by his research demonstrates both the need for this and the obvious difficulty of finding consensus.

Towards a consistency of approach: the Criminal Justice Act 1991

The Criminal Justice Act 1991 represented a major turning point in sentencing policy in England and Wales (for detailed commentary see Wasik and Taylor 1991; for background to the passage of the Act see Windlesham 1993). The government recognised that there was a serious lack of uniformity in sentencing practice that needed to be addressed. For the first time an Act of Parliament provided a framework for sentencers to operate within. The dominant, though not exclusive, determinant of sentence was to be retribution: unless the offence came within an exceptional category, any sentence had to be proportionate to the offender's culpability. Rehabilitation and incapacitation were given minor supporting roles whilst deterrence did not feature in the legislation (although it was quickly resurrected as a legitimate aim by the Court of Appeal). What is striking with hindsight is how rapidly the coherence of the Act was undermined.

In an attempt to preserve judicial independence, the government had intended the Court of Appeal to provide guidance to the lower courts on how to interpret the Act. The Court failed to provide the anticipated level of guidance to sentencers in lower courts (Dingwall 1997) thereby maintaining inconsistency. The Act was also compromised when the Court of Appeal reintroduced deterrence as a factor to be taken into account despite clear parliamentary intent to the contrary. Finally, after a sustained media onslaught, the government jettisoned the 'unit fine' system in the Criminal Justice Act 1993. This was of monumental importance given the extensive use that is made of the fine in the English system. Although the 1993 Act maintained a retributive basis for setting the amount of a fine, the failure to provide a uniform alternative mechanism plunged the penal system back into inconsistency.

Other problems were more foreseeable. One of the ubiquitous appeals of retribution is its apparent simplicity: how can anyone object to the notion that an offender gets the sentence which he deserves? How, though, does one calculate what an offender deserves? As subjective views vary widely, objective criteria need to be formulated for measuring both an offender's culpability and for attributing a proportionate sentence. The legislation though was deliberately evasive. A useful example is provided in s.1(2)(a), the main section determining the use of custody, which stated that a custodial sentence could only be imposed if 'the offence [was] so serious that only a custodial sentence [could] be justified'. Such a degree of generality was quite deliberate. The government had no wish to draft detailed sentencing guidelines of the type associated with several American states (for a critical evaluation of US sentencing guidelines see Stith and Cabranes 1998), in part because they knew that this would cause judicial indignation. The result of this was that the Court of Appeal were handed a daunting task as, in order to help sentencers in lower courts, they had to devise a way of measuring the seriousness of different types of criminal harm before calculating a proportionate penal response.

What happened was that the Court concentrated on comparatively serious offences. This was obviously important but was of no direct benefit to most sentencers as they would never have to deal with a case of that magnitude. These cases were also comparatively easy for the Court of Appeal in that there was usually no question that the offender was going to receive a custodial sentence, the only real issue being its length (Dingwall 1997). What the Court of Appeal appeared to do was avoid dealing with those offences where the choice of sanction was not obvious; the very offences which caused sentencers the most trouble.

Similarly, the Court of Appeal did not provide meaningful guidance on how sentencers were to deal with certain factors which are often pleaded in mitigation. Once again, there was no definitive statement on the impact that intoxication should have, although, again, the courts said that a readiness to accept and to address a drinking problem would be looked at favourably in deciding whether to impose a custodial sentence in borderline cases (*Howells* [1999] 1 WLR 307). One has to be careful of being overtly critical though as it has to be recognised that the task that the Court was given was something of a poison chalice, not least as the reflection it required would have been difficult in the context of the Court's everyday function and environment.

The retributive retreat

The 1991 Act is often represented as a high point in principled sentencing legislation in the UK (Northern Ireland and Scotland never had comparative legislation). Whether or not one agreed with its predominantly retributive underpinnings, one could not deny that the Act represented an attempt to provide penological coherence to the criminal justice system. Successive Acts in the 1990s restricted the importance of retribution by increasing the circumstances where utilitarian considerations were to be paramount. The role of retribution has been further undermined with the passing of the Criminal Justice Act 2003.

At first glance, retribution would appear to have become no more than one factor amongst many that sentencers are now bound to consider. Section 142(1) of the 2003 Act states that any court dealing with an offender must have regard to the punishment of offenders, the reduction of crime (including a specific mention to deterrence), rehabilitation, public protection and reparation in passing sentence. It is clear that utilitarian justifications have once again become both a central and a legitimate part of the equation. In the White Paper (Home Office 2002) which preceded the report, the government emphasised their desire for 'sentencers to consider the best way of preventing crime when they pass sentence' (para 5.4) and that the government would 'ensure that [the courts] base their sentencing practice on what has been shown to work in reducing reoffending . . .' (para 5.4). Commentators have concluded from this that the Act was designed to replace the retributive framework of the earlier legislation with a new framework designed to reduce reoffending (Baker and Clarkson 2002; Roberts 2002).

Yet closer examination of the Act shows that retributivism remains key in determining which form of punishment is appropriate. For example, s.152(2) states that:

> The court must not pass a custodial sentence unless it is of the opinion that the offence, or the combination of the offence and one or more offences associated with it, was so serious that neither a fine alone nor a community sentence can be justified for the offence.

Similar provisions can also be found with regard to community sentences (s.148(1)) and fines (s.164(2)). The Act also deals with some of the issues central to determining a sentence on retributive grounds. Section 143(1) states that, in order to assess the seriousness of any offence, the court 'must consider the offender's culpability in committing the offence and any harm which the offence caused, was intended to cause or might reasonably have caused'. The court must also treat any previous convictions as an aggravating factor if 'it can reasonably be so treated' having particular regard to the nature of the previous offence, its relevance to the current offence and the time that has elapsed between the two (s.143(2)). This provides more detail than the previous guidance in s.151(1) of the Powers of Criminal Courts (Sentencing) Act 2000 which blandly stated that the court may consider previous convictions when calculating the seriousness of the offence. The court is also under a duty to consider all of the information surrounding the offence, including any aggravating or mitigating factors (s.156(1)), and, in relation to determining the composition of a community sentence, may also take into account additional information about the offender (s.156(2)). Once again these provisions are stated in general terms and the onus has been put on the judiciary to interpret it.

When one looks at the list of factors outlined in the Act, one cannot avoid feeling that we have returned to a period of deep uncertainty. The White Paper gives little cause for optimism, merely stating that:

> Sentencers will be required to consider these purposes when sentencing and how the sentence they impose will provide the right balance between the purposes set out above, given the circumstances of the offence and the offender ... (para 5.9)

How is a sentencer to decide which factors are of primary importance in determining sentence? There would appear to be nothing to stop different sentencers coming up with individualised hierarchies depending on their personal penological preferences. We can realistically expect a continuation of disparity in how sentencers deal with intoxication. The situation is exacerbated as sentencers not only have to still contend with insufficient guidance on intoxication but they also lack guidance on how they are to balance potentially conflicting sentencing aims in the first place.

Explaining the compromise

How can one best explain this shift away from the relatively coherent approach found in the Criminal Justice Act 1991? In an international context the relative theoretical purity of the 1991 Act was always something of an oddity. Most comparable jurisdictions have legislation that is more akin to the 2003 Act. For example, the US federal sentencing guidelines state that all of the justifications discussed so far are relevant to sentencing (United States Sentencing Commission 1992), likewise the federal provisions in Australia (Crimes Act 1914, s.16A) and more recent reforms in Canada (see comment by Roberts and von Hirsch 1998) and New Zealand (Sentencing Act 2002; see comment by Roberts 2003).

Like governments in other jurisdictions, the Labour administration has had to balance competing criminal justice concerns. The manifesto on which they were initially elected famously stated an intention to be 'tough on crime, tough on the causes of crime'. The first part was probably a political necessity (Garland 1990: 80): throughout the 1990s there was an overriding mood of 'popular punitiveness' (Bottoms 1995: 40) both in the UK and elsewhere. In the British context this mood was wholeheartedly embraced by both a centre-left government keen to avoid being labeled 'soft on crime' and an increasingly desperate Conservative opposition who saw endlessly reactionary Law and Order policies as a way of clawing back much needed support (for general background see Downes and Morgan 1997; James and Raine 1998; Matthews and Young 2003). The result was that the two main British political parties were locked in a battle to be seen as the party of Law and Order but, in reality, their approaches were broadly consistent (Brownlee 1998). This is hardly surprising when one considers the potential popular and political consequences of introducing any reform that could be perceived and portrayed as unduly lenient on the offender. As Freiberg notes:

> Public policy makers ignore public feelings at their peril. Politicians are more adept than the academics in ensuring that their analyses are understandable to the public who understand street crime more readily than they understand regression coefficients. (2003: 255)

Immediately after taking office, Tony Blair's government fulfilled this part of its promise by introducing a number of reactionary criminal justice reforms (Driver and Martell 1998: 117). One group that was specifically targeted were problem drinkers. It will be recalled that, before the election, the Shadow Home Secretary insisted that Labour would 'reclaim the streets' from the 'aggressive begging of winos, addicts and squeegee merchants' (quoted in Anderson and Mann 1997: 256). After election to office he continued in a similar vein, talking of communities wanting to 'reclaim their street corners from prostitutes, their pavements from the vagrants and their parks from drunks and drug users' (quoted in Bowling 1999: 533).

Some of the government's early criminal justice proposals demon-strated a desire to be seen as 'tough on crime'. A particularly notable example relates to alcohol. After a section of English supporters at the Euro 2000 soccer finals caused national disgrace, the government attributed a politically embarrassing rise in reported crimes of violence to a culture associated with excessive drinking in pubs and clubs (*The Guardian* 18/07/00). The stakes were upped further when the American broadcasting network CNN claimed (misleadingly) that the UK had become a more violent society than the USA. In a panic move, Tony Blair promised to introduce a system of 'on the spot' fines for disorderly conduct. Within hours the idea was abolished as senior police officers, who had not even been consulted, expressed concerns about the practicalities of taking drunk individuals to cash machines so that they could pay their fines. Then, days later, the Prime Minister's 16 year old son was found drunk and incapable by police in central London after celebrating the end of his school examinations. Even without the familial twist, Tony Blair did not come out of the incident well.

There was though an added dimension to the Labour Party's policy. Unlike the Conservatives, the government had also committed itself to being 'tough on the causes of crime' (Downes and Morgan 1997: 100–101). Not everyone in the party agreed with a policy of ever-escalating punitiveness. To those individuals crime could be dealt with more effectively if attempts were made to rehabilitate those who offended or to incapacitate those who posed a particularly high risk of reoffending. To utilitarians, the just desert philosophy could not be justified on the basis that it was not designed to lead to future harm reduction. It is clear from the White Paper that preceded the Act (Home Office 2002) that the government were sympathetic to this view.

Why then didn't the government introduce sentencing legislation that clearly prioritised utilitarian justifications? The government was certainly not lacking in political confidence: this was, after all, the government that pioneered devolution in the UK. There is no doubt that the Labour government was in a sufficiently strong position to have introduced a principled sentencing package as opposed to the eclectic compromise that the 2003 Act represents.

By adding the caveat that they would not only be 'tough on crime' but 'tough on the causes of crime', the government were to some extent architects of their own misfortune. How could they introduce measures that would be effective from a utilitarian perspective in reducing crime without being seen as 'soft on crime'? Their manifesto catchphrase may have been a welcome departure (albeit a partial one) from mindless penality, but the fact that it had to accommodate a sense of popular puniveness meant that the 2003 legislation was destined to be a compromise. The Conservatives had made no such grand claims; the 1991 Act was designed in large measure to punish.

When the coherence of the 1991 Act unraveled due to a combination of judicial interpretation and media hostility, both the Conservative and then the Labour government felt required to make changes to sentencing policy with alarming frequency. With each cosmetic operation the 1991 Act became less and less recognisable. Against the popular background outlined above and the varied concerns of the judiciary and different criminal justice agencies, it is probably understandable that the 2003 Act takes the form that it does. International comparisons suggest it would be surprising were it otherwise. What is perhaps more unexpected is that the following summary of the position prior to the 2003 Act comes not from a hostile media source or an opposition party but from the government itself:

> The public are sick and tired of a sentencing system that does not make sense. They read about dangerous, violent, sexual and other serious offenders who get off lightly, or are not in prison long enough for the length of their sentence. There is no real clarity for magistrates and judges in sentencing and the system is so muddled the public do not always understand it or have confidence in it. (Home Office 2002: para 5.2)

The government may have wanted sentencers to move away from determining sentence only on the basis of retribution, but they did not want anyone to be under the illusion that the reintroduction of utilitarian considerations was going to dampen their enthusiasm to be tough on crime.

Conclusion

It is hardly surprising that there has been little consistency of approach when it comes to sentencing those who offend whilst intoxicated. Some of this is due to more general problems of sentencing. There has largely been a lack of a dominant sentencing rationale with the result that sentencers could chose the basis on which they passed sentence. This choice, and the resulting disparity, has largely been reinstated with the passing of the Criminal Justice Act 2003. An Act which provides a list of conflicting sentencing aims which sentencers must have regard to will do little to aid a consistency of approach.

Similarly, there have been ongoing problems about providing sentencers with sufficient guidance on how to sentence. It is clearly difficult to ensure that guidance from either an appellate court or another body is sufficiently detailed to be of value, especially in a climate where the judiciary are wary of outside interference. The primary technique employed so far – the guideline judgment – has been found wanting. Although they may have been helpful for certain serious offences, they have often failed to consider difficult 'disposition threshold' cases such as criminal damage or more minor offences of violence, where intoxication is often a factor, or, more generally, the effect, if any, that certain potentially mitigating factors should have. It is to be hoped that the new mechanisms for providing guidance introduced in the Act will prove more successful. The new Sentencing Advisory Panel (2004: para 1.22) has provided a list of factors that should either increase or decrease an offender's culpability. Some of these already have or are due to have a statutory basis so it is understandable that the Panel do not discuss them further. What is not acceptable is their unwillingness to explain why certain more contentious factors – including intoxication (see pp. 157–158) – have been classified in a particular manner.

There is a further factor worth bearing in mind. Not only do the justifications for punishment vary but so does the way in which lawyers plead intoxication in mitigation. After undertaking detailed court observation, Rumgay concluded that:

> There is no single intoxication excuse, crudely applied to all alcohol-related offences and offenders. Rather, there is a plurality of intoxication excuses, capitalising on the plurality of lay beliefs about alcohol, selectively and powerfully applied to explain and attribute responsibility for different kinds of criminality. The reach of these lay beliefs, and their moral connotations, is such that even the absence of alcohol from the circumstances of an offence is worthy of mention. (1998: 164)

Not only can intoxication be pleaded as mitigation, but so can sobriety. What this shows, as Rumgay's quote makes clear, is that the sheer number of lay beliefs about alcohol makes intoxication a nebulous yet useful form of mitigation due to its sheer adaptability. A clearer sense of why it might be relevant is needed unless one wants to perpetuate the disparity of approach found by Potas (1994).

How then should intoxication impact on sentencing? First, should it be treated as a mitigating factor? As was explained earlier, for intoxication to count as mitigation, one has to plausibly argue that the offender's culpability was somehow reduced by the fact that he was intoxicated. This is a retributive argument. It is certainly not universally shared. Nonetheless, it does not seem unreasonable to give some credit to those who offend whilst intoxicated *and who have not done so before*. Why is this caveat necessary? Simply because, as von Hirsch (1986) makes clear, tolerance is initially given due to the fallibility of individuals to succumb to pressures and temptations, of which intoxication is one. Thereafter the tolerance is withdrawn. What this means in effect is that someone who offends whilst intoxicated for the first time will receive a lesser sentence than if the offence had been committed whilst sober. Intoxication would then be treated as a neutral factor if there was a repetition.

This suggestion is hampered in practice by an unfortunate section of the Criminal Justice Act 2003. Section 143(2) states that courts should treat any previous convictions as an aggravating factor if '[they] can reasonably be so treated having particular regard to the nature of the previous offence, its relevance to the current offence and the time that has elapsed between the two'. Sentencers are likely to feel bound to regard a previous offence committed whilst intoxicated as an aggravating factor if they are sentencing someone who has committed a later offence after drinking.

Section 143(2) is, for a number of reasons, highly unsatisfactory. It undermines notions of proportionality by focusing attention away from the actual offence towards the offender's previous record. With regards to my proposal it undermines a principled attempt to arrive at a proportionate sentence. It is, in practice, too much to hope that a court would hold that a previous conviction for an offence committed whilst intoxicated could not reasonably be treated as an aggravating factor because it had no relevance to the current offence (although the Sentencing Advisory Panel believe that the section allows courts 'the flexibility to make their own judgments': 2004: para 51). What appears more likely to happen is that intoxication could provide the 'relevant' link between two offences which otherwise would have little in common. Whereas a sentencer may conclude that a previous sentence for theft should have no bearing on a sentence for an offence against the person, would there be no relevance between the offences if the offender had been drunk on both occasions?

Of course the section was not designed to make intoxication an aggravating factor. Its aim was to make 'relevant' previous convictions have this effect. However, as intoxication may supply the missing link between two otherwise disparate offences, the practical effect of s.143(2) may be that offenders who have a record of offending whilst intoxicated are likely to get a longer sentence on the basis of repetition than those who re-offend whilst sober.

For reasons that have been outlined earlier, I have reservations about treating previous convictions as an aggravating factor. Section 143(2) is to be regretted not just for the effect that it may have with regard to those who offend whilst intoxicated but, more generally, for the way in which sentencing will become increasingly removed from the offence in question.

A further complication is that courts are now bound by virtue of s.172 of the Criminal Justice Act 2003 to have regard to the recent decision by the Sentencing Guidelines Council (2004: para 1.22) that the offender's culpability is increased if the offence was committed 'under the influence of alcohol or drugs'. This decision has serious ramifications and, given that it does not appear to accord with current practice, deserved justification in the report. Although courts must 'have regard' to sentencing guidelines (Criminal Justice Act 2003, s.172), they are equally bound to take account of matters that 'in the opinion of the court, are relevant in mitigation' (Criminal Justice Act 2003, s.166(1)). What happens if the court remains of the opinion that intoxication is relevant in mitigation in the particular case before them? It would appear that, having regard to the guidance, they could still mitigate. What would though appear to be more problematic would be to have a general policy of treating intoxication as a neutral or mitigating factor. Quite simply that would require revised guidelines.

The government has also stated a position, though again without any conceptual analysis. This appears to differ from the Sentencing Guidelines Council in that, rather than arguing that intoxication should be treated as an aggravating factor, they argue that it should not be a mitigating factor:

> Individuals need to understand that if as a result of irresponsible drinking they commit offences these will not be treated as somehow of only minor importance because they were under the influence of alcohol. (Department for Culture, Media and Sport *et al.* 2005: para 4.1)

Not only does the 2003 Act cause problems with regard to the effect that previous convictions should have on sentencing but, as it includes a number of other factors that need to be taken into account along with retribution, it is necessary to comment on how intoxication should bear on these factors.

It is clear from judgments about criminal liability that the courts are mindful of the potential deterrent effects of a policy that inculpates intoxication. Yet evidence from other jurisdictions which have allowed juries the option of acquitting on the basis of intoxication suggests that the case can easily be overstated (Orchard 1993; Skene 1983; Smith 1981). This should not come as a surprise as deterrent policies assume a degree of popular knowledge about the criminal law which is unrealistic and a rationality on the part of offenders (von Hirsch *et al.* 1999) which is naïve, especially if they have been drinking. Unproven assumptions should not inform sentencing policy, particularly if there is evidence both to suggest that deterrent policies have met with little general success and that alternative strategies to dealing with intoxication have not led to an upsurge in drunken offending.

In contrast both incapacitation and rehabilitation have a useful role to play in sentencing those who offend whilst intoxicated. A number of potential sentences could be proportionate to the offender's culpability. It makes sense, particularly in the context of non-custodial sentences, to choose the options most likely to help the offender and potentially to remove him from areas where he has offended. The increase in available options is therefore to be welcomed.

These are tentative suggestions and represent a personal opinion about the priorities that should be followed in sentencing offenders. If it stimulates debate then its purpose will have been served. What is clear is that the current haphazard, unprincipled system of sentencing those who offend whilst intoxicated should not be allowed to continue. It is to be hoped that the government's apparent desire to respond to drink-related offending will not ignore these difficult philosophical issues.

Chapter 7

Conclusion

In the introduction it was noted that this was an opportune time to consider the link between alcohol and crime and the way that the state responds to offending by those who had been drinking alcohol. From the way the government talk about the issue, one could be mistaken for thinking that the problem was becoming worse, even if research suggests that the opposite is the case (Budd 2003). This should not surprise us as there are many examples of criminal justice 'crises' that generated sustained media coverage and which, on closer inspection, were found to lack originality.

There certainly is nothing new about the belief that the consumption of alcohol can lead to criminality. In fact, what is perhaps most remarkable is the length of time that the issue appeared to slip away from popular consciousness. Criminological research had noted for a while that many offenders had been drinking before offending (e.g. Wolfgang and Strohm 1956). These conclusions supported widely held popular beliefs, but the popular belief goes beyond that: not only is it believed that many offenders had drunk alcohol before offending but it is believed that alcohol, if not the direct cause of the offence, was highly significant in its commission. This additional causality belief is hardly surprising in a society where dire warnings about the consequences of overindulging hark back to biblical times and beyond. Indeed, it may be the case that the degree of popular acceptance that alcohol and crime are linked led to an atmosphere where additional research would have seemed to be either stating the obvious or patently flawed, depending on its conclusion.

Wolfgang and Strohms (1956) findings have been replicated on many occasions. Research has consistently shown that alcohol use is present in a high proportion of offences (Budd 2003; Maguire and Nettleton 2003; Richardson and Budd 2003). This relates both to drinking by the offender and to drinking by the victim if the offence in question is one of violence (Budd 2003). Such findings are not unique to the UK – the prevalence of alcohol in criminal events appears to be nearly universal (Bureau of Justice Statistics 1998; Greenfield and Weisner 1995; Yarvis 1994). It has also been shown that problem drinkers commit a disproportionate amount of crime (Allan *et al.* 2001; Platz 1994). People then are right to be concerned about a possible link between alcohol and crime, not least because the link appears to be strongest with respect to violent offences (Bureau of Justice Statistics 1998; Cookson 1992; Farabee *et al.* 2001; National Institute of Justice 1991; Thornton *et al.* 1990).

Given the above findings, the fact that the government have ordered a 'blitz' on alcohol-related crime is welcome. Whether the ensuing strategy deserves support depends largely on how the government interpret the existing data and, crucially, what changes to criminal justice policy follow. This concluding chapter will address these points in turn. Finally, some observations will be made about how strategies designed to respond to alcohol-related offending relate to more general shifts in criminal justice policy in recent years.

The government response

The official policy towards alcohol and crime could not be more 'New Labour' in tone: '[rights] and responsibilities are at the heart of the government's approach to alcohol' (Department for Culture, Media and Sport *et al.* 2005: para 1.1). The responses to this type of offending are also consistent with the broader Labour strategy of being 'tough on crime, tough on the causes of crime' (Downes and Morgan 1997). Increased punishment and more rigorous enforcement strategies co-exist with a range of crime prevention measures in the Licensing Act 2003, the primary legislative response to 'alcohol-related' crime. The holistic approach has involved both a number of different initiatives (Department for Culture, Media and Sport *et al.* 2005) and a variety of different government departments (ibid.: para 1.4; Prime Minister's Strategy Unit 2003). Moreover, local government, the police, health professionals, the drinks industry and local communities all have a role to play in combating intoxicated crime and disorder (Department for Culture, Media and Sport *et al.* 2005: para 1.4). The government's overriding aim is ambitious:

> We need to achieve a fundamental change in attitude, so that binge and underage drinking are no longer regarded as socially acceptable because of the problems which can follow in their wake. So we must no longer focus simply on containing or managing the disorder so often associated with excessive drinking but seek to eradicate it. (ibid.: para 1.2)

This quote reveals a number of things. It shows a belief that previous strategies were designed to merely contain or 'manage' the problem of offending by those who had been drinking. There is no intention of abandoning this aim, but it should form part of a larger project which is designed to change the acceptability of binge and underage drinking. One can see that recent initiatives have been designed both to lead to attitudinal change and to contain and manage disorder which the government believes to be 'alcohol-related'. It can be difficult to differentiate between measures in the Licensing Act which are designed to lead to cultural change and measures which are designed to help manage crime and disorder. Some provisions clearly are reactive and only have the latter aim. However, the most widely reported change in the legislation, the abolition of fixed permitted opening hours, could have both effects if successful; in the long run attitudinal change could lead to a reduction in crime and disorder and, in the short term, people leaving premises at different times might make it easier to manage crime and disorder. These claims, as we shall see, are controversial. Before considering the possible effects of the Act, the government's case for the changes will be outlined.

The government's case for reforming the licensing system

The Licensing Act 2003 is central to the government's strategy on alcohol and crime. Aspects of the Act will be discussed later in this chapter when consideration is given to 'managing' the problem of 'alcohol-related' offending, but this section will consider the most radical changes brought about by the Act – the abolition of automatic fixed closing times. Although this measure might lead to attitudinal change the government also justify it on the basis of managing the existing problem. Citing one study (Marsh and Fox Kibby 1992), the White Paper (Home Office 2000) which preceded the Act claimed that:

> [Research] indicates that spreading the period during which cus-
> tomers leave should produce five key outcomes:
> ✓ A more gradual, and orderly, pattern of dispersal of peak
>   densities between the hours of 11pm–12 midnight, and 2am–
>   3am in urban centres
> ✓ Significant reductions in reports of drink related offences and
>   in arrests for such offences
> ✓ Reductions in binge drinking and drunkenness on the streets
> ✓ Increased availability of refreshment and transportation facili-
>   ties due to more evenly spread demand
> ✓ A decrease in reports of nuisance and noise in direct propor-
>   tion to the lower densities at any given time. (para 64)

It is not proposed to allow all licensed premises to stay open all of the time. Instead, the Act provides a system whereby the licensing authorities can consider opening hours as part of the conditions attached to licensing premises (Bowes 2004a; 2004b).

The Licensing Act 2003: key provisions

Under the new licensing framework both premises and those who act as the premises' supervisor will have to be licensed. The introduction of premises licences is a new idea and is designed to facilitate the overall objectives of licensing, including the reduction of crime and disorder. Applications for premises licenses must be accompanied by an 'operating schedule' (s.17(3)(a)) which details, amongst other matters, the proposed licensed activities (s.17(4)(a)), the proposed times of these activities (s.17(4)(b)), information about the premises' supervisor (s.17(4)(e)) and the steps which the establishment would take to comply with the overall licensing objectives (s.17(4)(g)). This would, therefore, require detail on what measures would be introduced to combat crime and disorder.

The licensing authority are under a duty to grant the license application, subject to mandatory conditions set out in ss.19–21 of the Act, unless relevant representations are made by responsible authorities, such as the police, or by interested parties, such as local residents. This means that there is a presumption that premises' applications will be accepted. If relevant representations are made, a hearing must be convened to consider those representations, unless specified people agree. The licensing authorities have the power to grant the license subject to modifications necessary for the promotion of the licensing objectives (s.18(4)(a)(i)), or to exclude any of the licensable activities in the operating schedule (s.18(4)(b)), to refuse to allow the person specified in the operating schedule to act as premises supervisor (s.18(4)(c)) or to reject the application (s.18(4)(d)). One thing worth noting is that there is a specific provision relating to door stewards in the Act. If a premises license includes a condition that individuals are to be employed 'to carry out a security activity', all such individuals must be licensed by the Security Industry Authority (s.21(1)).

A premises license has effect either until it is revoked under s.52 of the Act or, if the licence is for a specified period, that period expires (s.26(1)). Clearly then the powers to revoke a license under s.52 are important. The section allows premises licences to be reviewed by interested parties. If the licensing authority believe that the premises are not promoting the licensing objectives adequately then they can modify the conditions of the license (s.52(4)(a)), exclude a licensable activity from the scope of the license (s.52(4)(b)), remove the designated premises supervisor (s.52(4)(c)), suspend the licence for a period not exceeding three months (s.52(4)(d)) or revoke the licence (s.52(4)(e)).

Part 6 of the Act provides the framework for personal licences. These licences operate in tandem with premises licenses and will allow individuals with a licence to move between premises with a licence. A personal licence only allows the licensee to supply alcohol from premises which have a premises license. Designated premises supervisors will have to hold a personal licence under the Act, other staff may do so but will not be under a requirement to obtain one. However, alcohol can only be supplied in a venue with a premises license if someone with a personal licence is acting in a supervisory capacity. It seems reasonable to assume that larger premises will employ a number of individuals with personal licences so that all shifts and periods of staff absence can be covered adequately.

Criticisms of the Licensing Act 2003

Most of the criticism of the 2003 Act has been directed towards the decision to abolish permitted drinking hours. Although it has sometimes been claimed that this will lead to a 24 hour drinking culture, the White paper argued that the likely result will be a considerable variation in opening hours depending on the type of premises and its location (Home Office 2000: para 61). The licensing authorities, for example, might be more willing to restrict the hours of a premises in the suburbs or in a village on the basis that this would reduce nuisance to local residents.

Concerns have been expressed about the way in which the government argued the case for abolishing standard hours. In the White Paper, the government were quite unequivocal that abolishing existing permitted opening hours for licensed premises would have a beneficial effect on crime and disorder:

> It should be noted that the Government's claims are completely unqualified. The Government does not say that abolishing permitted hours may in some circumstances have beneficial effects. It does not concede that there will be any exceptions. It says that everywhere in England and Wales, irrespective of the circumstances, abolishing permitted hours will of itself produce significant reductions in binge drinking and drunkenness, in crime and disorder and in arrests. (McNeill 2005: 7)

Is such a conclusion justified? The government cite two studies to support their stance, but do not mention a number of other studies which would suggest that a note of caution might have been appropriate.

McNeill (2005) refers to the experience in a number of different jurisdictions from Iceland to New Zealand. Iceland serves as a useful example as it shows that, whilst abolishing fixed licensing hours might have the effect of staggering the times at which people leave bars making policing easier, the experiment in Reykjavik also resulted in increases both in the number of police call outs and in the number of alcohol-related accidents and assaults dealt with by local hospitals. After two years, the city council re-introduced fixed opening hours. Problems of a similar nature had also emerged in New Zealand. There the solution appears to be the setting of unofficial fixed closing times through the use of planning restrictions and other measures (ibid.).

Closer to home, the Scottish position is worth reviewing. The government have argued that since the licensing laws were liberated in Scotland a number of positive benefits have accrued. Deehan (1999: 31) has argued that more liberal licensing laws there 'changed the masculine binge drinking culture to a slower drinking, female-friendly environment'. It is difficult to reconcile this conclusion with the statistics in the first chapter of this book which showed that Scottish men were more likely than their counterparts south of the border to 'binge' drink. It will also be recalled that Scottish women were those most likely to 'binge' drink in the UK. One has to question both how extending the licensing hours has had the effect of making Scottish pubs more 'female-friendly' – McNeill (2005) asks whether Scottish women only visit pubs after 11pm – and, if this is indeed the case, whether the price was worth paying.

A Scottish report (Scottish Executive Social Research 2003: para 4.6), which preceded changes to the licensing system in that jurisdiction (for background see Scottish Executive 2003), concluded that '[longer hours of alcohol sales] may be linked to increased problems with alcohol-related crime and disorder, as well as alcohol problems more generally'. Whilst the report acknowledged that 'the evidence from the UK and Scotland is mixed' (ibid.), it seems strange that the government in England and Wales are so ready to cite Scotland as a successful example of abolishing permitted hours when the Scottish Executive has arrived at a more circumspect conclusion.

The Republic of Ireland extended licensing hours in 2000 (McNeill 2005), although the reforms fell short of abolishing fixed drinking hours. According to crime statistics, there were increases in the number of public order offences in the year following the change (ibid.: 19). The Republic of Ireland has also recently reviewed its licensing laws (Commission on Liquor Licensing 2003). The Intoxicating Liquor Bill 2005 is consistent with the conclusions of the Commission which reviewed the adequacy of the existing law and concluded that:

In spite of the arguments put forward in favour of easing restrictions as a means of combating excessive consumption, the Commission considers that such a move would be unlikely to assist in combating alcohol-related harm and would not be in the public interest. (ibid.: 18)

At the same time though, they argued that '[simply] reverting to pre-2000 trading hours will not solve the problems either' (ibid.: 18). The whole tenor of the report is that simplistic solutions to Ireland's problematic increase in alcohol consumption throughout the 1990s are unlikely to succeed due to the range of factors which led to the increase. However, other jurisdictions, including Italy, Germany and Portugal have restricted opening hours during the 1990s (Scottish Executive Social Research 2003: para 2.17). It is interesting that the experiences of these countries have not been reviewed in any of the recent governmental reports in any of the jurisdictions which are in the process of reforming their licensing laws.

Returning to England and Wales, professional bodies have also expressed concerns about the proposal to abolish permitted hours. The Royal College of Physicians (2005) argue that, given present patterns of 'binge' drinking, the more likely effects will be 'a rise in alcohol misuse, drunkenness, medical damage, violence and public disorder'. They further caution that the premises which are most likely to take advantage of the liberalisation will not be 'local, neighbourhood pubs' but 'large, anonymous, urban establishments with a young clientele', in other words those most likely in the Royal College's opinion to encourage the most trouble.

Senior police officers are equally unconvinced by the government's rationale for abolishing permitted hours. The Association of Chief Police Officers (2005) have expressed 'considerable concerns' about the new scheme, believing that the likely result will be 'more people under the influence of alcohol or drunk, [leading] to more crime and disorder'. In turn this will have significant implications for the police in that 'officers will have to be diverted from other policing priorities'.

Two important points need to be made. The first is that, despite the way in which the media often report the issue, 24 hour opening will not be the norm. Many licensees simply will not apply for a premises license which significantly extends the current permitted hours as it would not make financial sense to keep the premises open for that extended period. It will also have to be seen how willing licensing authorities are to give licenses which significantly extend current hours. It is not unreasonable to conclude that the Act will mean that some premises will stay open later than at present, but that many will not and those which do stay open later will do so for periods which may be shorter than that commonly assumed. A combination of market forces and the criteria for objecting to an operating schedule mean that a further bifurcation between opening hours in large, city centre establishments and other, smaller premises in housing areas is likely.

The second point is one which the government are keen to emphasise; abolishing permitted opening hours is but part of the legislation. As has been mentioned in other chapters, the Act includes a range of offences designed to deter underage drinking and the supply of alcohol to those who are drunk. These measures largely build on existing offences and therefore have not been subject to much comment either in the academic literature or in the popular press.

The legal response

One thing which the government have elected not to address as part of this 'blitz' on 'alcohol-related' crime is the legal response towards those who commit offences whilst intoxicated. In one sense this is not surprising. The government's primary objective has been one of reducing such incidents in the first place. To this end, the measures which have been introduced have been designed to make policing this type of activity more effective or, more ambitiously, to try and change deeply ingrained cultural attitudes to 'binge' drinking. This approach is holistic in character and draws heavily on the Problem Oriented Policing model outlined in Chapter 4.

The problem is that, despite these initiatives, the courts still have to deal with large numbers of individuals who offend after drinking on a daily basis. To respond properly to this type of crime you need strategies not only for reducing its incidence but also for dealing with those who commit it. This part of the strategy remains lacking. Other than a brief remark praising the stance taken recently by the Sentencing Advisory Panel (Department for Media, Culture and Sport *et al.* 2005), it is noticeable that the government have not considered the various options regarding imposing criminal liability on those who were intoxicated. This is regrettable because, even if it is debatable whether convicting and sentencing individuals has a direct impact on subsequent crime rates (see Chapter 6), justice demands that those who offend are treated fairly.

It will be evident from the analysis in the last two chapters that there are a number of concerns that can be expressed about the current legal response to alcohol-induced offending. It is convenient to consider the legal response as involving two separate stages; first, a determination about what effect (if any) intoxication should have on an individual's criminal responsibility and, second, what effect (if any) intoxication should have on an individual's sentence. The first, determination is sometimes portrayed as an all-or-nothing decision. The defendant is either criminally responsible or not. Most legal systems have the same rule regardless of offence, although the approach in England and Wales is offence-specific. I will return to this point later. The second determination again might appear to lend itself to a definitive ruling on whether intoxication should be treated as a mitigating, a neutral, or an aggravating factor at the sentencing stage. Many sentencers would resist this on the basis that no two cases are alike and, consequently when you are trying to calculate an offender's culpability, you need to recognise that intoxication cannot be treated in a uniform manner.

The current position in England and Wales can be summarised in the following way. In an attempt to provide adequate protection for the public (the leading case of *Majewski* [1977] AC 443 was in no doubt that this was the overriding concern: see pp. 476, 495 and 498), evidence of intoxication can be taken into account in determining whether the defendant had the required *mens rea* for some offences, but not for others. It is essentially a compromise and an unsatisfactory one at that. Although case law has established which offences fall into which category, the tests employed to aid classification vary (compare the approaches of Lord Edmund-Davies, Lord Elwyn Jones and Lord Simon in *Majewski*) and, to compound matters further, do not appear to be applied correctly (Smith 1976). They also appear to be based on essentially meaningless linguistic distinctions (Williams 1983).

More concerning, however, is the fact that the approach rests on a presumption: namely that proof of intoxication is proof of basic intent (Healy 1994). Is this convincing? Some have tried to argue that intoxication can act as some kind of substitute for recklessness (Lord Edmund-Davies in *Majewski* [1977] AC 443 at 496; Stroud 1914). This is highly problematic. Recklessness is being used in far too loose a manner. The criminal law ordinarily requires a recklessness about causing the particular harm that materialised. In the words of the Canadian Supreme Court:

> It simply cannot be automatically inferred that there would be an objective foresight that the consequences of voluntary intoxication would lead to the commission of the offence. (*R v Daviault* [1994] 3 SCR 63 at 91)

With intoxication the recklessness would appear to be about getting oneself intoxicated. This may be undesirable conduct and may be worthy of moral censure. But it does not disguise the fact that the causal connection usually required in the criminal law between foresight and consequence is not there. Many of these flaws are widely recognised yet, given that most practitioners think that the system is 'workable' (Law Commission 1995), and that any government who introduced a reform which could be interpreted as being unduly lenient towards those who offend whilst intoxicated would be pilloried in the current political climate, reform seems unlikely.

The current lack of an approach towards sentencing those who offend whilst intoxicated is equally unsatisfactory. It is true that no two cases are wholly alike yet that does not mean that it is acceptable to have no guidance whatsoever on how to respond to one of the most frequently used pleas in mitigation (Rumgay 1998; Shapland 1981). What little guidance there has been from the higher courts suggests that intoxication should have no bearing on sentence (e.g. *R v Bradley* (1980) 2 Cr.App.R.(S.) 12). There are though exceptional cases where intoxication in combination with previous good character has acted as mitigation (e.g. *Spence* (1982) 4 Cr.App.R.(S.) 175). The rationale, however, is not fully developed in these judgments (which anyway are dated in terms of authority). What I propose in this regard is not inconsistent with these cases but will be justified more fully on the basis of penal theory.

A suggested legal response

It is one of the most fundamental principles of English law that the prosecution (generally) have the burden of proving all of the constituent elements of the offence against the defendant (*Woolmington v DPP* [1935] AC 462). Yet, if the offence is one of basic intent, the prosecution do not have to prove the *mens rea* was satisfied if the defendant claims to have been intoxicated at the time (in practice a defendant would be ill advised to do so for he or she would in effect be conceding *mens rea*). As courts elsewhere in the common law world have recognised (most notably in *Kamipeli* [1975] 2 NZLR 610; *R v O'Connor* (1980) 146 CLR 64), the English approach, as exemplified by *Majewski*, offends against the underlying principle that the prosecution have to prove that the defendant had the requisite *mens rea* for the offence.

One bold, but principled, alternative would be to say that evidence of intoxication can be considered in all cases of either basic or specific intent in determining whether the defendant had *mens rea*. Such a decision would be politically brave but would have the benefit of being consistent with the general principles of criminal liability. The approach would, no doubt, be subject to savage press criticism – that has certainly been the case at times in Australia and Canada – but, at least if Australian experience is anything to go by, would not result in masses of undeserved acquittals (Orchard 1993; Skene 1983; Smith 1981). The point needs to be made again that the degree of intoxication required for an acquittal is extreme and the danger with putting such evidence before a jury is that they will see the intoxication as an explanation for uncharacteristic behaviour rather than evidence of someone acting in a state akin to automatism. Such an approach would not therefore expose the public to considerable harm as predicted by *Majewski*. This, however, is arguably only one relevant consideration.

Healy (1994) asks the correct question when he asks whether one acquittal in such circumstances can be justified? How does one answer this? There are many factors that could be taken into account in determining whether certain conduct should be criminalised. Two particularly pertinent issues are the culpability of the individual involved and the harm caused by his or her conduct. If someone gets sufficiently intoxicated that they cannot form any *mens rea* and subsequently causes harm it does not seem unreasonable to say that the individual deserves to be punished. The public would quite rightly feel that justice had not been served if the individual escaped punishment. This was recognised in *Majewski* but the solution was wrong. Obviously the court did not have the authority to create a new offence (and there was judicial support in the judgment for the creation of such an offence). What is needed is a specific offence designed to cover those who cause harm whilst intoxicated. This is not an offence that would come into operation every time a defendant had been drinking prior to the offence taking place. On the contrary, it would apply in those rare cases where the intoxication was sufficiently extreme that it could not be proved that the defendant had the requisite *mens rea*. In political terms, the government could justifiably state that the creation of such an offence is consistent with their belief that intoxicated offenders deserve to be punished. Moreover, they could also claim that this approach ensures that such offenders are punished regardless of whether the offence had previously been categorised as one of 'basic' or 'specific' intent.

Admittedly the offence would be difficult to draft. In particular one would have to be careful not to make the offence so wide that it could only be enforced in a very selective manner (Leader-Elliott 1994). Nonetheless drafting has not proven to be impossible in other jurisdictions which operate such an approach.

Sentencing

Given the large number of defendants who raise intoxication as a mitigating factor at the sentencing stage, the paucity both of a guiding approach and of academic attention to the issue is alarming. For the reasons outlined in the last chapter the need for proper consideration of how intoxication should impact on sentencing is more pressing than reform of the substantive law.

As a general rule, because of the consequences for those involved, sentencing should not be allowed to happen without any form of guidance. Individuals need to be confident that there will be a similarity of approach. This is not the same thing as removing all discretion from sentencers. Rather it is a question of requiring sentencers to use that discretion in a particular manner.

In the previous chapter I argued that, generally speaking, intoxication should not be treated as a mitigating factor unless the offender had never offended whilst intoxicated before. This is similar to the general presumption that a first-time offender deserves credit. Such an approach recognises human frailty (von Hirsch 1986) – a position that appears equally valid to someone who offends after drinking. My argument is not that such an offender should merely receive a sentence discount for never having offended before. Rather it is that an individual who has not offended whilst drunk previously deserves some degree of mitigation *because* of the intoxication. Thereafter though any benefit caused by intoxication is lost on the basis that it is reasonable to expect the offender to modify his or her drinking in light of the previous incident.

There is though an important limitation to this. Such an approach does not warrant the offender's intoxication to be treated as an aggravating factor if there are subsequent repetitions. To do this one would need to either base the increase on specific deterrence grounds, and it was argued in the last chapter that there are insufficient grounds to base a sentencing policy on deterrence as yet (see Beyleveld 1979; Home Office 2001a; von Hirsch *et al.* 1999), or on a version of retribution which held that each repetition increased the offender's culpability and hence legitimated an increase in sentence. Whilst the latter may appear superficially attractive, there are two problems with it.

First, it supposes that at some point the individual who repeatedly offends whilst intoxicated becomes more morally culpable than his or her sober counterpart who commits the same offence. My argument is that this is not the case. The first-time drunken offender lacks the culpability of his or her sober counterpart on the basis that the results of his or her conduct were less foreseeable. Any repetition merely removes that difference; the results become more foreseeable and more analogous to the position of the sober offender.

Second, allowing intoxication to count as aggravation raises the perennial problem for desert theorists: sentencing decisions would increasingly become dependent not on the harm caused but on the offender's record (Wasik and von Hirsch 1994).

The approach which I have advocated is unashamedly retributive in character. As a consequence, incorporating it into the current sentencing framework is not wholly straightforward. Recent legislation states that sentencers are to take account of a range of sentencing objectives (Criminal Justice Act 2003, s.142(1)). Retributive considerations accordingly should form part, but only part, of the decision making process. Nonetheless, given my belief that one justification has to take priority, the above proposal offers an improvement over the haphazard current approach.

There are other reasons why the proposed approach may be considered consistent with the 2003 Act. Section 143(1) states that, when it comes to assessing the seriousness of the offence, the court 'must consider the offender's culpability in committing the offence and any harm which the offence caused, was intended to cause or might reasonably have caused'. An assessment of culpability, therefore, remains absolutely central to all sentencing decisions. In order to do this consistently guidance has to be provided about how to deal with factors which might affect culpability. Research (Shapland 1981; Rumgay 1998) shows that intoxication is the issue most frequently raised by defendants. It requires fuller consideration on this basis.

Nor should it be said that the proposal totally excludes other justifications for punishment. Once the appropriate level of punishment is calculated on a retributive basis, it is perfectly acceptable to choose from within the range of options of that severity one which will meet the needs of the offender in question (von Hirsch 1993: 60).

Responses to alcohol-related offending as part of the larger picture

The statistics paint an interesting picture. In the last decade alcohol consumption in the UK has risen (particularly with regard to women and young people) and a significant minority of people engage in 'binge' drinking (Office for National Statistics 2004; Prime Minister's Strategy Unit 2003). Yet, at the same time, according to successive British Crime Surveys, crime has fallen in the UK. In her review of the relevant data, Budd (2003) concluded that the proportion of respondents who claimed to have been assaulted and who claimed that the assailant had been drinking remained constant throughout successive sweeps. Not only had there been a decrease in the number of respondents who reported being a victim of violence but there had been a decrease in the number of respondents who reported being assaulted by someone who had been drinking *despite* a rise in the average *per capita* consumption of alcohol during the same period.

Why then has the government sought to act now and in the manner it has? There is, after all, nothing new about research findings which show that significant proportions of offenders had been drinking prior to committing the offence and nothing new about the popular belief in a causal link between alcohol and crime. Ironically, what has become more certain in the academic literature is an awareness of how problematic it is to find this causality which the public so readily assume (Bushman and Cooper 1990; Marsh and Fox Kibby 1992; Parker 1996; Rumgay 1998; Wincup 2005). To explain the government's actions I think two more general points need to be made.

'Managing' the 'problem'

Responding to what the government has termed 'alcohol-related' offending can be seen as part of a shift in methods of social control. Criminologists have identified a move towards the state 'managing' the problem caused by crime. This stems from a realisation that state criminal justice policies cannot impact on crime rates to the extent that is commonly imagined. Instead, the state empowers an ever more diverse range of actors to provide criminal justice services. These actors are set targets to meet by the government. Central government can thus be seen to be responding seriously and efficiently to crime, whilst, at the same time, the government can partially absolve itself of some of the accountability inherent in a more central model. Popular concern can be deflected away, at least partially, from the government towards other agencies that are failing to deliver on their commitments.

It is possible to portray such a move as a cynical abandonment by governments of their key responsibility for administering criminal justice. Equally it could be argued that such a model is more realistic and allows for a more co-ordinated approach. Space precludes a more detailed examination of the trend, but suffice to say that it is observable in many western criminal justice systems, as well as in England and Wales. With regards to the current strategy for responding to intoxicated crime we can see that the government has devolved aspects of the strategy to local government, the police, other criminal justice agencies, as well as the drink's industry. Building on the Cardiff experience (Maguire and Nettleton 2003), the government clearly see a multi-faceted, multi-agency approach as the way forward (Prime Minister's Strategy Unit 2004). No-one can accuse the government of apathy, but the approach does mean that the government are in a position to blame specific agencies if the strategy is, or, as crucially, appears to be, unsuccessful.

Nor is this trend towards managerialism unique to the criminal justice sphere. Parallel trends can be observed in other areas of social policy, including alcohol policy (Thom 1999). With regard both to alcohol policy and criminal justice, what can broadly be discerned in the post-war period is a move away from a treatment model to a managerial model. There has also been significant recent interplay between the two spheres. Recent harm reduction strategies relating to alcohol are often formed in conjunction with criminal justice agencies. Many of the preventative strategies which were discussed in Chapter 4 such as CCTV, the banning of alcohol consumption in public places and Zero Tolerance Policing are indicative of such a stance.

Governmental statements have also talked about reducing the harm associated with problem drinking. To this end, there has been an interesting move towards co-ordinating the government's response to problem drinking as exemplified by the Prime Minister's Strategy Unit coming onboard. Prior to this, different departments had different responsibilities. This split was most notable between the two key departments: the Department of Health, which had a focus on the health needs of people with drinking problems, and the Home Office, whose primary concern was with law and order issues arising from drinking. One of the government's present aims is to provide a co-ordinated, coherent response to the problems posed by alcohol.

The remaining normative dimension

Managerialism, however, does not operate in a normative void. 'Solutions' have to be evaluated not just in terms of whether they 'work' but in terms of whether they can be justified if they satisfy this first criterion. Chapter 4 considered the case of CCTV and banning the consumption of alcohol in public places. Both of these may have the potential to reduce crime, but, as they both pose restrictions to individual liberty, one has to be careful that crime prevention does not become the sole determinant for a measure's use. At times the government is well aware of such concerns, for example when it comes to the contribution made by the drink's industry to the British economy (Prime Minister's Strategy Unit 2003), but, at other times, difficult issues are avoided.

It is important that managing the problem, which the government acknowledge is important (Department for Culture, Media and Sport *et al.* 2005), includes a realisation that this means dealing with enduring, and complex, normative questions. These relate to crime prevention and policing issues as well as how the criminal law responds to those who offend after drinking alcohol. Given the experience in Canada, it is not surprising that the government would not wish to be seen to be adopting measures which could be portrayed as unduly lenient by the opposition and by the media. Yet, there is a way in which the government could address popular concerns about intoxicated offending. Just because the problem is not new and its causes are complex, does not mean that it should be accepted. What it does mean is that measures which are introduced to deal with it can be justified and are proportionate. On balance, some of the recent initiatives fulfil both criteria, some lack sufficient justification or are disproportionate whilst other pressing issues remain to be addressed.

References

Abel, E.L. and Zeidenberg, P. (1985) 'Age, alcohol and violent death: a post-mortem study', *Journal of Studies on Alcohol*, 46(3): 228.

Abel, E.L. (1987) 'Drugs and homicide in Erie County, New York', *International Journal of the Addictions*, 22(2): 195.

Ahlström, S., Bloomfield, K. and Knibbe, R.A. (2001) 'Gender differences in the drinking patterns in nine European countries: descriptive findings', *Substance Abuse*, 22(1): 69.

Alcohol Concern (2005) *Alcohol and Men*. London: Alcohol Concern.

All Party Group on Alcohol Misuse (1995) *Alcohol and Crime: Breaking the Link*. London: Alcohol Concern.

Allan, A., Roberts, M.C., Allan, M.M., Pienaar, W.P. and Stein, D.J. (2001) 'Intoxication, criminal offences and suicide attempts in a group of South African problem drinkers', *South African Medical Journal*, 91(2): 145.

Anderson, K. and Plant, M. (1996) 'Abstaining and carousing: substance use among adolescents in the Western Isles of Scotland', *Drug and Alcohol Dependence*, 41(2): 189.

Anderson, P. and Mann, N. (1997) *Safety First: The making of New Labour*. London: Granta.

Andreasson, S., Allebeck, P., Brandt, L. and Romelsjo, A. (1992) 'Antecedents and covariates of high alcohol consumption in young men', *Alcoholism: clinical and experimental research*, 16(4): 708.

Ashworth, A. (1975) 'Reason, logic and criminal liability', *Law Quarterly Review*, 91: 102.

Ashworth, A. (2000) *Sentencing and Criminal Justice* (3rd edn). London: Butterworths.

Ashworth, A. [2004] 'Criminal Justice Act 2003 (2) criminal justice reform: principles, human rights and public protection', *Criminal Law Review*: 516.

Association of Chief Police Officers (2005) *ACPO Position on the Licensing Act*, Press Release 04/05. London: Association of Chief Police Officers.

Atkins, S., Hussain, S. and Storey, A. (1991) *The Influence of Street Lighting on Crime and Fear of Crime*. Crime Prevention Unit Paper 28. London: Home Office.

Australian Institute of Criminology (2004) *Understanding Problem-Oriented Policing*. Canberra: Australian Institute of Criminology.

Baddely, A. and Della Sala, S. (1998) 'Working memory and executive control', in A.C. Roberts, T.W. Robbins and L. Weiskrantz (eds) *The Prefrontal Cortex: executive and cognitive functions*. New York: Oxford University Press.

Bagaric, M. (2000a) 'Proportionality in sentencing: Its justification, meaning and role', *Current Issues in Criminal Justice*, 12(2): 143.

Bagaric, M. (2000b) 'Incapacitation, deterrence and rehabilitation: flawed ideals or appropriate sentencing goals?', *Criminal Law Journal*, 24(1): 21.

Bagaric, M. (2001) *Punishment and Sentencing: A rational approach*. London: Cavendish Publishing.

Baker, E. and Clarkson, C. [2002] 'Making punishments work? an evaluation of the Halliday Report on sentencing in England and Wales', *Criminal Law Review*: 81.

Bayley, D.H. (1996) 'What do police do?', in W. Saulsbury, J. Mott and T. Newburn (eds) *Themes in Contemporary Policing*. London: Independent Inquiry into the Roles and Responsibilities of the Police.

Bayley, D.H. and Shearing, C. (1996) 'The future of policing', *Law and Society Review*, 30(3): 585.

Bean, P. (2004) *Drugs and Crime*. Cullompton: Willan Publishing.

Beaumont, S.J. (1976) 'Drunkenness and criminal responsibility – recent English experience', *Canadian Bar Review*, 54: 777.

Becher, H., Boreham, R. and Shaw, A. (2001) *Smoking, Drinking and Drug Use among Young People in England in 2000*. London: HMSO.

Beinart, S. Anderson, B., Lee, S. and Utting, D. (2002) *Youth at Risk? A national survey of risk factors, protective factors and problem behaviour among young people in England, Scotland and Wales*. London: Communities that Care.

Bennett, R.M., Buss, A.H. and Carpenter, J.A. (1969) 'Alcohol and human physical aggression', *Quarterly Journal of Studies on Alcohol*, 30: 870.

Bergman, B. and Brismar, B. (1994) 'Characteristics of violent alcoholics', *Alcohol and Alcoholism*, 29(4): 451.

Bettencourt, A.B. and Miller, N. (1996) 'Gender differences in aggression as a function of provocation: a meta-analysis', *Psychological Bulletin*, 119(3): 422.

Beyleveld, D. (1979) 'Deterrence research as a basis for deterrence policies', *Howard Journal of Criminal Justice*, 18(3): 135.

Bianchi, H. and van Swaaningen, R. (eds) (1986) *Abolitionism: Towards a non-repressive approach to crime* Amsterdam: Free University Press.

Blackstone, W. (1769) *Commentaries on the Laws of England Volume 4*.

Blount, W.R., Silverman, I.J. and Sellers, C.S. (1994) 'Alcohol and drug use among abused women who kill, abused women who don't, and their abusers', *Journal of Drug Issues*, 24(2): 165.

Blum, R.H. (1981) 'Violence, alcohol, and settings: an unexplored nexus', in J.J. Collins (ed.) *Drinking and Crime: perspectives on the relationships between alcohol consumption and criminal behavior*. New York: The Guildford Press.

Bochel, D. (1981) *Probation and After-care: Its development in England and Wales*. Edinburgh: Scottish Academic Press.

Bond, A. and Lader, M. (1986) 'The relationship between induced behavioural aggression and mood after the consumption of two doses of alcohol', *British Journal of Addiction*, 81: 65.

Bondy, S. and Rehm, J. (1998) 'The interplay of drinking patterns and other determinants of health', *Drug and Alcohol Review*, 17(4): 399.

Borges, G., Cherpitel, C.J. and Rosousky, H. (1998) 'Male drinking and violence-related injury in the emergency room', *Addiction*, 93: 103.

Bottoms, A. (1995) 'The philosophy and politics of punishment and sentencing', in C. Clarkson and R. Morgan (eds) *The Politics of Sentencing Reform*. Oxford: Clarendon Press.

Bowes, D. (2004a) 'Alcohol, violence and the new licensing law: Part 1', *Justice of the Peace*, 168(20): 368.

Bowes, D. (2004b) 'Alcohol, violence and the new licensing law: Part 2', *Justice of the Peace*, 168(22): 411.

Bowker, L.H. (ed.) (1998) *Masculinities and Crime*. London: Sage.

Bowling, B. (1999) 'The rise and fall of New York murder: zero tolerance or crack's decline?', *British Journal of Criminology*, 39(4): 531.

Bradfield, R. (1999) 'Attorney-General's reference No.1 of 1996 *re: Weiderman*', *Criminal Law Journal*, 23(1): 41.

Brantingham, P. and Faust, F. (1976) 'A conceptual model of crime prevention', *Crime and Delinquency*, 22: 284.

Bratton, W.J. (1997) 'Crime is down in New York city: blame the police', in N. Dennis (ed.) *Zero Tolerance: Policing a free society*. London: Institute for Economic Affairs.

Breeze, E. (1985) *Women and Drinking*. London: HMSO.

Brismar, B. and Bergman, B. (1998) 'The significance of alcohol for violence and accidents', *Alcohol: clinical and experimental research*, 22(7): 299.

British Medical Association (2004) *Alcohol – Young People*. London: British Medical Association.

Britton, A. and McPherson, K. (2001) 'Mortality in England and Wales attributable to current alcohol consumption', *Journal of Epidemiology and Community Health*, 55(6): 383.

Bromley, D.F.B. and Nelson, A.L. (2002) 'Alcohol-related crime and disorder across urban space and time: evidence from a British city', *Geoforum*, 33(2): 239.

Brownlee, I. (1998) *Community Punishment: A critical introduction*. Harlow: Longman.

Buchan, B. (2002) 'Zero tolerance, mandatory sentencing and early liberal arguments for penal reform', *International Journal of the Sociology of Law*, 30(3): 201.

Budd, T. (2003) *Alcohol-Related Assault: findings from the British Crime Survey*. London: Home Office.

Bureau of Justice Statistics (1998) *Alcohol and Crime*. Washington DC.: United States Department of Justice.

Bushman, B.J. (1997) 'Effects of alcohol on human aggression: validity of proposed explanations', in M. Galanter (ed.) *Recent Developments in Alcoholism: alcohol and violence*. Volume 13. New York: Plenum.

Bushman, B.J. and Cooper, H.M. (1990) 'Effects of alcohol on human aggression: an integrative research review', *Psychological Bulletin*, 107(3): 341.

Cain, P. (2002) 'NT tops nation for grog violence, study', *Northern Territory News*, 29 April.

Canadian Sentencing Commission (1987) *Sentencing Reform: A Canadian approach*. Ottawa: Government Publishing Centre.

Cavender, S.J. (1989) 'The Lords against *Majewski* and the law', *Bracton Law Journal*, 21: 9.

Chalmers, J. [2001] 'Surviving without *Majewski*', *Criminal Law Review*: 258.

Cherek, D.R., Schnapp, W., Moeller, F.G. and Dougherty, D.M. (1996) 'Laboratory measures of aggressive responding in male parolees with violent and nonviolent histories', *Aggressive Behavior*, 22(1): 27.

Chermack, S.T. and Giancola, P.R. (1997) 'The relationship between alcohol and aggression: an integrated biopsychosocial conceptualization', *Clinical Psychology Review*, 17(6): 621.

Cherney, A. and Sutton, A. (2003) 'Crime prevention and reduction', in A. Goldsmith, M. Israel and K. Daly (eds) *Crime and Justice: An Australian textbook in Criminology* (2nd edn). Pyrmont, New South Wales: Law Book Co.

Chikritzhs, T., Jonas, H., Heale, P., Dietze, P., Hanlin, K. and Stockwell, T. (1999) *Alcohol-Caused Deaths and Hospitalisations in Australia, 1990–1997*. National Alcohol Indicators Bulletin No.1. Perth, Western Australia: National Drug Research Institute.

Christie, N. (1977) 'Conflicts as property', *British Journal of Criminology*, 17(1): 1.

Christie, N. (1981) *Limits to Pain*. London: Martin Robertson.

Chiu, A.Y., Perez, P.E. and Parker, R.N. (1997) 'Impact of banning alcohol on outpatient visits in Barrow, Alaska', *The Journal of the American Medical Association*, 278(21): 1775.

Clarke, R.V. (1995) 'Situational Crime Prevention', in M. Tonry and D. Farrington (eds) *Building a Safer Society: Strategic approaches to crime prevention*. Chicago: The University of Chicago Press.

Clarke, R.V. (ed.) (1997) *Situational Crime Prevention: Successful case studies* (2nd edn). New York: Harrow and Heston.

Clarkson, C.M.V. (1978) 'Drunkenness, constructive manslaughter and specific intent', *Modern Law Review*, 41(4): 478.

Cochrane, J.K., Rowan, K., Blount, W.R., Heide, K.M. and Sellers, C.S. (1999) 'Beer joints and badasses: an aggregate-level assessment of alcohol availability and violent crime', *Criminal Justice Policy Review*, 9(3–4): 465.

Cochrane, R. and Howell, M. (1995) 'Drinking patterns of Black and White men in the West Midlands', *Social Psychiatry and Psychiatric Epidemiology*, 30(3): 139.

Coke upon Littleton (1817) *The Third Part of the Institutes of the Law of England*.

Collier, R. (1998) *Masculinities, Crime and Criminology*. London: Sage.

Collins, J. (1981) 'Alcohol careers and criminal careers', in J. Collins (ed.) *Drinking and Crime*. New York: The Guilford Press.

Collins, J.J. and Schlenger, W.E. (1988) 'Acute and chronic effects of alcohol use in violence', *Journal of Studies on Alcohol*, 49(6): 516.

Colvin, E. (1981) 'A theory of the intoxication defence', *Canadian Bar Review*, 59: 750.

Commission on Liquor Licensing (2003) *Final Report*. Dublin: Department of Justice, Equality and Law Reform.

Committee on Mentally Abnormal Offenders (England and Wales) (1975) *Report of the Committee on Mentally Abnormal Offenders*, Cmnd. 6244. London: HMSO.

Confederation of British Industry (2004) *Counting the Costs: 2002 absence and labour turnover study*. London: Confederation of British Industry.

Connell, R.W. (1995) *Masculinities*. Cambridge: Polity Press.

Connors, G.J. and Maisto, S.A. (1988) 'The alcohol expectancy construct: overview and clinical application', *Cognitive Therapy Research*, 12: 487.

Cook, P.J. and Moore, M.J. (1993a) 'Economic perspectives on reducing alcohol-related violence', in S.E. Martin (ed.) *Alcohol and Interpersonal Violence: fostering multidisciplinary perspectives*. Rockville, MD: National Institute on Alcohol Abuse and Alcoholism.

Cook, P.J. and Moore, M.J. (1993b) 'Violence reduction through restrictions on alcohol availability', *Alcohol Health and Research World*, 17(2): 151.

Cookson, H. (1992) 'Alcohol use and offence type in young offenders', *British Journal of Criminology*, 32(3): 352.

Cope, N. (2004) 'Intelligence led policing or policing led intelligence? Integrating volume crime analysis into policing', *British Journal of Criminology*, 44(2): 188.

Cordilia, A. (1985) 'Alcohol and property crime: exploring the causal nexus', *Journal of Studies on Alcohol*, 46(2): 161.

Cordner, S.M., Ainley, C.G. and Schneider, M.A. (1979) 'Rape and rapists in Victoria', *Australian and New Zealand Journal of Criminology*, 12: 41.

Cornish, D.B. and Clarke, R.V. (2003) 'Opportunities, precipitators and criminal decisions: a reply to Wortley's critique of situational crime prevention', in M. Smith and D.B. Cornish (eds) *Theory for Situational Crime Prevention*. Cullompton: Willan Publishing.

Costanza, S.E., Bankston, W.B. and Shihadeh, E. (2001) 'Alcohol availability and violent crime rates: a spatial analysis', *Journal of Crime and Justice*, 24: 71.

Crawford, A. (1998) *Crime Prevention and Community Safety: Politics, policies and practices*. London: Longman.

Criminal Law Revision Committee (England and Wales) (1980) *Offences Against the Person*, Cmnd. 7844. London: HMSO.

Dar, K., Chandry, Z.A., Mirza, J. and Alam, F. (2002) 'Ethnicity, patterns of substance misuse and criminality: a comparative study of White and Asian patient populations', *Journal of Substance Use*, 7(4): 244.

Dashwood, A. [1977] 'Logic and the Lords in *Majewski*', *Criminal Law Review*: 532.

Davies, P. (1999) 'The probation service in a rural area: problems and practicalities', in G. Dingwall and S.R. Moody (eds) *Crime and Conflict in the Countryside*. Cardiff: University of Wales Press.

Deehan, A. (1999) *Alcohol and Crime: taking stock*. London: Home Office.

Deehan, A. (2001) 'Policing alcohol-related crime in the UK – would a public health approach in alcohol-related crime reduction strategies help maximise success?', *Crime Prevention and Community Safety*, 3(4): 47.

Denscombe, M. and Drucquer, N. (1997) 'Diversity within ethnic groups: alcohol consumption and tobacco consumption by young people in the East Midlands', *Health Education Journal*, 59(4): 340.

Department for Culture, Media and Sport, Home Office and Office of the Deputy Prime Minister (2005) *Drinking Responsibly: the government's proposals*. London: Department for Culture, Media and Sport.

Department of Health and Royal College of General Practitioners (1992) *Women and Alcohol*. London: HMSO.

Dillon, M. (2004) 'Intoxicated automatism is no defence: *Majewski* is law in Ireland', *Irish Criminal Law Journal*, 14(3): 7.

Dingwall, G. (1997) 'The Court of Appeal and guideline judgments', *Northern Ireland Legal Quarterly*, 48(2): 143.

Dingwall, G. (1998) 'Selective incapacitation after the Criminal Justice Act 1991: a proportional response to protecting the public?', *Howard Journal of Criminal Justice*, 37(2): 177.

Dingwall, G. (2003) 'Alcohol, alcoholism and the criminal justice system in England and Wales', in I. O'Donnell and S. Kilcommins (eds) *Alcohol, Society and Law*. Chichester: Barry Rose.

Dingwall, G. and Harding, C. (1998) *Diversion in the Criminal Process*. London: Sweet and Maxwell.

Ditton, J., Chadee, D., Farrall, S., Gilchrist, E. and Bannister, J. (2004) 'From imitation to intimidation: a note on the curious and changing relationship between the media, crime and fear of crime', *British Journal of Criminology*, 44(4): 595.

Dodd, T., Nicholas, S., Povey, D. and Walker, A. (2004) *Crime in England and Wales 2003/2004*. London: Home Office.

Doherty, S.J. and Roche, M. (2003) *Alcohol and Licensed Premises: best practice in policing*. Payneham, South Australia: Australian Centre for Policing Research.

Dougherty, D.M., Cherek, D.R. and Bennett, R.H. (1996) 'The effects of alcohol on the responding of women', *Journal of Studies on Alcohol*, 57: 178.

Downes, D. and Morgan, R. (1997) 'Dumping the hostages to fortune? the politics of law and order in post-war Britain', in M. Maguire, R. Morgan and R. Reiner (eds) *The Oxford handbook of Criminology* (2nd edn). Oxford: Clarendon Press.

Driver, S. and Martell, L. (1998) *New Labour: Politics after Thatcherism*. Cambridge: Polity Press.

Duff, R.A. and Marshall, S.E. (2000) 'Benefits, burdens and responsibilities: some ethical dimensions of situational crime prevention', in A. von Hirsch, D. Garland and A. Wakefield (eds) *Ethical and Social Perspectives on Situational Crime Prevention*. Oxford: Hart Publishing.

Duffy, J.C. and De Moira, A.C.P. (1996) 'Changes in licensing law in England and Wales and indicators of alcohol-related problems', *Addiction Research*, 4(3): 245.

Engineer, R., Phillips, A., Thompson, J. and Nicholls, J. (2003) *Drunk and Disorderly: a qualitative study of binge drinking among 18 to 24 year olds*. Home Office Research Study No.262. London: Home Office.

Ensor, T. and Godfrey, C. (1993) 'Modelling the interactions between alcohol, crime and the criminal justice system', *Addiction*, 88(4): 477.

Erens, B., Primatesta, P. and Prior, G. (eds) (2001) *Health Survey for England: the health of minority ethnic groups*. London: HMSO.

Ettorre, E. (1997) *Women and Alcohol: a private pleasure or a public problem?*. London: The Women's Press.

Evans, C.M. (1986) 'Alcohol and violence: problems relating to methodology, statistics and causation', in P.F. Briain (ed.) *Alcohol and Aggression*. London: Croom Helm.

Fagan, J. and Davies, G. (2001) 'Street stops and broken windows', *Fordham Urban Law Review*, 28(4): 457.

Fagan, J.A., Hansen, K.V. and Jang, M. (1983) 'Profiles of chronically violent delinquents: an empirical test of an integrated theory of violent delinquency', in J. Kleugal (ed.) *Evaluating Juvenile Justice*. California: Sage.

Fairall, P.A. (1980) '*Majewski* banished', *Criminal Law Journal*, 4(5): 264.

Fallon, P (1975) *Crown Court Practice: sentence*. London: Butterworths.

Farabee, D., Joshi, V. and Anglin, M.D. (2001) 'Addiction careers and criminal specialization', *Crime and Delinquency*, 47(2): 196.

Farmer, L. (1996) *Criminal Law, Tradition and Legal Order: Crime and the genius of Scots law 1747 to the present*. Cambridge: Cambridge University Press.

Farrier, D. (1976) 'Intoxication: legal logic or common sense?', *Modern Law Review*, 39(5): 578.

Farrington, D.P., Langan, P.A. and Wilkström, P-O. (1994) 'Changes in crime and punishment in America, England and Sweden in the 1980s and 1990s', *Studies in Crime Prevention* 3: 104.

Farrington, D.P. and Loeber, R. (1999) 'Transatlantic replicability of risk factors in the development of delinquency', in P. Cohen, C. Slomkowski and L.N. Robins (eds) *Historical and Geographical Influences on Psychopathology*. Mahwah, New Jersey: Lawrence Erlbaum Associates.

Fergusson, D.M. and Horwood, L.J. (2000) 'Alcohol abuse and crime: a fixed-effects regression analysis', *Addiction*, 95(10): 1525.

Fergusson, D.M., Lynskey, M.T. and Horwood, L.J. (1996) 'Alcohol misuse and Juvenile Offending in Adolescence', *Addiction*, 91: 483.

Field, S. (1990) *Trends in Crime and Their Interpretation: A study of recorded crime in post-war England and Wales*, Home Office Research Study 119. London: HMSO.

Fingarette, H. (1974) 'Diminished mental capacity as a criminal law defence', *Modern Law Review*, 37: 264.

Fletcher, G. (1978) *Rethinking Criminal Law*. Boston, Massachussets: Little, Brown.

Flewelling, R.L., Paschall, M.J. and Ringwalt, C. (2004) 'The epidemiology of underage drinking in the United States: an overview', in R.J. Bonnie and M. O'Connell (eds) *Reducing Underage Drinking: a collective responsibility*. Washington DC: National Academy Press.

Fossey, E., Loretto, W. and Plant, M. (1996) 'Alcohol and youth', in L. Harrison (ed.) *Alcohol Problems in the Community*. London: Routledge.

Fox, R.G. (1999) 'Competition in sentencing: the rehabilitative model versus the punitive model', *Psychiatry, Psychology and Law*, 6(2): 153.

Freiberg, A. (2003) 'The four pillars of justice: a review essay', *Australian and New Zealand Journal of Criminology*, 36(2): 233.

Gardner, S. (1994) 'The importance of *Majewski*', *Oxford Journal of Legal Studies*, 14(2): 279.

Garland, D. (1990) *Punishment and Modern Society: A study in social theory*. Oxford: Clarendon Press.

Gerson, L.W. (1978) 'Alcohol-related acts of violence: who was drinking and where the acts occurred', *Journal of Studies on Alcohol*, 39(7): 1294.

Ginacola, P.R. and Zeichner, A. (1997) 'The biphasic effects of alcohol on human physical aggression', *Journal of Abnormal Psychology*, 106: 598.

Giancola, P.R. and Zeichner, A. (1995) 'An investigation of gender differences in alcohol-related aggression', *Journal of Studies on Alcohol*, 56: 573.

Gibbs, J.J. (1986) 'Alcohol consumption, cognition and context: examining tavern violence', in A. Campbell and J.J. Gibbs (eds) *Violent Transactions*. New York: Basil Blackwell.

Giesbrecht, N. and Nesbitt, S. (2001) 'Alcohol and crime: from understanding to effective intervention', *Journal of Substance Use*, 6(4): 215.

Gilyeat, D. (1994) *A Companion Guide to Offence Seriousness*. Ilkley: Owen Wells Publisher.

Goddard, E. and Higgins, V. (1999) *Smoking, Drinking and Drug Use among Young Teenagers in 1998*. London: Office for National Statistics.

Goldman, M.S., Brown, S.A. and Christiansen, B.A. (1987) 'Expectancy theory: thinking about drinking', in H.T. Blaine and K.E. Leonard (eds) *Psychological Theories of Drinking and Alcoholism*. New York: Guilford Press.

Goldman, M.S. and Rather, B.C. (1995) 'Inferring cognitive processes associated with alcohol-related behavior: reply to Kerby'. *Experimental and Clinical Psychopharmacology*, 3: 310.

Goldstein, H. (1977) *Policing a Free Society*. Cambridge, Massachussets: Ballinger.

Goldstein, H. (1979) 'Improving policing: a problem-oriented approach', *Crime and Delinquency*, 25: 236.

Goldstein, H. (1990) *Problem-Oriented Policing*. New York: McGraw-Hill.

Goodman, R.A., Mercy, J.A., Loya, F., Rosenberg, M.L., Smith, J.C., Allen, N.H., Vargas, L. and Kolts, R. (1986) 'Alcohol use and interpersonal violence: alcohol detected in homicide victims', *American Journal of Public Health*, 76(2): 144.

Gorman, D.M., Speer, P.W., Gruenewald, P.G. and Labouvie, E.W. (2001) 'Spacial dynamics of alcohol availability, neighborhood structure and violent crime', *Journal of Studies on Alcohol*, 62: 628.

Gottlieb, P., Kramp, P., Lindhardt, A. and Christensen, O. (1990) 'The social background of homicide', *International Journal of Offender Therapy and Comparative Criminology*, 34: 115.

Gough, S. (1996) 'Intoxication and criminal liability: the law commission's proposed reforms', *Law Quarterly Review*, 112: 335.

Gough, S. [2000] 'Surviving without *Majewski*?', *Criminal Law Review* 719.

Graham, K. (1980) 'Theories of intoxicated aggression', *Canadian Journal of the Behavioural Sciences*, 12: 141.

Graham, K. (2003) 'The yin and yang of alcohol intoxication: implications for research on the social consequences of drinking', *Addiction*, 98(8): 1021.

Grant, I. (1996) 'Second chances: Bill C-72 and the Charter', *Osgoode Hall Law Journal*, 33(2): 379.

Greenberg, S.W. (1981) 'Alcohol and crime: a methodological critique of the literature', in J. Collins (ed.) *Drinking and Crime*. New York: The Guilford Press.

Greene, J. (1999) 'Zero tolerance: a case study of police policies and practices in New York city', *Crime and Delinquency*, 45: 171.

Greenfield, L.A. and Henneberg, M.A. (2001) 'Victim and offender self-reports of alcohol involvement in crime', *Alcohol Research and Health*, 25(1): 20.

Greenfield, T.K. and Weisner, C. (1995) 'Drinking problems and self-reported criminal behavior, arrests and convictions: 1990 US alcohol and 1989 county surveys', *Addiction*, 90(3): 361.

Guntjahr, E., Gmel, G. and Rehm, J. (2001) 'Relation between average alcohol consumption and disease: an overview', *European Addiction Research*, 7(3): 117.

Gustafson, R. (1991) 'Aggressive and nonaggressive behavior as a function of alcohol intoxication in women', *Alcoholism: clinical and experimental research*, 15: 886.

Hafemeister, T.L. and Jackson, S.L. (2004) 'Effectiveness of sanctions and law enforcement practices targeted at underage drinking not involving operation of a motor vehicle', in R.J. Bonnie and M. O'Connell (eds) *Reducing Underage Drinking: a collective responsibility*. Washington DC: National Academy Press.

Hale, Sir M. (1736) *A History of the Pleas of the Crown Volume 1*.

Hale, C. (1996) 'Fear of crime: a review of the literature', *International Review of Victimology*, 4: 79.

Hall, G. (1987) *Hall on Sentencing in New Zealand*. Wellington: Butterworths.

Hanly, C. (2003) 'The impact of alcohol on sentencing', in I. O'Donnell and S. Kilcommins (eds) *Alcohol, Society and Law*. Chichester: Barry Rose.

Hannaford, A. [2002] 'A night with the cops', *Evening Standard*, 11 October.

Harnett, R., Thom, B., Herring, R. and Kelly, M. (2000) 'Alcohol in transition: towards a model of young men's drinking styles', *Journal of Youth Studies*, 3(1): 61.

Harrington, V. (2000) *Underage Drinking: findings from the 1998–99 youth lifestyles survey research*. London: Home Office.

Harrison, L. and Gardiner, E. (1999) 'Do the rich really die young? Alcohol-related mortality and social class in Great Britain, 1988–94', *Addiction*, 94(12): 1871.

Hawkins (1716) *Pleas of the Crown Book 1*.

Hawkins, J.D., Catalano, R.F. and Miller, J.Y. (1992) 'Risk and protective factors for alcohol and other drug problems in adolescence and early adulthood: implications for substance abuse prevention', *Psychological Bulletin*, 112: 64.

Health and Safety Executive (1998) *Don't Mix It! A guide for employers on alcohol and work*. Sudbury: Health and Safety Executive.

Healy, P. (1990) 'R v *Bernard*: difficulties with voluntary intoxication', *McGill Law Journal*, 35: 610.

Healy, P. (1994) 'Intoxication in the codification of Canadian criminal law', *Canadian Bar Review*, 73: 515.

Heather, N. and Robertson, I. (2004) *Problem Drinking* (3rd edn). Oxford: Oxford Medical Publications.

Heidensohn, F. (1985) *Women and Crime*. London: Macmillan.

Heim, D., Hunter, S.C., Ross, A.J., Bakshi, N., Davies, J.B., Flatley, K.J. and Meer, N. (2004) 'Alcohol consumption, perceptions of community responses and attitudes to service provision: results from a survey of Indian, Chinese and Pakistani young people in Greater Glasgow, Scotland, UK', *Alcohol and Alcoholism*, 39(3): 220.

Herz, A. and Kania, H. (2002) 'Everyday perceptions of crime', *European Journal of Crime, Criminal Law and Criminal Justice*, 10(4): 276.

Hibell, B., Andersson, B., Ahlström, S., Balakireva, O., Bjarnason, T., Kokkevi, A. and Morgan, M. (2000) *The 1999 ESPAD Report. The European school survey project on alcohol and other drug use among students in 30 European countries*. Stockholm: The Swedish Council for Information on Alcohol and Other Drugs.

Hingson, R. and Howland, J. (1993) 'Alcohol and non-traffic unintended injuries', *Addiction*, 88: 877.

Hingson, R. and Kenkel, D. (2004) 'Social, health, and economic consequences of underage drinking', in R.J. Bonnie and M. O'Connell (eds) *Reducing Underage Drinking: a collective responsibility*. Washington DC: National Academy Press.

Hoaken, P.N.S., Giancola, P. and Pihl, R.O. (1998) 'Executive cognitive functions as mediators of alcohol-induced aggression', *Journal of Studies on Alcohol*, 59: 599.

Hoaken, P.N.S. and Pihl, R.O. (2000) 'The effects of alcohol intoxication as aggressive responses in men and women', *Alcohol and Alcoholism*, 35(5) 471.

Hobbs, D., Hadfield, P., Lister, S. and Winlow, S. (2002) 'Door lore: the art and economics of intimidation', *British Journal of Criminology*, 42(2): 352.

Hobbs, D., Hadfield, P., Lister, S. and Winlow, S. (2003) *Bouncers: violence and governance in the night-time economy*. Oxford: Oxford University Press.

Hogg, P.W. and Bushell, A.A. (1997) 'The charter dialogue between courts and legislatures', *Osgoode Hall Law Journal*, 35: 75.

Holcomb, W.R. and Anderson, W.P. (1983) 'Alcohol and multiple drug abuse in accused murderers', *Psychological Reports*, 52: 159.

Hollis, W.S. (1974) 'On the etiology of criminal homicides: the alcohol factor', *Journal of Police Science and Administration*, 2(1): 50.

Home Office (1966) *Residential Provision for Homeless Discharged Offenders: report of the working party on the place of voluntary service in after-care.* London: HMSO.

Home Office (1971) *Habitual Drunken Offenders: report of the working party.* London: HMSO.

Home Office (2000) *Time for Change: proposals for the modernisation of our licensing laws.* London: HMSO.

Home Office (2001a) *Making Punishments Work: report of a review of the sentencing framework for England and Wales.* London: Home Office.

Home Office (2001b) *Criminal Justice and Police Act 2001 – alcohol consumption in public places*, guidance letter to police chiefs and chief executives of local authorities, 24 August.

Home Office (2002) *Justice for All.* London: HMSO.

Home Office (2003) 'What works reducing reoffending', http://www.crimereduction.gov.uk/workingoffenders1.htm#evidence

Home Office (2004) 'Alcohol blitz – building on success', press release 349. London: Home Office.

Homel, R. (1994) 'Can police prevent crime?', in K. Bryett and C. Lewis (eds) *Un-Peeling Tradition: contemporary policing.* Melbourne: Macmillan.

Homel, R., Tomsen, S. and Thommeny, J. (1992) 'Public drinking and violence: not just an alcohol problem', *The Journal of Drug Issues*, 22(3): 679.

Honess, T., Seymour, L. and Webster, R. (2000) *The Social Contexts of Underage Drinking.* London: Home Office.

Hopkins Burke, R. (2002) 'Zero tolerance policing: new authoritarianism or new liberalism?', *Nottingham Law Journal*, 11(1): 20.

Horder, J. (1993) 'Pleading involuntary lack of capacity', *Cambridge Law Journal*, 52(2): 298.

Horder, J. (1995) 'Sobering Up? The Law Commission on criminal intoxication', *Modern Law Review*, 58(4): 534.

Hore, B.D. (1988) 'Alcohol and crime', *Alcohol and Alcoholism*, 23(6): 435.

Hough, M. (1985) 'Organisation and resource management in the uniformed police', in K. Heal, R. Tarling and J. Burrows (eds) *Policing Today.* London: HMSO.

Hough, M. (1995) *Anxiety About Crime: findings from the 1994 British Crime Survey* Home Office Research Study No.147. London: Home Office.

Hough, M. and Roberts, J.V. (2002) 'Public knowledge and public opinion of sentencing: findings from five jurisdictions', in N. Hutton and C. Tata (eds) *Sentencing and Society: International Perspectives.* Aldershot: Ashgate.

Howard, M. (2004) 'Restoring respect – cutting crime', speech in Middlesbrough, 10 August (available at http://www.conservatives.com/tile.do?def=news.story.page&obj_id=113496&speeches=1).

Huang, B., White, H.R., Kosterman, R., Catalano, R.F. and Hawkins, J.D. (2001) 'Developmental associations between alcohol and interpersonal aggression during adolescence', *Journal of Research in Crime and Delinquency*, 38(1): 64.

Hudson, B. (2003) *Understanding Justice: an introduction to ideas, perspectives and controversies in modern penal theory* (2nd edn). Milton Keynes: Open University Press.

Hull, J.G. and Bond, C.F. (1986) 'Social and behavioral consequences of alcohol consumption and expectations: a meta-analysis', *Psychological Bulletin*, 99: 347.

Hume, D. (1797) *Commentaries on the Law of Scotland Respecting the Description and Punishment of Crimes* (reprinted 1987). Edinburgh: Butterworths.

Hupkens, C.L.H., Knibbe, R.A. and Drop, M.J. (1993) 'Alcohol consumption in the European Community: uniformity and diversity in drinking patterns', *Addiction*, 88(10): 1391.

Innes, J. (2004) 'Drinking is "out of control"', *The Scotsman*, 15 March.

Innes, M. (1999) 'An iron fist in an iron glove? The zero tolerance policing debate', *Howard Journal of Criminal Justice*, 38(4): 397.

Institute of Alcohol Studies (2004) *Alcohol and Mental Health*. St. Ives: Institute of Alcohol Studies.

Institute of Alcohol Studies (2005a) *Women and Alcohol*. St. Ives: Institute of Alcohol Studies.

Institute of Alcohol Studies (2005b) *Alcohol Consumption and Harm in the UK and EU*. St. Ives: Institute of Alcohol Studies.

Ireland, C.S. and Thommeny, J.L. (1993) 'The crime cocktail: licensed premises, alcohol and street offences', *Drug and Alcohol Review*, 12(2): 143.

Ito, T.A., Miller, N. and Pollock, V.E. (1996) 'Alcohol and aggression: a meta-analysis on the moderating effects of inhibitory cues, triggering events, and self-focused attention', *Psychological Bulletin*, 120: 60.

James, A. and Raine, J. (1998) *The New Politics of Criminal Justice*. Harlow: Longman.

Jefferson, T. (1997) 'Masculinities and crime', in M. Maguire, R. Morgan and R. Reiner (eds) *The Oxford Handbook of Criminology* (2nd edn). Oxford: Clarendon Press.

Jeffs, B. and Saunders, W. (1983) 'Minimising alcohol related offences by enforcement of the existing licensing legislation', *British Journal of Addiction*, 78: 67.

Jernigan, D. and Mosher, J. (2001) 'Making the link: a public health approach to preventing alcohol-related violence and crime', *Journal of Substance Use*, 6(4): 273.

Jones, T.H. and Christie, M.G.A. (1992) *Criminal Law*. Edinburgh: W. Green.

Karmen, A. (2000) *New York Murder Mystery: the true story behind the crime crash of the 1990s.* New York: New York University Press.

Keller, M. (1976) 'Problems with alcohol: an historical perspective', in W.J. Filstead, J.J. Rossi and M. Keller (eds) *Alcohol and Alcohol Problems: new thinking and new directions.* Cambridge, Massachussets: Ballinger Publishing Co.

Kelling, G. and Coles, C. (1997) *Fixing Broken Windows: restoring order and reducing crime in our communities.* New York: New York University Press.

Kingma, J., Oskam, J., Klaver-Branderhorst, A. and Klasen, H.J. (1992) 'Alcoholconsumptie en Geweldsslachtoffers: Een Trendonderzoek over de Periode 1970 t/m 1991 (Alcohol consumption and victims of violence: a trend study of the 1970–1991 period)', *Tijdschrift-voor-Alcohol, Drugs en Andere Psychotrope Stoffen*, 18(4): 197 cited in K. Pernanen and S. Brochu (1997) *Attributional Fractions for Alcohol and Other Drugs in Relation to Crimes in Canada: literature search and outline of data banks.* Ottawa: Canadian Centre on Substance Abuse.

Kleinig, J. (2000) 'The burdens of situational crime prevention: an ethical commentary', in A. von Hirsch, D. Garland and A. Wakefield (eds) *Ethical and Social Perspectives on Situational Crime Prevention.* Oxford: Hart Publishing.

Knox, F. (2001) 'Clarifying zero tolerance', *Police Journal*, 74(4): 292.

Koch, B.C.M. (1998) *The Politics of Crime Prevention.* Aldershot: Ashgate.

Koffman, L. (1996) *Crime Surveys and Victims of Crime.* Cardiff: University of Wales Press.

Kroll, B. and Taylor, A. (2002) *Parental Substance Misuse and Child Welfare.* London: Jessica Kingsley.

Labour Party (1997) *Because Britain Deserves Better.* London: The Labour Party.

Lader, D. and Meltzer, H. (2002) *Drinking: adult's behaviour and knowledge in 2002.* London: HMSO.

Lang, A.R., Goeckner, D.J., Adesso, V.J. and Marlatt, G.A. (1975) 'The effects of alcohol on aggression in male social drinkers', *Journal of Abnormal Psychology*, 84: 508.

Langan, P.A. and Farrington, D.P. (1998) *Crime and Justice in the United States and England and Wales, 1981–96.* Washington DC: Bureau of Justice.

Lash, B. (2002) *Young People and Alcohol: some statistics on the possible effects of lowering the drinking age.* Wellington: Ministry of Justice.

Law Commission (England and Wales) (1993) *Intoxication and Criminal Liability*, Consultation Paper No. 127. London: HMSO.

Law Commission (England and Wales) (1995) *Intoxication and Criminal Liability*, Law Commission Report No. 229. London: HMSO.

Law Reform Commission (Victoria) (1986) *Criminal Responsibility: intention and gross intoxication.* Melbourne, Vic: Government Printers.

Law Reform Commission (Victoria) (1999) *Criminal Liability for Self-Induced Intoxication*. Melbourne, Vic: Government Printers.

Layton Mackenzie, D. (2002) 'Criminal justice and crime prevention', in L. Sherman, D. Farrington, B. Welsh and D. Layton Mackenzie (eds) *Evidence-Based Crime Prevention*. London: Routledge.

Leader-Elliott, I. (1994) 'Intoxication and criminal responsibility: law and law reform', in *National Symposium on Alcohol Misuse and Violence: report 6B*. Canberra: Australian Government Publishing Service.

Leifman, H. (2001) 'Homogenisation in alcohol consumption in the European Union', *Nordic Studies on Alcohol*, 18: 15.

Leifman, H. (2002) 'A comparative analysis of drinking patterns in six EU countries in the year 2000', *Contemporary Drug Problems*, 29(3): 501.

Leigh, B.C. (1989) 'In search of the seven dwarves: issues of measurement and meaning in alcohol expectancy theory', *Psychological Bulletin*, 105(3): 361.

Lenke, L. (1982) 'Alcohol and crimes of violence: a causal analysis', *Contemporary Drug Problems* 11: 355.

Leonard, K.E. and Quigley, B.M. (1999) 'Drinking and marital aggression in newlyweds: an event-based analysis of drinking and the occurrence of husband marital aggression', *Journal of Studies on Alcohol*, 60(4): 96.

Levi, M. (1997) 'Violent crime', in M. Maguire, R. Morgan and R. Reiner (eds) *The Oxford Handbook of Criminology*. Oxford: Oxford University Press.

Lewis, D.E. (1986) 'The general deterrent effect of longer sentences', *British Journal of Criminology*, 26(1): 47.

Light, R. (1994) 'Questioning the link between alcohol and crime', in E. Stanko (ed.) *Perspectives on Violence*. London: Quartet Books.

Lightfoot, L.O. and Hodgins, D. (1988) 'A survey of alcohol and drug problems in incarcerated offenders', *International Journal of the Addictions*, 23(7): 687.

Lipsey, M.W., Wilson, D.B., Cohen, M.A. and Derzon, J.H. (1997) 'Is there a causal relationship between alcohol use and violence?', in M. Galanter (ed.) *Recent Developments in Alcoholism: alcohol and violence* Vol.13. New York: Plenum.

Lipton, R. and Gruenewald, P.J. (2002) 'The spacial dynamics of violence and alcohol outlets', *Journal of Studies on Alcohol*, 63: 187.

Lister Sharp, D. (1994) 'Underage drinking in the United Kingdom since 1970: public policy, the law and adolescent drinking behaviour', *Alcohol and Alcoholism*, 29: 5.

Livingstone, S. (1996) 'On the continuing problem of media effects', in J. Curran and M. Gurevitch (eds) *Mass Media and Society*. London: Arnold.

Lowe, G., Foxcroft, D.R. and Sibley, D. (1993) *Adolescent Drinking and Family Life*. Reading: Horwood Academic.

Loza, W. and Clements, P. (1991) 'Incarcerated alcoholics' and rapists' attributions of blame for criminal acts', *Canadian Journal of Behavioural Science*, 23(1): 76.

Lumb, R.C. (1996) 'Community attitudes regarding police responsibility for crime control', *Police Journal*, 69(4): 319.

Lynch, A.C.E. [1982] 'The scope of intoxication', *Criminal Law Review*: 139.

Macdonald, E. (1986) 'Reckless language and *Majewski*', *Legal Studies*, 6(3): 239.

MacMillan-Brown, H. (1995) 'No longer *Leary* about intoxication: in the aftermath of *R v Daviault*', *Saskatchewan Law Review*, 59: 312.

Maguire, M. and Nettleton, H. (2003) *Reducing Alcohol-Related Violence and Disorder: an evaluation of the 'TASC' project*. London: Home Office.

Maisto, S.A., Connors, G.J. and Sachs, P.R. (1981) 'Expectation as a mediator in alcohol intoxication: a reference level model', *Cognitive Therapy and Research*, 5: 1.

Makela, P. (1999) 'Alcohol-related mortality as a function of socio-economic status', *Addiction*, 94(6): 867.

Makkai, T. (2001) 'Alcohol and disorder in the Australian community: some results from the national drug strategy household survey', in P. Williams (ed.) *Alcohol, Young Persons and Violence*. Canberra, ACT: Australian Institute of Criminology.

Manning, P.K. (2001) 'Theorizing policing: the drama and myth of crime control in the NYPD', *Theoretical Criminology*, 5(3): 315.

Marsh, H.L. (1991) 'A comparative analysis of crime coverage in newspapers in the United States and other countries from 1960–1989: a review of the literature', *Journal of Criminal Justice*, 19(1): 67.

Marsh, P. and Fox Kibby, K. (1992) *Drinking and Public Disorder: a report of research conducted for the Portman Group by MCM Research*. London: The Portman Group.

Martin, C., Earleywine, M., Musty, R., Perrine, M. and Swift, R. (1993) 'Development and validation of the biphasic alcohol effects scale', *Alcoholism: clinical and experimental research*, 17: 140.

Martin, S.E. and Bachman, R. (1998) 'Contribution of alcohol to the likelihood of completion and severity of injury in rape incidents', *Violence Against Women*, 4(6): 694.

Martinson, R. [1974] 'What works – questions and answers about prisoner reform', *The Public Interest*: 22.

Martinson, R. (1979) 'New findings, new views: a note of caution regarding sentencing reform', *Hofstra Law Review*, 7: 243.

Mason, G. and Wilson, P.R. (1989) *Alcohol and Crime*, Trends and Issues in Crime and Criminal Justice No. 18. Canberra, ACT: Australian Institute of Criminology.

Matthews, R. (1992) 'Replacing "broken windows": crime, incivilities and urban change', in R. Matthews and J. Young (eds) *Issues in Realist Criminology*. London: Sage.

Matthews, R. and Young, J. (eds) (2003) *The New Politics of Crime and Punishment*. Cullompton: Willan Publishing.

Matthews, S., Chikritzhs, T., Catalano, P., Stockwell, T. and Donath, S. (2002) *Trends in Alcohol-Related Violence in Australia, 1991/92–1999/00* National Alcohol Indicators Bulletin No. 5. Perth, Western Australia: National Drug Research Institute.

Mawby, R.I. (2000) 'Core policing: the seductive myth', in F. Leishman, B. Loveday and S. Savage (eds) *Core Issues in Policing* (2nd edn). Harlow: Pearson.

May, C. (1992) 'A burning issue? Adolescent alcohol use in Britain 1970–1991', *Alcohol and Alcoholism*, 27: 109.

McAuley, F. (1997) 'The intoxication defence in criminal law', *Irish Jurist*, 32: 243.

McCall Smith, R.A.A. and Sheldon, D. (1997) *Scots Criminal Law* (2nd edn). Edinburgh: Butterworths.

McClory, C.B. (2001) 'A re-assessment of *Brennan* v *HMA* and the problems of non-insane automatism', *Scottish Law Gazette*, 69(6): 187.

McConville, B. (1995) *Women under the Influence: alcohol and its impact.* London: Rivers Oram Press.

McCord, D. (1992) 'The English and American history of voluntary intoxication to negate mens rea', *Journal of Legal History*, 11: 372.

McGuire, J. (ed.) (1995) *What Works? Reducing reoffending.* Chichester: Wiley.

McKeigne, P.M. and Karmi, G. (1993) 'Alcohol consumption and alcohol-related problems in Afro-Caribbeans and South Asians in the United Kingdom', *Alcohol and Alcoholism*, 28(1): 1.

McMahon, J., Jones, B.T. and O'Donnell, P. (1994) 'Comparing positive and negative alcohol expectancies in male and female social drinkers', *Addiction Research*, 1: 349.

McMurran, M. and Hollin, C.R. (1989) 'Drinking and delinquency: another look at young offenders and alcohol', *British Journal of Criminology*, 29(4): 386.

McNeill, A. (2005) *Crime and Disorder, Binge Drinking and the Licensing Act 2003.* St. Ives: Institute of Alcohol Studies.

Measham, F. (1996) 'The "Big Bang" approach to sessional drinking: changing patterns of alcohol consumption among young people in North West England', *Addiction Research*, 4(3): 283.

Messerschmidt, J.W. (1993) *Masculinities and Crime.* Langham, MD: Rowman and Littlefield.

Mewett, A.W. and Manning, M. (1985) *Criminal Law* (2nd edn). Toronto: Butterworths.

Miller, B.A. and Welte, J.W. (1986) 'Comparisons of incarcerated offenders according to use of alcohol and/or drugs prior to offense', *Criminal Justice and Behavior*, 13(4): 366.

Miller, P.M., Smith, G.T. and Goldman, M.S. (1990) 'Emergence of alcohol expectancies in childhood: a possible critical period', *Journal of Studies on Alcohol*, 51: 343.

Mitchell, C. (1988) 'The intoxicated offender – refuting the legal and medical myths', *International Journal of Law and Psychiatry*, 11: 77.

Moller-Madsen, B., Dalgaard, J.B., Charles, A.V., Grymer, F., Hedeboe, J., Jensen, S.E., Moller, B.N., Nielson, J. and Sommer, J. (1986) 'Alcohol involvement in violence: a study from a Danish community', *Journal of Legal Medicine*, 97(2): 141.

Muir, W.K. (1977) *The Police: street corner politicians*. Chicago: Chicago University Press.

Munro, C. (1992) 'Judicial independence and judicial functions', in C. Munro and M. Wasik (eds) *Sentencing, Judicial Discretion and Training*. London: Sweet and Maxwell.

Murphy, C.M. and O'Farrell, T.J. (1996) 'Marital violence among alcoholics', *Current Directions in Psychological Science*, 5: 183.

Murphy, C.M., O'Farrell, T.J., Fals-Stewart, W. and Feehan, M. (2001) 'Correlates of intimate partner violence among male alcoholic patients', *Journal of Consulting and Clinical Psychology*, 69: 528.

Nagin, D. and Paternoster, R. (1991) 'The preventive effects of perceived risk of arrest', *Criminology*, 29: 561.

National Centre for Social Research and Department of Epidemiology and Public Health at the Royal Free and University Medical College (2001) *The Health of Minority Ethnic Groups*. London: Office for National Statistics.

National Institute of Justice (1991) *Drug Use Forecasting: drugs and crime 1990 annual report*. Washington, DC: United States Department of Justice.

Nazroo, J.Y. (1997) *The Health of Britain's Ethnic Minorities: findings from a national survey*. London: Policy Studies Institute.

Nelson, A.L., Bromley, R.D.F. and Thomas, C.J. (2001) 'Identifying micro and temporal patterns of violent crime and disorder in the British city centre', *Applied Geography*, 21: 249.

Neve, R.J.M., Lemmens, P.H. and Drop, M.J. (1997) 'Gender differences in alcohol use and alcohol problems: mediation by social rules and gender-role attitudes', *Substance Use and Misuse*, 32(11): 1439.

Newburn, T. (2002) 'Atlantic crossings: policy transfer and crime control in England and Wales', *Punishment and Society*, 4(2): 165.

Newburn, T. (2003) *Crime and Criminal Justice Policy* (2nd edn). Harlow: Longman.

Newburn, T. and Shiner, M. (2001) *Teenage Kicks? Young people and alcohol: a review of the literature*. York: Joseph Rowntree Foundation.

Norris, C. and Armstrong, G. (1999) *The Maximum Surveillance Society: the rise of CCTV*. Oxford: Berg.

Norström, T. (1993) 'Familjevåld och totalkonsumtionen av alcohol (family violence and the per capita consumption of alcohol)', *Nordisk Alkoholtidskrift*, 10: 311, cited in K. Pernanen and K. Brochu (1997)

Attributable Fractions for Alcohol and Other Drugs in Relation to Crimes in Canada: literature search and outlines of data banks. Ottawa: Canadian Centre on Substance Abuse.

Norton, A. (1998) 'Alcohol-related crime: the good practice of the magistrates' courts', *Alcohol and Alcoholism*, 33: 78.

O'Donnell, I. and O'Sullivan, E. (2002) 'The politics of intolerance – Irish style', *British Journal of Criminology*, 43(1): 41.

O'Donnell, M. and Sharpe, S. (2000) *Uncertain Masculinities: youth, ethnicity and class in contemporary Britain.* London: Routledge.

Oei, T.P.S. and Baldwin, A.R. (1994) 'Expectancy theory: a two process model of alcohol use and abuse', *Journal of Studies on Alcohol*, 55: 525.

Oei, T.P.S., Fergusson, S. and Lee, N.K. (1998) 'The differential role of alcohol expectancies and drinking refusal self-efficacy in problem and nonproblem drinkers', *Journal of Studies on Alcohol*, 59(6): 704.

O'Farrell, T.J. and Murphy, C.M. (1995) 'Marital violence before and after alcoholism treatment', *Journal of Consulting and Clinical Psychology*, 63(2): 256.

Office for National Statistics (2003) *Living in Britain: results from the 2002 General Household Survey.* London: HMSO.

Office for National Statistics (2004) *Living in Britain: results from the 2003 General Household Survey.* London: HMSO.

Orchard, G. (1980) 'Criminal responsibility and intoxication – the Australian rejection of *Majewski*', *New Zealand Law Journal*, 23: 532.

Orchard, G. [1993] 'Surviving without *Majewski* – a view from down under', *Criminal Law Review*: 426.

Osgood, D.W. (1994) 'Drugs, alcohol and adolescent violence', paper presented at the annual meeting of the American Society of Criminology, Miami, cited in B. Huang, H.R. White, R. Kosterman, R.F. Catalano and J.D. Hawkins (2001) 'Developmental associations between alcohol and interpersonal aggression during adolescence, *Journal of Research in Crime and Delinquency*, 38(1): 64.

Painter, K. (1988) *Lighting and Crime Prevention: the Edmonton project.* London: Centre for Criminology and Police studies, Middlesex University.

Parker, H. (1996) 'Young adult offenders, alcohol and criminological cul-de-sacs', *British Journal of Criminology*, 36(2): 282.

Parker, R.N. and Auerhahn, K. (1998) 'Alcohol, drugs and violence', *Annual Review of Sociology*, 24: 291.

Parker, R.N. and Cartmill, R.S. (1998) 'Alcohol and homicide in the United States, 1935–1995 – or one reason why US rates of violence may be going down', *Journal of Criminal Law and Criminology*, 88(4): 1369.

Parker, R.N. and Rebhun, L.A. (1995) *Alcohol and Homicide: a deadly combination of two American traditions.* Albany, New York: State University of New York Press.

Paton, E. [1995] 'Reforming the intoxication rules: the Law Commission's report', *Criminal Law Review*: 382.

Pease, K. (2002) 'Crime reduction', in M. Maguire, R. Morgan and R. Reiner (eds) *The Oxford Handbook of Criminology*. Oxford: Oxford University Press.

Pernanen, K. (1991) *Alcohol in Human Violence*. New York: Guildford Press.

Pernanen, K. and Brochu, S. (1997) *Attributable Fractions for Alcohol and Other Drugs in Relation to Crimes in Canada: literature search and outlines of data banks*. Ottawa: Canadian Centre on Substance Abuse.

Pihl, R.O., Paylan, S.S., Gentes-Hawn, A. and Hoaken, P.N.S. (2003) 'Alcohol affects executive functioning differentially on the ascending versus descending limb of the blood alcohol concentration curve', *Alcoholism: clinical and experimental research*, 27(5): 773.

Plant, M. (1990) *Women and Alcohol: a review of international literature on the use of alcohol by females*. Geneva: World Health Organisation.

Plant, M. (1997) *Women and Alcohol: contemporary and historical perspectives*. London: Free Association Books.

Platz, W.E. (1994) 'Empirical data for the purpose of multidimensional analysis of alcohol delinquency related behaviour', *Wiener Klinische Wochenschrift*, 106(3): 80, referred to in K. Pernanen and S. Brochu (1997) *Attributable Fractions for Alcohol and Other Drugs in Relation to Crimes in Canada: literature search and outlines of data banks*. Ottawa: Canadian Centre on Substance Abuse.

Poldrugo, F. (1998) 'Alcohol and criminal behaviour', *Alcohol and Alcoholism*, 33(1): 12.

Potas, I. (1994) 'Alcohol and sentencing of violent offenders', in *National Symposium on Alcohol Misuse and Violence: Report 6A*. Canberra: Australian Government Publishing Service.

Prime Minister's Strategy Unit (2003) *Alcohol Harm Reduction Project: interim analytical report*. London: Prime Minister's Strategy Unit.

Prime Minister's Strategy Unit (2004) *Alcohol Harm Reduction Strategy for England*. London: Prime Minister's Strategy Unit.

Purser, R., Johnson, M., Orford, J. and Davis, P. (1999) *Drinking in Second and Subsequent Generation Black and Asian Communities in the English Midlands*. London: Alcohol Concern.

Quigley, T. (1987a) 'Reform of the intoxication defence', *McGill Law Journal*, 33: 1.

Quigley, T. (1987b) 'Specific and general nonsense?', *Dalhousie Law Journal*, 11: 75.

Quigley, T. and Manson, A. (1989) '*Bernard* on intoxication: principle, policy and points in between – two comments', 67 C.R. (3d) 168.

Raistrick, D., Hodgson, R. and Ritson, B. (eds) (1999) *Tackling Alcohol Together*. London: Free Association Books.

Ramsay, M. (1991a) *Lagerland Lost? An experiment in keeping drinkers off the streets in central Coventry and elsewhere*, Crime Prevention Unit Paper 22. London: Home Office.

Ramsay, M. (1991b) *The Effect of Better Street Lighting on Crime and Fear: a review*, Crime Prevention Unit Paper 29. London: Home Office.

Ramstedt, M. and Hope, A. (2004) *The Irish Drinking Culture – drinking and related harm, a European comparison*. Dublin: Health Promotion Unit, Department of Health and Children.

Rashbaum, W.K. [2002a] 'In new focus on quality of life, city goes after petty criminals', *New York Times*, 22 May.

Rashbaum, W.K. [2002b] 'Falling crime in New York defies trend', *New York Times*, 29 Novenber.

Reiner, R. (2002) 'Media made criminality: the representation of crime in the mass media', in M. Maguire, R. Morgan and R. Reiner (eds) *The Oxford Handbook of Criminology*. Oxford: Oxford University Press.

Rex, S. (2002) 'Reinventing community penalties: the role of communication', in S. Rex and M. Tonry (eds) *Reform and Punishment: the future of sentencing*. Cullompton: Willan Publishing.

Richardson, A. and Budd, T. (2003) *Alcohol, Crime and Disorder: a study of young adults*. London: Home Office.

Robbins, C. and Martin, S.S. (1993) 'Gender, styles of deviance, and drinking problems', *Journal of Health and Social Behavior*, 34: 302.

Roberts, J.V. (2002) 'Alchemy in sentencing: an analysis of sentencing reform proposals in England and Wales', *Punishment and Society*, 4: 445.

Roberts, J.V. (2003) 'Sentencing reform in New Zealand: an analysis of the Sentencing Act 2002', *The Australian and New Zealand Journal of Criminology* 36(3): 249.

Roberts, J.V. and Hough, M. (eds) (2002) *Changing Attitudes to Punishment: public opinion, crime and justice*. Cullompton: Willan Publishing.

Roberts, J.V. and von Hirsch, A. (1988) 'Conditional sentencing and the fundamental principle of proportionality in sentencing', *Criminal Reports*, 10: 222.

Rohsenow, D.J. (1983) 'Drinking habits and expectancies about alcohol's effects for self versus others', *Journal of Consulting and Clinical Psychology*, 51: 752.

Rohsenow, D.J. and Bachorowski, J.A. (1984) 'Effects of alcohol and expectancies on verbal aggression in men and women', *Journal of Abnormal Psychology*, 93: 418.

Room, R. and Rossow, I. (2001) 'The share of violence attributable to drinking', *Journal of Substance Use*, 6(4): 218.

Ross, S. and Polk, K. (2003) 'Crime in the streets', in A. Goldsmith, M. Israel and K. Daly (eds) *Crime and Justice: an Australian textbook in Criminology* (2nd edn). Pyrmont, NSW: Lawbook Co.

Royal College of Physicians (2005) *Changes to Licensing Laws – key issues*. London: Royal College of Physicians.

Royal Society for the Prevention of Accidents (1998) *Drownings in the UK*. London: Royal Society for the Prevention of Accidents.

Ruby, C.C. (1980) *Sentencing* (2nd edn). Toronto: Butterworths.

Rumgay, J. (1998) *Crime, Punishment and the Drinking Offender*. Basingstoke: Palgrave Macmillan.

Russell, J. (ed.) (1993) *Alcohol and Crime – proceedings of a Mental Health Foundation conference*. London: Mental Health Foundation.

Saunders, P. (1998) 'The good practice of the police: an alternative approach in dealing with offenders who abuse/misuse alcohol', *Alcohol and Alcoholism*, 33(1): 73.

Scarman, Lord (1982) *The Scarman Report: the Brixton disorders 1981*. Harmondsworth: Penguin.

Scarre, G. (1996) *Utilitarianism*. London: Routledge.

Schabas, P.B. (1984) 'Intoxication and culpability: towards an offence of criminal intoxication', *University of Toronto Faculty Law Review*, 42: 147.

Scottish Executive (2003) *The Nicholson Committee: review of liquor licensing law in Scotland*. Edinburgh: Scottish Executive.

Scottish Executive Social Research (2003) *Liquor Licensing and Public Disorder: review of literature on the impact of licensing and other controls/ audit of local initiatives*. Edinburgh: HMSO.

Scottish Office (1995) *Does Closed Circuit Television Prevent Crime? An evaluation of the use of CCTV surveillance cameras in Airdrie town centre*, Crime and Criminal Justice Research Findings No. 8. Edinburgh: Scottish Office.

Scottish Office (1999a) *A Safer Scotland: tackling crime and its causes*. Edinburgh: Scottish Office.

Scottish Office (1999b) *The Effect of Closed Circuit Television on Recorded Crime Rates and Public Concern about Crime in Glasgow*, Crime and Justice Research Findings No. 30. Edinburgh: Scottish Office.

Scribner, R.A., MacKinnon, D.P. and Dwyer, J.H. (1995) 'Relative risk of assaultive violence and alcohol availability in Los Angeles county', *American Journal of Public Health*, 85(3): 335.

Sellers, J. (1978) 'Mens rea and the judicial approach to "bad excuses" in the criminal law', *Modern Law Review*, 41(3): 245.

Sentencing Advisory Panel (2004) *New Sentences – Criminal Justice Act 2003*. London: Sentencing Advisory Panel.

Sentencing Guidelines Council (2004) *Overarching Principles: seriousness*. London: Sentencing Guidelines Council.

Shapland, J. (1981) *Between Conviction and Sentence: process of mitigation*. Routledge.

Shepherd, J. (1994) 'Violent crime: the role of alcohol and new approaches to the prevention of injury', *Alcohol and Alcoholism*, 29: 5.

Shepherd, J., Irish, M., Scully, C. and Leslie, I. (1989) 'Alcohol consumption among victims of violence and among comparable UK populations', *British Journal of Addiction*, 84(9): 1045.

Sherman, L. (1992) 'Attacking crime: policing and crime control', in M. Tonry and N. Morris (eds) *Modern Policing*. Chicago: University of Chicago Press.

Sherman, L. (1997) 'Policing for crime prevention', in L. Sherman *et al.* (eds) *Preventing Crime: what works, what doesn't, and what's promising.* Washington DC: National Institute of Justice.

Shiner, R. (1990) 'Intoxication and responsibility', *International Journal of Law and Psychiatry*, 13: 9.

Simmons, J. and Dodd, T. (2003) *Crime in England and Wales 2002/2003*. London: Home Office.

Singh, R.U. (1933) 'History of the defence of drunkenness in English criminal law', *Law Quarterly Review*, 49: 528.

Skene, L. (1983) 'Drunkenness and acquittals', *Law Institute Journal*, 57: 318.

Skogan, W. (1990) *Disorder and Decline: crime and the spiral of decay in American neighbourhoods*. New York: Free Press.

Smith, D.I. and Burvill, P.W. (1987) 'Effect on juvenile crime of lowering the drinking age in three Australian states', *British Journal of Addiction*, 82(2): 181.

Smith, G. (1981) 'Footnote to *O'Connor's* case', *Criminal Law Journal*, 5: 270.

Smith, J.C. [1976] 'Comment on *Majewski*', *Criminal Law Review*: 375.

Smith, J.C. (1987) 'Intoxication and the mental element in crime', in P. Wallington and R. Merkin (eds) *Essays in Honour of F.H. Lawson*. London: Sweet and Maxwell.

Smith, J.C. and Hogan, B. (1992) *Criminal Law* (7th edn). London: Butterworths.

Smith, K.J.M. and Wilson, W. (1993) 'Impaired voluntariness and criminal responsibility', *Oxford Journal of Legal Studies*: 69.

Smith, S. (1984) 'Crime in the news', *British Journal of Criminology*, 24: 289.

South, N. (2002) 'Drugs, alcohol and crime', in M. Maguire, R. Morgan and R. Reiner (eds) *The Oxford Handbook of Criminology*. Oxford: Oxford University Press.

Speer, P.W., Gorman, D.M., Labouvie, E.W. and Ontkush, M.J. (1998) 'Violent crime and alcohol availability relationships in an urban community', *Journal of Public Health Policy*, 19: 303.

Spencer, K. (2005) 'The intoxication "defence" in Ireland', *Irish Criminal Law Journal*, 15(1): 2.

Spunt, B., Goldstein, P., Brownstein, H., Fendrick, M. and Langley, S. (1994) 'Alcohol and homicide: interviews with prison inmates', *The Journal of Drug Issues*, 24(1): 143.

Steele, C.M. and Joseph, R.A. (1990) 'Alcohol myopia: its prized and dangerous effects', *American Psychologist*, 45: 921.

Steele, C.M. and Southwick, L. (1985) 'Alcohol and social behavior I: the psychology of drunken excess', *Journal of Personality and Social Psychology*, 48: 18.

Stets, J.E. (1990) 'Verbal and physical aggression in marriage', *Journal of Marriage and the Family*, 43: 721.

Stevenson, R.J., Lind, B. and Weatherburn, D. (1999) 'The relationship between alcohol sales and assault in New South Wales, Australia', *Addiction*, 94(3): 397.

Stith, K. and Cabranes, J.A. (1998) *Fear of Judging: sentencing guidelines in the federal courts*. Chicago: University of Chicago Press.

Stockwell, T., Vallis, R., Phillips, A. and Hollins, P. (1998) 'Attitudes to health promotion in licensed premises', *Journal of the Royal Society of Health*, 108(6): 209.

Stroud, D.A. (1914) *Mens Rea*. London: Sweet and Maxwell.

Stroud, D.A. (1920) 'Constructive murder and drunkenness', *Law Quarterly Review*, 36(3): 273.

Subhra, G. (2002) *Drinking in Black and Minority Ethnic Communities. 100% proof: research for action on alcohol*. London: Alcohol Concern.

Sullivan, G.R. (1994) 'Involuntary intoxication and beyond', *Criminal Law Review*: 272.

Tardif, G. (1968) 'Alcoholism and violence', *Toxicomanies*, 1(2): 125.

Taylor, R. (1988) 'Half prison intake has drink problem: report', *The West Australian*, 10 November.

Taylor, S.P. and Leonard, K.E. (1983) 'Alcohol and human physical aggression', in R.G. Green and E.I. Donnerstein (eds) *Aggression: theoretical and empirical reviews*. New York: Academic Press.

Thom, B. (1999) *Dealing With Drink: alcohol and social policy from treatment to management*. London: Free Association Books.

Thom, B. and Francome, C. (2001) *Men at Risk: risk taking, substance use and gender*. London: Middlesex University.

Thomas, D.A. (1979) *Principles of Sentencing* (2nd edn). London: Heinemann.

Thornton, D., Cookson, H. and Clark, D. (1990) 'Profiles of the youth custody population: dependencies, delinquencies and disciplinary infractions', in The British Psychological Society Criminological and Legal Psychology Division (ed.) *Applying Psychology to Imprisonment: young offenders*. London: British Psychological Society.

Tolmie, J. (1999) 'Intoxication and criminal liability in New South Wales: a random patchwork?', *Criminal Law Journal*, 23(4): 218.

Tolmie, J. (2001) 'Alcoholism and criminal liability', *Modern Law Review*, 64(5): 688.

Tonry, M. and Farrington, D.P. (1995) *Building a Safer Society: strategic approaches to crime prevention*. Chicago, Illinois: University of Chicago Press.

United States Department of Health and Human Services (2000) *10th Special Report to the US Congress on Alcohol and Health: highlights from current research.* Washington DC: US Department of Health and Human Services.

United States National Research Council (1978) *Deterrence and Incapacitation: estimating the effects of criminal sanctions on crime rates.* Washington DC: National Research Council.

United States Sentencing Commission (1992) *Guidelines Manual.* Washington, DC: United States Sentencing Commission.

Van Dijk, J. and De Waard, J. (1991) 'A two dimensional typology of crime prevention projects: with a bibliography', *Criminal Justice Abstracts,* 23: 483.

Velleman, R. and Templeton, L. (2003) 'Alcohol, drugs and the family: results from a long running research programme within the UK', *European Addiction Research,* 9(3): 103.

Virgo, G. [1993] 'The Law Commission consultation paper on intoxication and criminal liability part 1: reconciling principle and policy', *Criminal Law Review*: 415.

Von Hirsch, A. (1986) *Past or Future Crimes: deservedness and dangerousness in the sentencing of criminals.* Manchester: Manchester University Press.

Von Hirsch, A. (1993) *Censure and Sanctions.* Oxford: Clarendon Press.

Von Hirsch, A. (2002) 'Record-enhanced sentencing in England and Wales', in S. Rex and M. Tonry (eds) *Reform and Punishment.* Cullompton: Willan Publishing.

Von Hirsch, A. and Ashworth, A. (eds) (1998) *Principled Sentencing: theory and policy* (2nd edn). Oxford: Hart Publishing.

Von Hirsch, A., Bottoms, E., Burney, E. and Wilkström, P.O. (1999) *Criminal Deterrence and Sentencing Severity.* Oxford: Hart Publishing.

Wacquant, L. (2003) 'Towards a dictatorship over the poor? Notes on the penalization of poverty in Brazil', *Punishment and Society,* 5(2): 197.

Walker, N. (1991) *Why Punish?* Oxford: Oxford University Press.

Walker, N. and Padfield, N. (1996) *Sentencing: theory, law and practice* (2nd edn). London: Butterworths.

Walklate, S. (1995) *Gender and Crime.* Hemel Hempstead: Harvester Wheatsheaf.

Wanigaratne, S., Unntham, S. and Strang, J. (2001) 'Substance misuse and ethnic minorities: issues for the UK', in D. Bhugra and R. Cochrane (eds) *Psychiatry in Multicultural Britain.* London: Gaskell.

Wanigaratne, S., Dar, K., Abdulrahim, D. and Strang, J. (2003) 'Ethnicity and drug use: exploring the nature of particular relationships among diverse populations in the United Kingdom', *Drugs – Education Prevention and Policy,* 10(1): 39.

Ward, A.R. (1986) 'Making some sense of self-induced intoxication', *Cambridge Law Journal,* 45(2): 247.

Wasik, M. (1999) 'Is intoxication a mitigating factor in sentencing?', *Justice of the Peace,* 163(37): 724.

Wasik, M. (2001) *Emmins on Sentencing* (4th edn). London: Blackstone Press Ltd.

Wasik, M. and Taylor, R.D. (1991) *Blackstone's Guide to the Criminal Justice Act 1991*. London: Blackstone Press.

Wasik, M. and von Hirsch, A. [1994] 'Section 29 revised: previous convictions in sentencing', *Criminal Law Review*: 409.

Waterson, J. (1996) 'Gender divisions and drinking problems', in L. Harrison (ed.) *Alcohol Problems in the Community*. London: Routledge.

Watson, M. and Burleigh, J. [2000] 'Why the Met can't match NYPD', *Evening Standard*, 2 October.

Weaver, T., Renton, A., Stimson, G. and Tyrer, P. (1999) 'Severe mental illness and substance misuse', *British Medical Journal*, 318: 137.

Welsh, B.C. and Farrington, D.P. (2002) *Crime Prevention Effects of Closed Circuit Television: a systematic review*. Home Office Research Study 252. London: Home Office.

Welte, J.W. and Aber, E.L. (1989) 'Homicide: drinking by the victim', *Journal of Studies on Alcohol*, 50: 197.

White, H.R. and Gorman, D.M. (2000) 'Dynamics of the drug-crime relationship', in G. LaFree (ed.) *Criminal Justice 2000: the nature of crime*. Washington DC: United States Department of Justice.

White, R. and Boyer, K. (1985) 'Alcoholism amongst the Tasmanian population: research note', *Australian and New Zealand Journal of Criminology*, 18: 109.

White, S. [1989] 'Offences of basic and specific intent', *Criminal Law Review*: 271.

Wichstrom, L. (1988) 'Alcohol intoxication and the school drop-out', *Drug and Alcohol Review*, 17: 413.

Wieczorek, W.F. and Welte, J.W. (1994) 'Alcohol involvement in serious crime', paper presented at the American Society of Criminology Conference, Miami, cited in J.W. Welte, L. Zhang and W.F. Wieczorek (2001) 'The effects of substance use on specific types of criminal offending in young men', *Journal of Research in Crime and Delinquency*, 38(4): 416.

Wieczorek, W.F., Welte, J.W. and Abel, E.L. (1990) 'Alcohol, drugs and murder: a study of convicted homicide offenders', *Journal of Criminal Justice*, 18(3): 217.

Wiley, J.A. and Weisner, C. (1995) 'Drinking in violent and nonviolent events leading to arrest: evidence from a survey of arrestees', *Journal of Criminal Justice*, 23(5): 461.

Wilkins, C., Casswell, S., Bhatta, K. and Pledger, M. (2002) *Drug Use in New Zealand: national surveys comparisons 1998 and 2001*. Auckland: Alcohol and Public Health Research.

Williams, G. (1983) *Textbook of Criminal Law* (2nd edn). London: Stevens.

Williams, K.S. (2004) *Textbook on Criminology* (5th edn). Oxford: Oxford University Press.

Williams, K.S., Goodwin, M. and Johnstone, C. (2000) 'Closed circuit television (CCTV) surveillance in urban Britain: beyond the rhetoric of crime prevention', in J.R. Gold and G. Revill (eds) *Landscapes of Defence*. Harlow: Prentice Hall.

Williams, K.S. and Johnstone, C. (2000) 'The politics of the selective gaze: closed circuit television and the policing of public space', *Crime, Law and Social Change*, 34: 183.

Williams, P. and Dickson, J. (1993) 'Fear of crime: read all about it? The relationship between newspaper crime reporting and fear of crime', *British Journal of Criminology*, 33(1): 33.

Wilsnack, R.W., Vogeltanz, N.D. and Wilsnack, S.C. (2002) 'Gender differences in alcohol consumption and adverse drinking consequences: cross-cultural patterns', *Addiction*, 95: 251.

Wilson, D. and Sutton, A. (2003) *Open Street CCTV in Australia*, Trends and Issues 271. Canberra, ACT: Australian Institute of Criminology.

Wilson, J.Q. (1968) *Varieties of Policing Behavior*. Cambridge, Massachussets: Harvard University Press.

Wilson, J.Q. and Kelling, G. [1982] 'Broken windows: the police and neighbourhood safety', *Atlantic Monthly* 29.

Wilson, W. (1995) 'Involuntary intoxication: excusing the inexcusable?', *Res Publica*, 1(1): 25.

Wincup, E. (2005) 'Drugs, alcohol and crime', in C. Hale, K. Hayward, A. Wahidin and E. Wincup (eds) *Criminology*. Oxford: Oxford University Press.

Windlesham, Lord (1993) *Responses to Crime: penal policy in the making*. Oxford: Oxford University Press.

Wolfe, B.M. and Baron, R.A. (1971) 'Laboratory aggression related to aggression in naturalistic social situations: effects of an aggressive model on the behaviour of college student and prisoner observers', *Psychonomic Science*, 24: 193.

Wolfgang, M.E. and Strohm, R.B. (1956) 'The relationship between alcohol and criminal homicide', *Quarterly Journal of Studies on Alcohol*, 17: 411.

World Health Organisation (2000) *International Guide for Monitoring Alcohol Consumption and Related Harm*. Geneva: World Health Organisation.

World Health Organisation (2002) *World Health Report: reducing risks, promoting healthy life*. Geneva: World Health Organisation.

Wright, K.N. (1993) 'Alcohol use by prisoners', *Alcohol Health and Research World*, 17(2): 157.

Yarvis, R.M. (1994) 'Patterns of substance abuse and intoxication among murderers', *Bulletin of the American Academy of Psychiatry and the Law*, 22(1): 411.

Zedner, L. (2003) 'The concept of security: an agenda for comparative analysis', *Legal Studies*, 23(1): 153.

Zhu, L., Gorman, D.M. and Horel, S. (2004) 'Alcohol outlet density and violence: a geographical analysis', *Alcohol and Alcoholism*, 39(4): 369.

Zimring, F.E. and Hawkins, G. (1995) *Incapacitation: penal confinement and the restraint of crime*. New York: Oxford University Press.

Cases

New Zealand

Northern Ireland

Republic of Ireland

Scotland

South Africa

Index